TAV

D0349378

Monty's Greatest Victory

MONTY'S GREATEST VICTORY

THE DRIVE FOR THE BALTIC APRIL–MAY 1945

CHARLES WHITING

LEO COOPER

First published in 1989 by The Crowood Press.

Reprinted in 2002 by
LEO COOPER
an imprint of Pen & Sword Books Ltd
47 Church Street
Barnsley
South Yorkshire
S70 2AS

© Charles Whiting 1989, 2002

ISBN 0 85052 909 3

A CIP catalogue for this book is
available from the British Library

Printed and bound in England by
CPI UK

NORFOLK LIBRARY AND INFORMATION SERVICE	
SUPP	FARR
INV. NO.	C735015
ORD DATE	01/03/05
940.5421	

Contents

Acknowledgements 7
Introduction 15

BOOK ONE: DECISION ON THE ELBE
1 'You're on your way to Berlin!' 25
2 'Hier ist Bremen.' 42
3 'Holy catfish . . . what a mess!' 59
4 'You have twenty-four hours in which to decide.' 75
5 'I think how horrid my mother was to me.' 91

BOOK TWO: GOETTERDAEMMERUNG
1 'Come out and bloody well fight!' 109
2 'If only the British would hurry up and get across the Elbe.' 123
3 'We British always win!' 138
4 'Herr Leutnant, this is what we are fighting against!' 154
5 'My Führer, my loyalty to you will be unconditional.' 170

BOOK THREE: THE LONG SURRENDER
1 'It'll be a piece of frigging cake!' 187
2 'A proper Fred Karno's, this is!' 203
3 'We're celebrating. We're going
   to have bread and margarine tonight!' 220
4 'Now togedder, we fight the Russians!' 240
5 'A tin of corned beef means true love!' 257
6 'The only German secret weapon not used.' 274

ENVOI
Bibliography 289
Source Notes 291
Index 293

Acknowledgements

I suppose over the last fifty years I have met or corresponded with most of the chief actors in this book – from Doenitz, that last 'Führer', allowing himself to be interviewed in his blue pyjama jacket, very deaf, but as hard as nails still; through Speer, quick, vocal and eager even after twenty years in Spandau; down to those last-ditch fortress commanders who refused to surrender at first: Fahrmbacher, still proud of that telegram from the Führer awarding him the Knight's Cross of the Iron Cross, Frisius and the like – I met them.

With the Americans it was mostly by correspondence – General Gavin of the 82nd Airborne, who always maintained to me that there was a Russian spy at Eisenhower's HQ; tough old General Clarke of the 7th Armored Division; Lt Colonel John Eisenhower. Perhaps they didn't agree with my views but they were generous of their time, helping out the 'limey', although their military masters had long given up thinking very highly of the British.

Predictably, the British Generals were either delightfully off-beat or cagey – Sir Brian Horrocks, my old corps commander, giving me documents and saying carelessly, 'Better in your files than in my waste-paper basket'; Sir Kenneth Strong, Eisenhower's Chief of Intelligence, who had blotted his copybook in the British Army (wasn't he calling Montgomery 'a cad' in 1945?), trying 'to set the record straight' in that careful Scottish manner of his. 'Monty' himself I saw once only but that was a long time before. When it came time to talk to him, I was warned by Tom Howart, one of his former 'eyes and ears', an ex-Major and now High Master of Monty's old school St Paul's, that it was no use – 'the old man was completely ga-ga'.

But specifically now my greatest debt is to those who were at the sharp end, did the fighting, Chas Bedford of the 53rd Division, Fred Pettinger of Monty's old 'Iron Division', the Third, ex-Sergeant Jones of the 6th Airborne Division, and many others, for their recollections – and one other ex-infantryman fighting at the other end of the long

7

front, Tom Dickinson of the US 70th Infantry Division, now a pillar of New York City's library system.

To all of you – thanks!

Charles Whiting
York, England
2002

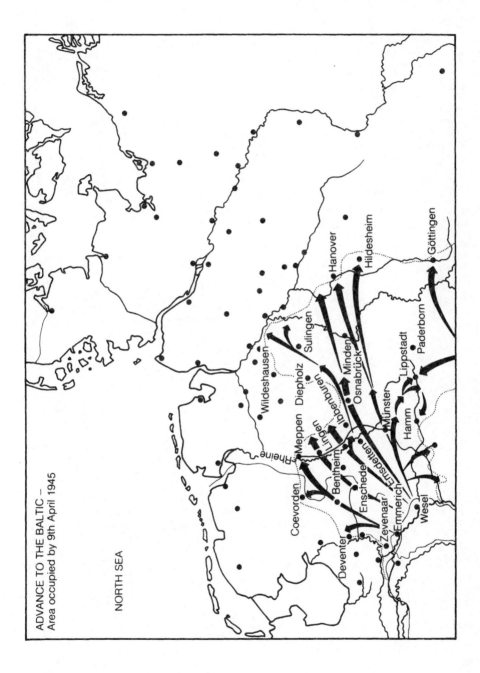

ADVANCE TO THE BALTIC –
Area occupied by 9th April 1945

NORTH SEA

Göttingen
Paderborn
Hildesheim
Hanover
Lippstadt
Minden
Sulingen
Münster
Osnabrück
Hamm
Diepholz
Wildeshausen
Ibbenbüren
Meppen
Lingen
Emsdetten
Bentheim
Rheine
Enschede
Wesel
Emmerich
Zevenaar
Coevorden
Deventer

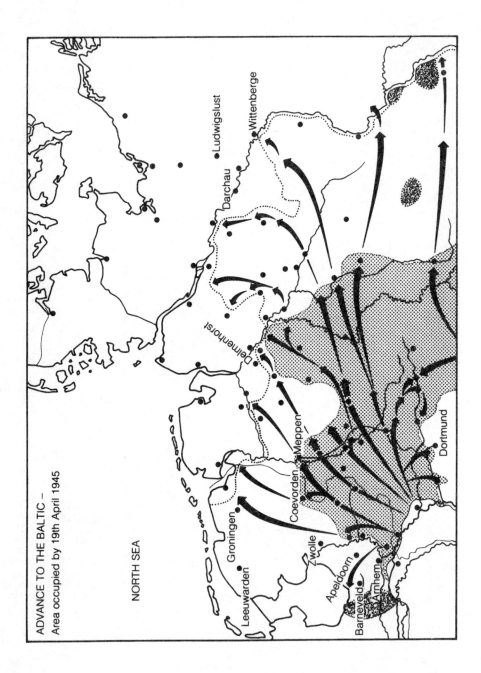

ADVANCE TO THE BALTIC –
Area occupied by 19th April 1945

NORTH SEA

Leeuwarden

Groningen

Zwolle

Apeldoorn

Barneveld

Arnhem

Coevorden

Meppen

Delmenhorst

Darchau

Ludwigslust

Wittenberge

Dortmund

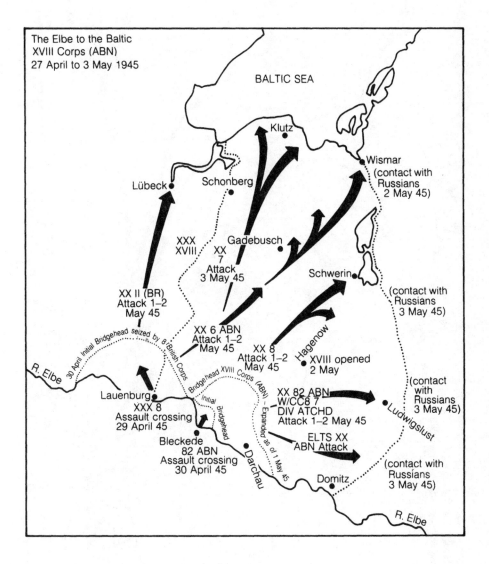

The Elbe to the Baltic
XVIII Corps (ABN)
27 April to 3 May 1945

BALTIC SEA

Klutz

Wismar
(contact with
Russians
2 May 45)

Lübeck

Schonberg

XXX
XVIII

XX
7
Attack
3 May 45

Gadebusch

Schwerin

(contact with
Russians
3 May 45)

X II (BR)
Attack 1–2
May 45

30 April Initial Bridgehead seized by 8 British Corps

XX 6 ABN
Attack 1–2
May 45

XX 8
Attack 1–2
May 45

Hagenow

XVIII opened
2 May

(contact
with
Russians
3 May 45)

R. Elbe

Lauenburg

Bridgehead XVIII Corps (ABN) – Expanded as of 1 May 45

XXX 8
Assault crossing
29 April 45

Initial
Bridgehead

XX 82 ABN
W/CC8 7
DIV ATCHD
Attack 1–2 May 45

Ludwigslust

Bleckede
82 ABN
Assault crossing
30 April 45

Darchau

ELTS XX
ABN Attack

Domitz

(contact with
Russians
3 May 45)

R. Elbe

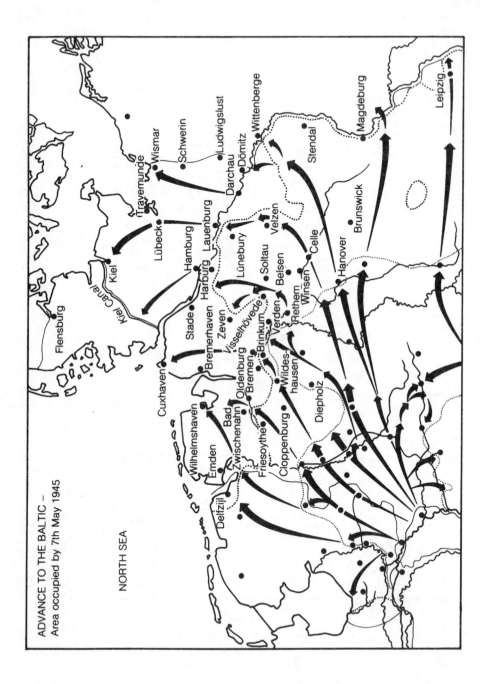

ADVANCE TO THE BALTIC –
Area occupied by 7th May 1945

NORTH SEA

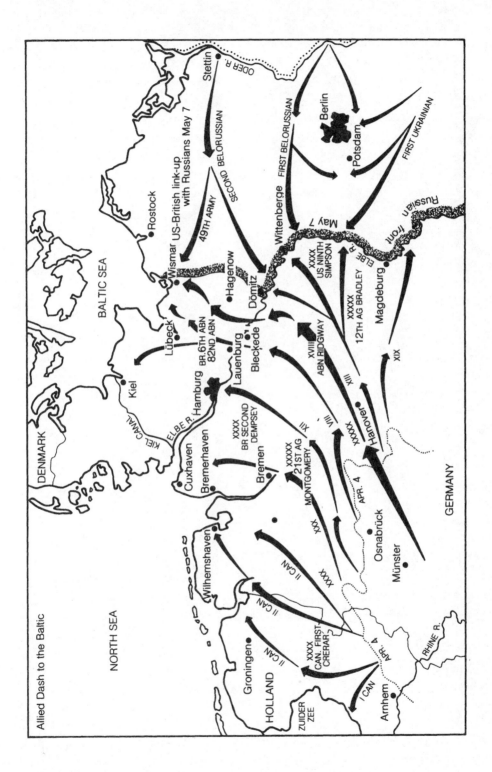

Allied Dash to the Baltic

INTRODUCTION

'He who holds Northern Germany holds Germany'

General Blumentritt, Montgomery's opponent, April 1945

Stomping the dunes that terrible dawn, Brigadier Barker was shocked by what he saw. For 10 long miles the whole beach at Dunkirk was a never-ending smudge of khaki: British soldiers packed tightly together, waiting. 'Bubbles' Barker, who this day would amputate a soldier's shattered arm with a jackknife and years later command the assault corps in that last battle, cried in anguish to his young aide, 'Good God, I never thought I'd see the British Army reduced to this!'

As the beaten British Army in France shuffled by the miles of abandoned trucks and carriers, past the wrecked guns, their barrels burst and spread outwards like celery sticks, it was clear not only to generals but private soldiers too that the BEF[1] was finished. Standing in the middle of a demoralised mob, Corporal Thomas Nicholls of the Worcester Yeomanry spotted the regiment's 'old sweat'. Cheerfully he called out, 'Hey, what about the thin red line now?'

'Fuck the thin red line,' the old sweat snorted. 'I'm off!'

They were all off. Most were orderly and behaved still like soldiers. Others were laden with loot they had stolen from French houses during the long retreat. Some were drunk and without rifles for they had thrown them away; they would fight no more.

Preparing to board the destroyer which would take him back to England, where he would attempt to re-form this beaten army, General Alan Brooke, who had commanded the BEF's 2nd Corps, felt a sense of guilt and of overwhelming, total despair. A little earlier he had met his commander, Lord Gort, for a last time. He had been too shaken to speak; the tragedy was appalling. The wooden-headed Guards officer, who had allowed this tragedy to happen to the British Army on account of his incompetent leadership, stared sombrely at his corps commander and pondered, 'I wonder what view history will take of the events that are happening now.' Brooke had not

1 British Expeditionary Force.

commented; his heart had been too full.

Now, feeling that he was betraying the men of his corps by leaving them this way, Brooke sought out the perky little commander of his 3rd Division, who was to take over the 2nd Corps. Somehow he groped through his final orders, while a newly promoted brigadier, Brian Horrocks, watched the two figures standing on the sand at some distance. Suddenly Brooke, who would soon command the whole of the British Army, could stand the emotional strain no longer. He laid his head on the shoulder of the little divisional general and began to sob, while the other officer patted his back gently like a mother might comfort a heart-broken little child. 'I remained a silent and interested spectator of this astonishing scene,' Horrocks recalled many years later. Then the newly promoted brigadier, who too would one day command a corps in that final battle, was called across. Unemotionally and without pathos, his new boss, one who would dominate his life for the next five years, started to rap out his orders for the day. Bernard Law Montgomery was in business . . .

Montgomery, who had always prided himself on being an un-swerving realist, did all he could to save what was left of his new corps. He had seen disaster from the moment the pitifully equipped BEF had moved to France. For him, 'the war was lost in Whitehall years before it began'. But he avoided any recriminations. He continued with his set routine, which prevented him from breaking down in the way that one other corps commander and several other divisional commanders did. All day he was on the beaches, accompanied solely by his one unwounded aide, young Charles Sweeney of the Ulster Rifles, but taking his meals at the usual time and turning in never later than ten o'clock after drinking his usual cup of hot milk.

He was tireless in his devotion to his troops until, on the afternoon of 1 June 1940, accompanied by his Chief of Staff Ritchie, yet another of his corps commanders in that last battle of years ahead, he boarded the destroyer which would take him home. Even now, when most of the rescued men simply slumped apathetically on the decks, his spirits didn't flag. Captain Stevens-Guille, the destroyer's captain, noted how the little General's spirits seemed to rise with every new wave of attacking German planes. 'Ah, another lot coming in now . . . What do you think their tactics are going to be? . . . I wouldn't come in all at once if I were them . . . If they came in one at a time I think they'd have a first-class chance of hitting us.' But the German dive-bombers didn't. Mopping his brow, Captain Stevens-Guille told himself he had never heard of Montgomery up to now, but it struck him that the little General was the 'coolest customer' he'd ever met.

Three days later Churchill warned the House of Commons that 'wars are not won by evacuation. We must be very careful not to assign to this deliverance the attribute of a victory.' But to the nation Dunkirk was seen as a victory. There were calls for a 'Dunkirk Medal' and some troops took to moving around with a flash inscribed 'Dunkirk' on their shoulders. The little General never saw Dunkirk that way. The British Army had failed in his opinion. It needed to be reformed drastically. Dunkirk was a defeat which one day he would avenge.

Five years later, Field Marshal Montgomery, now an army group commander, leading a force of two million Americans, Britons and Canadians, had achieved that aim. He had well and truly wiped out the stigma of Dunkirk. But in April 1945 he had almost reached the end of that long road which had led from Dunkirk, through El Alamein, Sicily and Italy, to Normandy, the Ardennes and the German Rhine. Now he was preparing to fight his last battle, perhaps the last great battle a British Army would ever fight.

But it would be a battle which would go strangely unnoticed by historians of the Second World War. Despite the fact that it ended in the capture of 2,500,000 German prisoners, brought about the liberation of Denmark and Norway and ensured the final surrender of what was left of the Third Reich, military historians and others have passed it by with the merest of mentions, a sentence or two, a couple of paragraphs, a page at the most.

John Toland, the popular American writer on the war, gently mocked the whole campaign in the north in *The Last Hundred Days*:

For the past few weeks Blumentritt [Monty's opponent on the River Elbe] had been waging a gentleman's battle with the British pulling back with as little bloodshed as possible. Since mid-April an informal liaison had been maintained between the adversaries, and that morning one of the liaison officers from Second British Army came to Blumentritt unofficially and said that since the Russians were closing in on Lübeck, His Majesty's Forces wondered if the Germans would allow them to take the Baltic port ahead of the Russians.

All very 'top-hole' and gentleman-like, as the Americans liked to see the British in those days.

The American Army Group Commander Bradley, Montgomery's comrade-in-arms (one could hardly call him friend) saw it in pretty much the same way in *A General's Life*:

Ridgway[2] positioned the British 6th Airborne in the van of his XVIII Airborne Corps so the British could have the honor and public acclaim of greeting the Russians at Wismar. As it turned out Gavin's[3] troops actually linked first, but we downplayed that union in order not to upstage the British . . .

Monty's last campaign from the Rhine to Lübeck was, on the whole, one of the most cautious and uninspired of the war. It began with flamboyant overkill at the Rhine in a typical Monty set-piece battle and petered out to his usual desultory pursuit and reluctance to go for the jugular, to make the kill, to take risks. Had we not primed Ridgway in advance and then rushed him to help Monty, the Russians would surely have reached the Danish border first and perhaps gone on to Copenhagen with possible damaging consequences in the post-war world.

In other words, a generous Bradley had allowed Montgomery to have the kudos of victory, but it was good old American get-up-and-go which had really brought that victory.

Like Bradley another American, Major-General Franklin, who fought in the last campaign as a major in Ridgway's American Airborne Corps, also distorted Montgomery's battle. In *Across the Rhine* he devoted one short paragraph to the start of Montgomery's last battle. The struggle for Bremen, the second greatest port in Germany, took four days and involved three British infantry divisions. But according to General Franklin, the surviving six thousand German defenders surrendered in one day – and without a fight. All patently untrue.

Even Montgomery's British biographers, who do not have the same nationalistic axe to grind as the Americans, have paid scant attention to this last campaign of Britain's most outstanding soldier of the twentieth century. R.W.Thompson and Alan Moorehead, both war correspondents who followed the campaign, and Ronald Lewin, who fought in it as an artillery officer, devote little space to what happened in those fateful last days of April and the early ones of May 1945. Even Nigel Hamilton, whose monumental three-volume biography of the 'Master' runs into thousands of pages, concerns himself more with Montgomery's depressed mood and anger with the Americans at the time that with that last battle itself.

Yet, with an army of some seventeen divisions engaged in active operations against the enemy, Montgomery would suffer 21,646 British and 6,380 Canadian casualties between the crossings of the Rhine and the Elbe in that month of April, out of a total of 191,219 (including the Canadians) for the campaign as a whole. In other words, the population of a small town had vanished in a matter of

---

2 General Matt Ridgway, commander of the 18th AB Corps.
3 General James Gavin, commander of the 82nd US AB Division.

weeks, in a campaign which, in the eyes of the Americans at least, was supposedly a walkover.

Why? Why has this, perhaps the last major campaign the British Army will ever fight in the twentieth century, been so neglected? Was Monty's last battle a kind of sideshow – as he seemed to think it himself right to that triumphant surrender of the German Army to him *personally* at Luneburg Heath, when his opinion changed considerably? Eisenhower's biographer, Stephen E. Ambrose, seemed to think so. In *Supreme Command*, he wrote of Eisenhower's attempts to convince Churchill – and Montgomery – of the importance of crossing the river Elbe and racing for the Baltic port of Lübeck in order to seal off the Baltic: 'By stressing Lübeck, he gave Twenty-First Army Group [i.e. Montgomery's command] a significant role to play, which hopefully would mollify the British.'

Or was there more beneath the veil that has seemingly been drawn over this last campaign of a huge British army in Europe? Have the writers about that time, and even the participants themselves, deliberately set about creating a picture of the end of the Second World War in Europe in which American generals, the representatives of the new emerging superpower, would be the recipients of the kudos of final victory over the Germans; while Montgomery, the detested representative of an empire on the decline, was fobbed off as a sideshow, hardly worthy of mention? As Major-General Essame, who took part in the battle himself as an infantry brigadier, has stated in *The Battle for Germany*:

The more popular section of the press at the time, both the British and American, tended to portray the Allied statesmen as if they were the leading actors in some gigantic play and the generals like jockeys engaged in a nightmare international steeplechase. Montgomery with his flair for personal publicity, his gift of concise and acid expression and built-in conviction that he had been selected by the Almighty to destroy Hitler and all he stood for, was the answer to the journalists' proverbial prayer. In consequence, Anglo-American clashes of opinion and personality during the campaign were exaggerated then and have been since.

Was it, then, all a matter of personal and national pride and Anglo-American rivalry, with Montgomery being, as usual, his own worst enemy, antagonising 'Ike', 'Brad' and 'Georgie'?[4] Did the Americans really decide that the pesky little Englishman, with his vanity and overweening ambition, should be deprived of the great final victory which the British thought was rightfully theirs after six years of total

4 Eisenhower, Bradley and Patton

war? Certainly Eisenhower went on record after the war as saying that Montgomery irritated him like 'a burr under a saddle'. Sir James Grigg, British Minister of War and a personal friend of Montgomery, warned him about his personal attacks on the Americans, writing to him in secret cipher and on a one-time pad: 'I beseech you in the Bowels of Christ to watch your step or at any rate your loudspeaker as long as SHAEF (Eisenhower's HQ) still exists. I have quite enough quarrels to cope with!'

But perhaps there was another dimension which helped to obscure this last British battle of the war in Europe. Of all the campaigns fought in 1945, Montgomery's was the most 'political'. For it was one waged under political conditions and objectives which could not be revealed to the general public – not to mention the British and American soldiers who fought it – for many years to come. Not only was the battle fought against the German enemy, but also against the erstwhile ally, Russia. Montgomery's orders were to beat the Germans, it is true. Yet at the same time he was also to beat the Russians in the race for the Baltic. The Red Army had to be prevented from getting a foothold in Germany's Schleswig-Holstein and Denmark, which would give them the control of the exit to the Baltic and, to a certain extent, control over the North Sea too.

Eisenhower, at the same time as he was leaning over backwards to accommodate the Russians by surrendering his good chances of taking Berlin and Prague before the Red Army, was also urging Montgomery to get moving: 'Our arrival in Lübeck before our Russian friends from Stettin would save a lot of argument later on. There is no reason why the Russians should occupy Denmark.' Churchill, for his part, was concerned with more than just that limited political objective. That April, Montgomery's political master was thinking the unthinkable. While the war with Germany was still not yet won, the War Office planners were, at Churchill's specific order, busily considering the possibility of how they might tackle Russia in the event of a new war. Under the leadership of that man who had sobbed on Dunkirk beach, they were making an urgent study of the subject in case, as Sir Alan Brookes (as he is now) phrased it delicately, 'trouble should arise in our future discussions with her [Russia]'. Thus a third and final element was added to this strange battle. If Churchill were going to fight the erstwhile ally, Russia, would he not one day need the manpower that the present enemy, Germany, might provide? Would it be wise, therefore, to batter her into the ground completely so that there would be no hope of ever incorporating her in any future western coalition? Could Montgomery salvage any form of political organisation from the wreck of the Third Reich with which he could deal in a possible future crisis?

Long after the war, the American historian Martin Blumenson, the partisan of Eisenhower and Patton, wrote of Montgomery: 'Well-schooled, well-trained, experienced, Montgomery was competent, adequate. He was not great . . . He is, I think, vastly overrated, the most overrated general of World War Two.' Well, in those last days of the Second World War in Europe, that 'vastly overrated general' was going to fight one of the strangest battles of the twentieth century: one which would involve beating the Germans, yet not beating them so soundly that they could not rally to the western cause, if the need arose; and which at the same time ensured without bloodshed that the Russian allies did not cross the line of the Elbe. In this battle, despite his weaknesses and limitations, Montgomery would show that he had every claim to be accepted, without cavil, as Wellington's heir.

BOOK ONE: DECISION ON THE ELBE

THURSDAY 12 APRIL – SUNDAY 22 APRIL 1945

'There is only one thing worse than fighting with allies –
and that is fighting *without* them!'

Winston Churchill, March 1945

1

'You're on your way to Berlin!'

I

The simple radio signal electrified the headquarters of the leading American division – the 2nd Armored, nicknamed 'Hell-on-Wheels'. At last on this Thursday night, the division had reached the final natural obstacle barring the Allies' path to the greatest prize of them all – the German capital, Berlin! Now all that stopped them from racing to the heart of the dying Reich was a mere couple of hundred yards of water. Final victory was within grasping distance.

On the high ground east of the little riverside town of Schoenebeck, the dust-covered American Sherman tanks ground to a halt. Gratefully the weary drivers switched off their engines. It had been a long day. They had been marching and fighting to achieve this objective ever since 6.30 that morning, taking 1,700 German prisoners in the process. Stiffly the men of the 2nd Division's Combat Command B , led by Colonel Paul A. Disney, got down from their vehicles and stared at the river, the angry burr of machine guns and the crack of enemy guns ahead.

While his men smoked and talked in hushed tones, the commander of the point, Major James Hollingsworth, studied the position through his binoculars. The Major looked like something out of a Hollywood B-movie, with his twin Colt pistols strapped low to his hips and a Thompson sub-machine-gun slung over his shoulder. But Hollingsworth's appearance was not all show. He had seen plenty of action in these last two years in Africa and Europe and it was said of him that he had personally killed 150 enemy soldiers. Only three hours before he had shot and killed two SS men who had had the audacity to attempt to hold up his advance. No, Hollingsworth was no mere poseur.

Now, tired as he was, he was excited by the sight of a bridge still

25

standing across the river. The enemy had not yet blown it because they were still using it themselves, urgently attempting to evacuate their own armour across it before it was too late. Hollingsworth stared hard at the single-span bridge, mind racing. It was packed with German troops in their vehicles, the tanks and wood-burning *Wehrmacht* trucks crawling along nose-to-tail, their shapes camouflaged from the greatly feared Allied fighter-bombers – *Jabos* the Germans called them. God, if he could only take that column of Krauts by surprise and capture the bridge! It would mean promotion and a decoration, he knew that for certain.

Only two days before, his CO, Colonel Disney, had been summoned to the forbidding presence of Divisional Commander-General Isaac White. White, the commander of the US Army's biggest armoured division, which formed a column 72 miles long when it moved, had not wasted words. Disney had barely had time to salute before White snapped, 'Right, take off east!'

Colonel Disney, who was accustomed to White's laconic orders, had been too worn after eleven days of constant fighting and marching to think straight. He had looked bleakly at the commanding general and stammered, 'But what's the objective, sir?'

White's answer had been equally laconic. 'Berlin!'

Now Hollingsworth, filled with White's and Disney's sense of urgency to be the first Allied troops to reach the German capital, wondered if he could not pull off the same sort of coup as the US 9th Armored Division had done on the Rhine the month before. The tankers of the Ninth had captured the railway bridge at Remagen on the run before the surprised German defenders had had time to blow it up. They had made it 'the most famous bridge in the world', as the correspondents had headlined the exciting news.

Standing there on the heights while his men rested, Hollingsworth realised that everything now depended upon speed. Hurriedly he briefed his two company commanders, Captains James Starr and Jack Knight. Hollingsworth did not know that the River Elbe had not been taken by storm for over a century and a half, but the knowledge would not have worried the tough Major. That April evening, history was unimportant; history was here and now.

'They're moving along the road running north to south into Bad Salzelmen,' he told his two subordinates. 'Then they swing east at the road junction, head into Schoenebeck and cross the bridge. Our only hope is to swing into Bad Salzelmen and grab the junction. Now here's what we'll do. When we get to the junction, your company,

Starr will peel off and block the road, holding the Germans coming up from the south.' Starr nodded his understanding. 'I'll join on the rear of the German column,' the Major continued, 'that has already swung east into Schoenebeck and follow it across the bridge ... Knight, you come up behind. We've got to get that bridge. *And by God, we're going to do it!.'*

'Turn 'em over!' Hollingsworth yelled into his tank mike as he stood in the turret of his Sherman five minutes later. All along the column his drivers gunned their engines. Blue flame spurted from the exhausts of the 30-ton monsters. There was a rusty creak. The tracks started to move. The first tank lurched forward. They were on their way. Now everything depended upon them capturing the Elbe bridge.

Hatches battened down, the gunners tensed behind their weapons in the green-glowing turrets, the American tanks hit Bad Salzelmen. Before the surprised Germans could react, the leading Shermans were already through. At the same time, Starr's men commenced their feint. Abruptly everything was noise and confusion.

On the bridge, the fleeing Germans began to speed up. They knew now that the 'Amis', as they called the Americans, were coming. But unknown to the alarmed enemy, the first of Hollingsworth's tanks were tucked in neatly at the rear of the German column. Would the daring attempt to fool them and seize the bridge by a *coup de main* succeed? Hollingsworth prayed that it would.

Hollingsworth's tank swung round a corner. Someone gasped. A German Mark IV tank was waiting for them there. But Staff Sergeant Cooley, Hollingsworth's gunner, was quicker. He jerked the electrically operated turret round. The Sherman trembled. A long yellow flame stabbed the darkness. A white blob, which was an armour-piercing shell, raced towards the German. The Mark IV slammed into the nearest wall as if propelled by some gigantic fist. Almost immediately it started to burn.

But it had served its purpose. As Hollingsworth's tank rattled by the burning German, the enemy began to react. German infantry armed with the one-shot, deadly enemy missile-launcher, the *Panzerfaust*, popped up from every alleyway and commenced firing at the Ami tanks. Here and there Shermans rolled to a halt, burning or with gleaming silver holes skewered in their metal hides.

Hollingsworth's luck held, however. The Sherman continued to roll ever forward. Now the single-span German bridge was only two

27

hundred yards away. He was going to do it. Peering from the observation slits in the turret, the Major could see that the entrance to the bridge was defended by a maze of 6-foot-high concrete walls. It was a primitive but effective means of defence. The walls would slow any attacking tank down to walking pace. The approach would be like some kind of deadly obstacle race.

Hollingsworth made a snap decision. He sprang from the turret. Pistol in one hand and outside mike in the other, he started directing his driver through the maze while at the same time directing Sergeant Cooley's fire. Yard by yard the lone tank, guided by the brave officer, started to crawl forward.

Suddenly a thin stab of flame split the growing darkness. Metal struck metal. A solid-shot shell howled off the cobbles to Hollingsworth's front. Razor-sharp slivers struck Hollingsworth in the face. He yelped with pain and reeled back, bleeding heavily and blinded by his own blood.

With an impatient jerk of the hand holding the pistol, the Major freed his eyes of the blood. He continued directing the tank. Abruptly a jeep loomed up out of the fog of war. Too late he attempted to get the driver to avoid it. To no avail. The Sherman smacked into the little vehicle. The road was effectively blocked.

Cursing angrily the Major abandoned the trapped tank. He whistled up his armoured infantrymen. Doggedly, leaning forward as if they were advancing against a stiff wind, they fought their way forward, fighting from barrier to barrier. But Hollingsworth's proverbial luck was beginning to run out now.

They were a mere 60 yards from the bridge. But the Germans were fighting back stubbornly. They, too, knew the vital importance of this bridge over the Elbe that led to Berlin. The night air was thick with sudden death. Fifty yards to go. Abruptly a pain like that of a red-hot poker bore into the Major's knee. Blinded by the blood pouring from his head wound, sickened by the agony of his new wound in the knee, feeling the strength ebbing from his body by the second, he carried on for another few paces. Then he couldn't take any more. His knees sagged weakly beneath him like those of a new-born foal. 'Fall back,' he commanded as his men hesitated before the wall of enemy fire.

They started to withdraw while Hollingsworth took a last look at the bridge, only 40 yards away now, though at that moment it might well have been four thousand miles off. If he had been able to capture it, the 2nd Armored Division would have been in the capital of Hitler's vaunted '1,000 Year Empire' in eleven short hours. But that wasn't to be. Sadly he fell back with the rest of his weary, beaten force.

Two hours later, just before dawn on Thursday 12 April 1945, the Germans blew up the last remaing bridge in the American sector of operations along the River Elbe . . .

But the men of the 'Hell-on-Wheels' division did not give up easily. Hollingsworth's boss, Brigadier-General Sidney Hinds, knew just how vital it was to get across that last river before Berlin. He knew well, too, just how tough Divisional Commander Isaac White could be with failures. White had a contingency plan worked out at HQ for a dash to Berlin once the Elbe had been crossed. There at Headquarters there was a top-secret map broken into six phases, all leading to a huge blue swastika superimposed on Berlin and the one word – 'GOAL'. And he, Sid Hinds, was not going to be the one who let White down.

Hurriedly, after he learned of the failure of Hollingsworth's *coup de main* at the bridge, Hinds worked out a plan for an assault crossing of the Elbe. As he saw it, he would throw a couple of battalions of infantry across at the little township of Westerhusen, south of the great city of Magdeburg. Once they had crossed successfully, his engineers could commence building a pontoon bridge to bring up the division's armour and artillery. Of course, he realised it was going to be a risky business. The infantry would have to go across without any heavy weapons, especially anti-tank guns. All they could take with them would be the machine-guns and mortars of the heavy weapons companies, plus the ineffective American missile launcher – the bazooka. Once the Krauts learned of the American's presence they would surely zero in with their heavy artillery. Then his bridge might be destroyed and his infantry left stranded on the enemy side of the river – and for the time being there would be no support for them from the air, the Allied tactical air force bases were too far to the rear. But it was a risk Hinds was prepared to take. Every hour he delayed, he knew, lessened the chance of the 2nd Armored Division beating the Russians to the German capital.

Thus it was that, as the light began to fade on 12 April, two battalions of infantry started to make their way quietly across the slow-flowing river towards the enemy-held bank. Hinds watched the men of the 1st and 3rd Battalions of the 41st Armored Infantry Regiment go, his stomach tormented into a tight knot, waiting for the first dry crack of a

German 88mm or the obscene howl of their multiple mortar, the 'screaming meemie'. None came. The Germans remained strangely silent. By eleven o'clock that night two battalions were across and a third was following. Now it was up the to the engineers.

At quarter to eleven, the divisional engineers started to build their pontoon bridge in total uneasy darkness. At first they had hoped to use a British invention, 'Monty's Moonlight' – a means of bouncing searchlight beams off clouds to create an artificial moonlight. But there were no clouds and the cursing, sweating engineers had to work in an inky blackness, each man tensing increasingly as the pontoons stretched ever closer to the enemy side of the river. For out there in the middle of the Elbe, with no artillery or aerial support, even the thickest of them knew they were sitting ducks.

Again the Americans' luck held. By now they were already half-way across and the enemy had not fired a single shot at them. They were going to do it. The bridge which was vital for the success of this first American bridgehead on the Elbe continued to grow. Here and there the men began to wonder aloud what they would call the makeshift structure when it was finished; American military engineers dearly loved giving their bridges grandiose names. Finally it was decided that the completed bridge would be named after brand new Commander-in-Chief, President Harry S. Truman, and be called 'Gateway to Berlin'.

But unknown to the sweating engineers of the 2nd Armored Division, they, nor any other Allied unit, would ever use the bridge as a 'gateway to Berlin'. Another future president of the United States would see to that . . .

At 45, General Wenck, tough and handsome in an arrogant Prussian manner, was Nazi Germany's youngest army commander, though his 'army' was composed of 200,000 men, without heavy weapons or armour, who were hastily organised into makeshift divisions. But the majority of the General's young men were from the Reich's training organisations, NCOs and officers who were battle-experienced and used to improvisation under combat conditions.

Now Wenck, who was still strapped into a metal corset and pale after suffering a serious motoring accident in the East, acted decisively when the startling news reached him that the Amis had crossed the Elbe in some force. From his command post at Rosslau on the Elbe, he ordered that all available German artillery should commence shelling the American bridgehead and, in particular, the 'Gateway to Berlin' bridge, now nearing completion. At the same time he commanded all German *Volkssturm* in the area to attack and drive the invaders back across the river, And to give the elderly German Home Guard units more muscle, he commanded, too, that the division *Scharnhorst*, named after one of Germany's heroes of the battle against Napoleon, should lend their support in the coming counter-attack.

The hastily assembled force went quickly into action, although most of the young German soldiers involved knew in their hearts that the Reich had already lost the war. Eager for their appointment with destiny and supported by some eight assault guns, they set off to throw the Amis back the way they had come.

In the meantime long-range German artillery had begun shelling the pontoon bridge itself. Deadly air burst exploded over the engineers while large shells slammed into the water, drenching them with spouts of spray. Men screamed and, flinging up their hands, as if in despair, disappeared over the side of the makeshift bridge. Others dropped their tools and cowered behind whatever shelter they could find.

Hurriedly the American commanders called upon counter-fire in order to blast the German guns from their position. Smoke pots were rapidly spread out along the bank and ignited. Thick clouds of black–white smoke started to rise in the dawn air. Abruptly all was chaos, confusion and sudden, violent death.

Now the eager young men of the *Scharnhorst* attacked with the desperate *élan* of their kind, prepared to sacrifice their young lives, even at this juncture for 'People, Fatherland and Führer'. They caught the Amis digging in and completely without anti-tank weapons. Swiftly they broke through the Americans' perimeter.

The defenders' resistance started to weaken. Here and there GIs sprang from their foxholes and ran to the rear. In the confusion a score of completely exhausted Americans surrendered. A battalion commander abandoned his men and was found later on the other bank, claiming the battalion had been wiped out. Relentlessly the Germans, protected by tanks and thrusting a dozen captured Americans in front of them at bayonet point as human shields, pressed home their attack.

At the very last moment the 2nd Division's own artillery thundered into action and broke up the German counter-attack before the enemy reached the trapped battalions' final perimeter. But now the survivors, some 1,200 men out of nearly 2,000 who had originally crossed, were boxed into a narrow strip of land along the river bank.

The Germans turned their attentions on the headquarters group commanding the operation from the eastern bank of the Elbe. With the pontoon bridge a mere 25 yards away from its goal, a lucky salvo fell on Colonel Disney's command post and wounded the most senior officer on the spot. The confusion increased.

Now even the ever-optimistic General Isaac White, back at divisional HQ was prepared to accept the fact that things were going wrong. Optimism started to fade rapidly. His Chief of Staff signalled corps HQ that the situation up front was 'pretty bad'. The attacking infantry had lost '3/41 AIR complete'.[1] An hour later the same officer radioed, 'We have never asked for air support urgently before, but we need it now!'

Despite the fact that the weather – sunny and cloudless – was perfect for flying, the request was turned down. The air bases were still too far back for the fighter-bombers to comply with that desperate plea for help. The attackers would have to keep on fighting without any kind of aerial support. Rapidly the position on the far bank of the Elbe was becoming untenable . . .

Just after midday, White gave in. The order was issued that the bridgehead should be abandoned. Some of the infantry were so eager to escape the deadly trap that they threw away their equipment and actually attempted to swim the broad river. Others waited with growing anxiety their turn to be evacuated in this 'mini-Dunkirk', as one of them called it after the war, while their own artillery fired a smoke barrage across the Elbe and their ferries were knocked out one by one by the Germans, until finally there was one single DUKW left to complete the evacuation.

By late afternoon all the survivors had returned save for one company commanded by a young lieutenant trapped on the other side, and the proud US 2nd Armored Division – 'The Hell-on-Wheels' – had suffered its first retreat of the long bloody campaign in North-West Europe.

II

While the 2nd Armored Division had fought deperately to cross the Elbe and maintain its position there, its running mate the 83rd Infantry Divison had had an easy time of it. Under the command of

---

1 3rd Battalion, 41st Armored Infantry Regiment.

General Macon, the 83rd Division had raced the 2nd Armored for two weeks for the honour of crossing the Elbe first. Pressing any kind of vehicle into use, even a captured German steamroller, it had reached the river barrier just after its rival division. After a nasty little skirmish at the township of Barby, a few mile upstream of Schoenebecke, the 'Rag Tag Circus' had commenced its crossing of the great natural barrier.

Early on the afternoon of Friday 13 April, General Macon sent two battalions of his infantrymen across the Elbe in assault boats under the cover of a heavy smokescreen and against no opposition. As one of them described the operation jubilantly afterwards, 'It was just like a Sunday afternoon picnic with no fire of any kind.' Excitedly the regiment commander directing the operation, Colonel Edwin Crabill, strode up and down the west bank exorting his men. 'Don't waste the opportunity of a lifetime,' he shouted. 'You are on your way to Berlin!'

Neither Colonel Crabill nor his army commander, General 'Big Simp' Simpson, commander of the US 9th Army, knew that they were not on their way to the German capital. Three weeks before at his headquarters in a former French technical college at Rheims – 'the little red schoolhouse' the GIs called it – the Allied Supreme Commander, General Dwight D. Eisenhower, had decided that he wouldn't attempt to capture Berlin. As he told an astonished and dismayed General 'Blood and Guts' Patton some time later, 'From a tactical point of view it is highly inadvisable for the American Army to take Berlin and I hope political influence won't cause me to take the city. It has no tactical or strategic value and would place upon the American forces the burden of caring for thousands and thousands of Germans, displaced persons and Allied prisoners of war.' Patton had looked at Eisenhower aghast and expressed the sentiments of many of those who knew about this top-secret decision, especially the British. 'Ike', he had blurted out, 'I don't see how you figure that out. We had better take Berlin and quick – and on to the Oder!'

Now fresh infantry streamed across the Elbe and Crabill urged them on, crying excitedly, 'Don't wait for someone to tell you what to do! Get over there in any shape you can! If you move now you can make it without a shot being fired.' An enthusiastic General Simpson called his superior, Army Group Commander General Bradley, to tell him the news.

As yet Simpson didn't know of the Supreme Commander's decision not to attempt to take Berlin and to leave it to the Russians. Later Simpson explained that he felt then that his 'bridgehead was opposed by a kind of crust of newly formed outfits that were putting up some opposition; but with another pontoon bridge and another division or two across, we could have broken through. I think we could have been in Berlin in twenty-four hours . . . What was left of the German armies were over there against the Russians except this little crust that was around me, and a good part of that was pulled away about the time I was halted.' Simpson felt Berlin was his for the taking.

But Bradley, who more than anyone had helped to form Eisenhower's new policy on Berlin, felt personally threatened by Simpson's exciting news. The lantern-jawed, bespectacled Army Group Commander had come a long way in the last two years. Then he had not had the faintest inkling that by 1945 he would be commanding forty divisions, advising the Supreme Commander on what to do next, or be receiving phone calls – as he had the day before – from the British premier Winston Churchill, pleading with him not to retreat from the Elbe. He, Churchill, wished to retain as much as possible of eastern Germany in order to use the area as a bargaining counter with the Russians. This April 1945, in spite of the inherent modesty which had earned him his nickname 'the GIs General', he was acutely conscious of his prestige as the second most important American soldier in Europe.

Now Simpson's call threatened his new-found status. If Berlin were once again to become the Allies' chief objective, as it had been for the last two years right up to Eisenhower's surprise decision of 28 March 1945, inevitably the advance to the German capital would be under Montgomery's command. Since his own awkward, hesitant handling of the American armies in the Belgian Ardennes in December 1944, when he had been caught completely off-guard by the surprise German counter-attack and Montgomery had taken over command of his two northern armies, he had come to hate the little Englishman more than he did 'the other fellow', as he invariably called the German army.

If Montgomery again took over his 9th Army under Simpson, as he had done right up to the beginning of April, the kudos of final victory in Berlin would go to the opinionated Britisher, whom Patton called contemptuously 'the little fart'. His own drive to central Germany and Bavaria might even be stopped, and once again his personal reputation and the prestige of the US Army would suffer as it had done during the surprise attack into the Ardennes. That he couldn't tolerate!

Now, as an impatient Simpson waited for a decison for his 9th Army, Bradley called Eisenhower and told him the news of the 83rd's firm bridgehead on the Elbe at Barby. To his alarm Eisenhower seemed to be in the process of changing his mind on the subject of Berlin, and Bradley knew the Supreme Commander well enough by now to realise that he could reverse decisions very easily. It was one of his bad habits. Now 'Ike' asked, 'Brad what do you think it might cost us to break through from the Elbe and take Berlin?'

Bradley did some quick thinking, his mind racing, the alarm bells jingling. 'I estimate', he said finally, 'that it might cost us 100,000 men.' Eisenhower was silent and Bradley guessed he was staring at the casualty chart which hung prominently in the L-shaped map room in the Supreme HQ.[2] It would show that the Allies were taking extremely light casualties in the drive east. Indeed they were the lightest of the whole campaign in North West Europe.

Hurriedly, as if trying to convince Eisenhower, Bradley added, 'It would be a pretty stiff price to pay for a prestige objective, especially when we know that we've got to pull back and let the other fellow take over.' He meant the Russian allies, who, it had been agreed, would take over East Germany as their zone of occupation after peace was declared.

The Supreme Commander did not comment. Instead, after exchanging a few more unimportant remarks, he finished the conversation and hung up, leaving Bradley a worried man. What was Eisenhower going to do now?

This indecision at the top was unknown to the men currently fighting on the other side of the Elbe and valiantly attempting to extend the bridgehead won by the 83rd Division. The 2nd Armored had sent other troops across. They had been followed by a regiment from the 35th Infantry Divison. By now the bridgehead had been extended to a depth of five miles and although the occasional German fighter came hurtling out of the sky, cannon and machine-guns blazi ,g, the American positions were not otherwise under attack. In the bridgehead nobody doubted that the 83rd Division would be able to break out and drive for Berlin at will. All the men needed was the green light from above.

But still that green light did not arrive. For already Eisenhower was reformulating his plans and once again they did not include Berlin. On Sunday morning Simpson was hurriedly summoned to Bradley's HQ in Wiesbaden. 'I've got something very important to tell you,' Bradley told 'Big Simp' over the scrambler phone, 'and I don't want

2   That chart is still there in 'the little red schoolhouse'.

to say it on the phone.' Mystified, Simpson boarded his own plane, leaving his 9th Army staff already working on an optimistic plan for the future attack on Berlin, which included the key phrase 'to enlarge the Elbe River bridgehead to include Potsdam'. (Potsdam is a suburb of Berlin.)

An hour later he arrived at Wiesbaden Air Field,[3] still littered with the wreckage of *Luftwaffe* Heinkels and Focke-Wulfs. Bradley was waiting for him. With surprising formality for two men who had known each other as junior officers for years before the war, Simpson saluted and then they shook hands.

Bradley got down to business immediately. 'You must stop on the Elbe,' he said baldly, though later Simpson thought his old comrade was oddly embarrassed. 'You are not to advance any further in the direction of Berlin . . . I'm sorry, Simp, but there it is.'

The tall lean commander of the Ninth Army, who kep his balding head closely shaven, could hardly believe his own ears. 'Where in hell did you get this?' he demanded hotly.

Bradley passed the buck neatly. He looked up at the other officer from his steel-rimmed GI glasses. 'From Ike,' he retorted.

Simpson was too stunned to remember much of what was said after that. 'All I could remember', he recalled later, 'was that I was heart-broken and I got back on the plane in a kind of a daze.'

As the plane flew northwards over the war-torn North German plain, all he could think of was 'How am I going to tell my staff, my corps commanders and my troops? Above all, how am I going to tell my troops?' By the time he reached his HQ the exceedingly tall, almost emaciated commander had composed himself somewhat. He told the war correspondents attached to his HQ, who had been alerted that something big was in the offing, 'Well, gentlemen, here's what's happened. I got orders to stop where we are. I cannot go to Berlin!'

There were murmurs of disbelief from the assembled journalists, followed by words of sympathy for the obviously shaken 9th Army commander. Someone exclaimed, 'That's a hell of a shame, sir!'

Simpson's face hardened. 'These are my orders,' he said, 'and I have no further comments to make.' Thereafter he fled to his own HQ.

Now he had to tell his men. An hour later he was on the Elbe himself, after informing his corps commanders what had transpired at Wiesbaden.

---

3 The same airfield is in US military hands to this very day.

On the Elbe he visited the headquarters of the weary 2nd Armored Division. Here he bumped into an exhausted Brigadier-General Hinds, who the day before had seen the cable of a cable-ferry he had had built across the great river snapped by an unbelievable million-to-one shot from a German artillery piece.

Hinds looked at a sombre-faced Simpson, worried that the latter might be angry at his command's slow progress over the Elbe. 'I guess we're all right now, General,' he said apologetically. 'We had two good withdrawals. There was no excitement and no panic and our Barby crossings are going good.'

'Fine,' Simpson said, repressing his rising emotions. 'Keep some of your men on the east bank if you want to.' Hinds looked up at him puzzled. Simpson explained. 'But they're not to go any further. This is as far as we're going.'

Hinds looked shocked. 'No sir,' he said stubbornly. 'That's not right! We're going to Berlin.'

As Hinds recalled after the war, Simpson seemed to struggle to control himself. He managed to do so; he had years of training in repressing his emotions. 'No,' he said finally, in a flat dead voice, 'we're not going to Berlin, Sid. This is the end of the war for us . . .'

'Big Simp' Simpson was right. His 9th Army would sit out the remaining three weeks of the Second World War, 300,000 thousand fighting men doing nothing while the Russians occupied Berlin, that capital which Eisenhower had once called 'the glittering prize'.

Now, the River Elbe and what lay beyond – Holland, North Germany, the Baltic, Denmark and Norway – would be left to the British Army and Field Marshal Bernard Law Montgomery.

III

In that second week of April 1945, when the American attack on the Elbe was finally called, Field Marshal Sir Bernard Law Montgomery, commander of the 21st British Army Group, located in his tiny tactical HQ in the middle of nowhere, was a slightly confused and a considerably angry man.

At the beginning of the month the small, beak-nosed Field Marshal, who had the British upper-class difficulty with his r's and whose sloppiness in military dress had occasioned criticism from King George VI himself, had thought that Berlin was to be the main objective of the Anglo-American final drive into the Reich. As his own forces, and Simpson's US 9th Army still under his command, were the closest to the enemy capital, he had assumed, too, that he undoubtedly would lead the attack. He had been in for a shock. For Eisenhower had startled him by writing that 'that place [Berlin] has become, as far as I am concerned, nothing but a geographical location'.

Four days after Eisenhower had informed him of his drastic change of strategy, which seemingly had not had the approval of the Joint Chiefs of Staff, Eisenhower had taken the US 9th Army from him. Abruptly his own forces had been reduced from seventeen British and Canadian divisions and one Polish division, which, as he noted cynically, had 'liberated a concentration camp of 1,700 Polish women south of Winschoten and have made very little progress since then'. While Simpson of the Ninth and his well-equipped troops were now to sit on the Elbe twiddling their thumbs and doing nothing, his armies were suddenly down to half their original size and – apparently – without a mission, save to guard the flank of the American armies further south. What was he to do?

'He was moody that month,' Major Howarth, the newest of 'the Master's' liaison officers, who had come to Montgomery's tactical HQ in February 1945 straight from his infantry regiment, recalled; 'not about little things, but about something big of which we were not aware. He rarely visited our mess as he had done of old and spend the evening chatting to us. He kept very much to himself in those last days.'

That moodiness, which spoiled for him even the attraction of the only 'home' he knew that year, – his small TAC HQ, with his adoring 'eyes and ears' (the name had given to his keen young liaison officers), the nightly chats where no punches were pulled on either side, and then to bed precisely at ten o'clock with a glass of warm milk – stemmed undoubtedly from the problems facing him.

But it also undoubtedly came from the unkind trick of fate which now seemed to exclude him and his armies from the final great victory, which he felt was his due as the 'Victor of El Alamein'. After three black years of defeat he had led Britain to a great victory in 1942 when 'Ike', 'Brad', and 'George'[4] had been obscure American one- and two-star generals. Now the Americans had squeezed him out of the limelight and given him what amounted to a sideshow in the final battle with the Germans, while their troops captured the headlines in central and southern Germany.

---

4 Eisenhower, Bradley and Patton.

Of course, Montgomery being Montgomery could not see that, in the eyes of the Americans, he had many defects, both professional and personal. As a soldier he had made several major mistakes during the campaign in Europe. At Caen, on the Scheldt and at Arnhem, his conduct of operations had drawn criticism from the American generals, who found him too slow, too stubborn, too set in his ways. In their eyes, he was always fighting the 'Second Battle of El Alamein', preferring the 'set-piece attack' and eternally bothered about 'tidying up' the battlefield before he would proceed to the next objective.

But it was the little Field Marshal's personality which roused the American generals' ire most and which had directly contributed to the uneviable position in which he now found himself. Though he could never see it himself, Montgomery was fated – and always had been since his days as a young officer-cadet at Sandhurst – to seek self-destruction through his high-handed, arrogant behaviour: a man simply made to be misunderstood and then finally hated.

Every war produces its own heroes. But it had taken three long years of black despair and defeat for Britain to produce its own military hero: Bernard Law Montgomery.

But the bishop's son, who neither drank, smoked nor womanised, was a different kind of general from the bemedalled, glittering, red-faced general officers that the British Army usually produced at that time: men addicted to blood sports, good food, port and skirt-chasing. Even the Russian Marshal Rokossovsky was surprised when the envoy he sent to Montgomery's HQ to find out the Field Marshal's tastes reported that the Englishman didn't like cigars, dancing girls or wine. 'What the devil does he do all day?' exploded Rokossovsky, who never fought his battles without a mistress permanently installed at his headquarters.

Skinny and small – 144 pounds and 5 foot 8 inches – he didn't even dress like the traditional general. Indeed he was decidedly careless about his appearance, often wearing corduroy trousers and civilian shoes instead of army-issue items. More than once he made a public appearance carrying a ragged old 'gamp' – an umbrella. He was inclined, too, to wear the distinguishing headgear of some favourite unit, instead of the traditional general's redbound cap – the red beret of the Airborne, the slouch hat of the Australians, the black beret of the Tank Regiment, and all adorned, quite contrary to army regulations, with several regimental badges.

Nor did he treat his soldiers like the average British general of the time did. His troops saw him and they heard him. He would gather them round him everywhere he went, dispensing with the usual 'bull' of such visits, and tell them 'the form', as he called it: what he wanted them to do, and how they were going to do it with the least number of casualties possible. Although he was a strict non-smoker himself, he always had packets of cigarettes ready to distribute among the fighting troops. He ensured, too, that his men had plenty of drink – and women as well. Indeed, right at the beginning of the war he had narrowly escaped being fired because he had instituted brothels for the men of his division in order to lower the VD rate.

His soldiers liked him well enough and, thanks to the BBC, the popular press and his own personal style which was always good for copy, so did the public back in the United Kingdom. Whenever he made an appearance there he was generally mobbed by the civilians. But it was a different thing altogether with many of his military contemporaries, both British and American.

At first, back at the height of his popularity in 1943–44, most of this dislike and resentment expressed itself in back-biting and malicious tales, told when the little General was out of earshot. 'Admiral Ramsey of the Royal Navy and Montgomery are both torpedoed', they related, 'and thrown into the Channel. Ramsey pleads with Monty not to tell anyone that he can't swim. He would be the laughing stock of the Navy if it came out. Monty answers that he won't tell, if Ramsey doesn't reveal that he, Monty, can't walk across the water!'. In 1944, when it was officially announced that the insufferable Montgomery, who had sacked so many elderly Blimps during the course of his wartime career, was to command all ground forces in the coming invasion of Normandy, it was widely commented in London's club-land that the 'gentlemen are all now out; now the players are in!'

But once the Americans, in particular, got to know Montgomery – 'that insufferable little man' as an exasperated Churchill once called him – better in the months that followed the invasion, they were less inclined to hide their bitterness and resentment in sarcastic comment or anecdotes. Patton, whom earlier in Normandy Montgomery had made wait outside his caravan and whittle a stick until 'the Master' was ready to receive him, habitually called the Britisher 'a little fart'. 'Montgomery', he sneered to his cronies, 'has never won a battle since he left Africa and only El Alamein there. I won Mareth for him.'

By Christmas 1944, General Bradley was telling Eisenhower, his boss, 'You must know, Ike, that I cannot serve under Montgomery. If he is put in command of all ground forces you must send me back home.' One month later Eisenhower himself was warning Montgomery's long-suffering Chief of Staff Freddie de Guingand that he should tell his chief that it was 'either him or me'. If Montgomery persisted in demanding that he should take over the role of senior ground commander in North-West Europe then he, Eisenhower, would request his own recall in Washington.[5]

By March 1945 Montgomery's abrasive attitude made Eisenhower feel 'like a horse with a burr under his saddle' and he was no longer talking to the Field Marshal. By then Eisenhower had at last overcome his initial respect and admiration for the victor of El Alamein. Thus it was not difficult for Eisenhower's old West Point comrades – Bradley and Patton – to convince him that the final victory in Europe must go not to Montgomery in the north but to Bradley's American armies to the south. The results of Montgomery's control of American troops in the Battle of the Bulge and the vicious clash of personalities between Montgomery and the Americans had changed the whole remaining course of the war on the Continent and would, for that matter, change the post-war balance of power in Europe permanently. 'I can out-fight that little fart Monty, anytime,' Patton had once boasted. Now Patton and all the rest of the American top brass were having their revenge. The 'little fart' was being left totally out in the cold . . .

---

5   The kind of person that Montgomery could be is illustrated by the fact that he did not invite his long-term Chief of Staff to the great 1946 Victory Parade in London. Nor did he take de Guingand with him when he moved back to the War Office in 1946. All the same, the every-loyal de Guingand played a large role thirty-five year later in setting up the fund which paid for Montgomery's statue in London.

2

'Hier ist Bremen.'

I

At dawn the Germans counter-attacked.

For days the British infantry, some battalions now reduced from eight hundred to two hundred men, and desperately tired after three weeks' combat, had been fighting their way northwards to the twin German cities which barred their way – Bremen and Hamburg. Now it was the enemy's turn.

At first light, just as the sky was flushing the ugly white of the false dawn, the rumble of artillery, the ever-present background music of war, started to rise in volume. Far to the rear the 'heavies' crashed into action. Closer to the front the 25-pounders joined in the thunder of death, followed by the thump of 3-inch British mortars. The Germans now took up the challenge. Their dreaded 88mm cannon tore the dawn apart with their flat ripping sound. A 'moaning Minnie', the enemy's six-barrelled mortar, added its obscene, stomach-churning howl to the murderous cacophony. Machine-guns commenced chattering. The battle for the river-line was about to begin.

In their slit trenches, the men of the 43rd Division's 1st Worcestershire Regiment waited expectantly. Like most of the British infantry regiments, there were only a few of the veterans left who had landed with the division in Normandy. The men who were now defending their positions along the bank of the River Lethe were teenagers, some with only six months' service, just like the German 18-year-olds soon about to attack them. Now the war in Germany was being fought by boys!

Suddenly, startlingly, air bursts started to explode above their bent heads. Razor-sharp chunks of gleaming hot metal scythed the air. Soil showered down upon their helmets like heavy tropical rain on a tin roof. Men yelped with pain. Here and there a 'man', who had hardly begun to shave in earnest, slumped to the bottom of his hole, wounded or dead.

For exactly five endless minutes the German bombardment lasted. It stopped abruptly. There was a sudden loud echoing silence. Shaking the mud and rubble off their helmets and shoulders, the Worcesters raised themselves. NCOs asked for reports of casualties. Officers hissed they were to 'stand to'. Rifle bolts were jerked back. Magazines on the Brens were tapped to ensure they were securely in place. Grenades were hastily placed handily on the lips of the trenches. Safety catches were released with fingers that trembled ever so slightly. *The Jerries were coming!*

They came down a hill to the north-west. There were two hundred or more of them. In front there were two Mark IV tanks, their superstructure camouflaged by fir branches. Like the snouts of predatory monsters seeking their prey, the tanks' long, overhanging cannon swung from left to right. Behind them the German infantry grouped, bent-shouldered, in what they called the *Traube* (the grape), seeking whatever protection they could.

They came forward slowly at a measured pace, like countrymen coming home after a long day in the fields, their weapons clutched to their hips, bodies tense and expectant. Here and there an officer, cap tilted cockily to one side, shouted an order. But the Worcesters couldn't hear. The rusty clatter of the tank tracks was too loud. Stolidly the Germans plodded on, ignoring the shower of soil and pebbles flung up at them by the tracks of the tanks.

Someone shouted an order in English. Abruptly the British line erupted into violent action. Brens commenced chattering frenetically. Clicking their bolts back and forth, the young riflemen started firing. Here and there an officer stood up and took a deliberate aim with his antiquated .38 calibre revolver, knowing as he did so that the bullet couldn't carry more than a hundred yards. Still the action encouraged the men. The Germans came on.

Then they were there. Inside the slit-trench line. The German force, hastily thrown into a battle-group by the German paratroop commander General Erdmann, might be the last scrapings of the barrel, but they were determined to die rather than submit. Men swayed back and forth on the parapets, cursing obscenely, sweating like pigs with the effort of trying to slaughter each other. Almost immediately the Worcesters' two forward platoons were overrun. Lieutenant Smith, not much older than the boys he commanded, fell dead in the mud. The Germans pressed home their attack. D Company's right flank crumbled and broke.

Here and there a Worcester, eyes wide, staring and blank with

43

unreasoning fear, started to scramble from his hole and head for the rear. Desperately Lieutenant Crossingham rallied what was left of D Company and fought back. The German attack faltered. For a moment Crossingham thought the enemy had had enough; the steam was going out of their assault. But he was wrong. Their young officers, hardened and brutalised in the bitter battles of the Ostfront brooked no hesitation. They waved their machine pistols, crying hoarsely at their soldiers, and came on yet again . . .

For two long hours the battle raged on the bank of that obscure German river. But the Germans simply could not penetrate the defences of Major Hall's A Company of the 1st Worcesters. The dead lay everywhere and the bursts of machine-gun fire were punctuated by the pathetic cries of the German wounded as they called 'Sanitaeter!' But no stretcher-bearers came.

Finally the British had had enough. The Worcesters had lost enough good men in the ten-month battle that had brought them to this place; they wanted to lose no more. An appeal went to the divisional artillery commander. He relayed it to the corps artillery commander. With a frightening hush, the whole weight of the British 30th Corps' artillery descended upon the doomed Germans. For days ammunition had been coming forward by the truckload. But demands for shells had been few. Now the gunners of General Horrocks's 30th Corps let the unseen Germans have everything they had, consuming hundred of pounds' worth of shells by the minute.

That finally did it, The survivors of the last German attack on the Worcesters in the Second World War fled, leaving their dead and dying behind, sprawled out in the grotesque postures of those killed violently in battle.

That Sunday morning of 15 April 1945, as the 1st Worcesters started to advance again, timid old German men and women began to emerge hesitantly from the shattered woods on both sides of the road. With the aid of dumb show and signs, the humble folk, mostly clad in rusty black, asked the British officers if they could take away the dead in the little wooden carts they towed behind them.

The officers gave their approval. Slowly the civilians started to collect the dead. Mostly they were boys, clad in camouflaged jackets, given a carbine or machine pistol and thrown into battle; others were family men in their late-forties. A few, men of the German 2nd Marine Division, were in their twenties, former sailors without ships hastily transformed into infantry. Now they were all dead, sprawled out in the muddy, shell-cratered fields, their bloody limbs already going stiff.

As the civilians moved among them, their clothes already stained with blood, they cried silently, tears rolling down their toil-hardened, sunken faces. It was a sombre scene, as one eyewitness recalled later, 'pathetic in its utter futility even to the battle-hardened troops of the Division'.

But on this war-torn Sunday there was little time to reflect upon the futility of war. The 43rd Division, like the other divisions of General Horrocks' 30th Corps, were probing forward, attempting to open a route to the Corps' last major objective – the port of Bremen. As the day advanced, the 43rd's Somerset Light Infantry, supported by the Sherman tanks of the 13/18th Hussars, took the lead. As smoke shells started to descend upon the fields surrounding the little German town of Alhorn, the infantry commenced their attack.

The lead platoon advanced across the damp, flat German fields, broken at regular intervals by the irrigation ditches of the area. Before them lay the positions of the enemy. There the Germans crouched in their holes, dug in the sandy soil beneath the birch trees. Alhorn boasted a *Luftwaffe* field and they had been told to hold it. The *Fliegerhorst* would be used by the new German jets which could shoot down anything the Allies could send against them. So the defenders waited in their grave-like holes, crouched behind the thin, perforated barrels of their machine-guns which could fire a thousand rounds a minute.

Then came the old ritual of death which the British infantry had come to know so well since they had landed in Normandy in what now seemed another age. The machine-guns hissed into cruel life, as the PBI – the poor bloody infantry – emerged from the smoke. Men fell heavily. Others started to run, cursing hoarsely, brown and white tea mugs springing up and down on their packs. British artillery opened up. Great gaping, steaming holes appeared suddenly to their front. The infantry ran on, bayonets levelled, a mad gleam in their eyes, carried away now by the crazy bloodlust of battle.

Minutes later it was all over. Here and there a German was too late in raising his hands in surrender and yelling, '*Kamerad!*' He got a kick in the backside or a rifle butt slammed home into his face for his tardiness. Leaving a few of their number to shepherd to the rear their scruffy prisoners, including two bemedalled and scared *Luftwaffe* officers conscripted into the infantry, the rest pushed on.

They fought their way into Alhorn. In the lead Sergeant Carroll of the Somerset Light Infantry found himself blundering into a telphone exchange which had been abandoned hastily, the floor strewn with broken glass. Interested in 'souvenirs', but wary of booby traps, the NCO's gaze fell upon two electrical sockets. One was labelled 'Bremen' and it was still plugged in. The young Sergeant hesitated. Was it some kind of fiendish Jerry booby trap? But his curiosity overcame him. He plugged in the other socket and summoned up his skimpy German vocabulary.

'*Wer da, bitte?*'[1] he said hoarsely into the mouthpiece, while outside rifles still cracked intermittently.

For a moment nothing happened. Then very faintly, but still distinctly, a female voice answered, '*Hier ist Bremen.*'

Montgomery's armies had made their first contact with their next objective. Bremen was now three miles away . . .

II

On that Sunday 15 April there was no rest for the British and Canadian troops advancing up the narrow corridor formed by the River Ems to the west and the River Weser to the east. It was a crazy, confused day with moments of brutality, even savagery, going hand in hand with moments of intense relief, even happiness.

On the previous day Lieutenant Colonel Wigle, the CO of the Canadian Argyll and Sutherland Highlanders, which belonged to the Canadian 2nd Corps, had been killed in a first-fire fight just outside his own HQ in the small town of Friesoythe. Now, on this 'day of peace', the dead Colonel's sorrowing soldiers determined to take their revenge. For they believed Colonel Wigle had been shot treacherously by a German sniper dressed in civilian clothes.

Four days before, when other Canadian soldiers had felt they had been fired upon by German civilians during the fight for Soegel, they had sent in the engineers after the place had been captured. The latter had systematically set about burning down the whole centre of the village. Now the Canadians did the same at Friesoythe. Hurriedly the unfortunate civilians were booted out of their homes, chased on their way by threats and harsh cries of '*raus*' and '*mach' schnell*'. Some pleaded to be allowed to take some treasured possession with them – a clock,

---

1 'Who is there, please?'

a pot, even one of the thick feather beds of the area. But the Canadians had hardened their hearts. The civilians were not allowed to take a single piece with them.

Then as the handful of old men, women and children cowered at a safe distance, the Canadians went from house to house, setting alight the half-timbered, red-brick farmhouses, in which animal and man had lived side by side under the same roof for centuries. On this Sunday, it seemed, God had given up on the human race and had abandoned it to its fate . . .

But the suffering was not all one-sided this Sunday. As Colonel Crozier of the Manchester Regiment noted in his diary, '158 and 160 Brigades [of the 53rd Division to which the Manchesters belonged] are just played out: some battalions are less than 200 strong and they are very tired.' In fact the infantry of Montgomery's divisions, all of which had been in action since Normandy,[2] were exhausted and depleted. On that Sunday, when the 53rd Division's Welch Regiment were asked to find a detachment to guard a recently captured bridge at Weitzmuhlen, they literally could not find enough men to do the job.

But then the men of the 1/5th Welch had suffered heavy losses during the fighting ever since the breakout from the Rhine bridgehead, including the action at Rethem five days before. The village, newly captured by the Welshmen, had been counter-attacked by the bold young teenagers of the training regiment of the 12th SS Panzer Division, 'Hitler Youth'.

The 'Hitler Youth' Division had been virtually wiped out defending Caen in 1944, then it had suffered grievous losses in the Battle of the Bulge and in later battles in Hungary in January and March of 1945. But the new recruits lacked none of the division's old élan. Clad in their camouflaged tunics and helmets, firing from the hip as they came, the SS men had swept down Rethem's main street, setting fire to houses on both sides and inflicting 50 per cent casualties on the defending Welshmen.

Now the SS brought up a quick-firing 20mm cannon and started pounding the remaining houses in British hands with a hail of glowing white tracer shells. It was too much for the survivors, many of whom were already wounded. They began to fling away their weapons and raise their arms in surrender. At this late stage of the war, few of them felt like throwing away their lives for the sake of this God-forsaken German village.

2 Save the 52nd (Lowland) Division, which had entered combat in October 1944.

One of the 1/5th Welch, however, decided he was not going into the 'bag', even though Allied victory was just around the corner. He was Private Parry, who lay in the debris-littered gutter of the road, feigning death, as the jubilant young Germans rounded up their prisoners, searching them for precious cigarettes and the chocolate they craved.

According to his own story related to the press later, fifteen of his comrades were dragged out of one of the shattered houses and lined up against the nearest wall. One of their captors, a great swaggering brute, thereupon picked up an abandoned British Bren-gun. Clasping the light automatic rifle to his right hip, he fired cold-bloodedly into the British prisoners. They fell, most of them dead before they hit the ground. Thereupon the German murderer dropped the Bren, went over to where Parry lay feigning death 25 yards away and slammed his cruelly shod jackboot into Parry's side. Fortunately the Welshman's ammunition pouch deadened the blow and he could prevent himself from yelling out with pain.

Satisfied that all the 'Tommies', as the Germans called the British still, were dead, the SS left. After a tense half-hour making sure that they had really gone, Parry rose and stole back to his own lines, to tell his story.

One of the press present was particularly impressed by the sole survivor's account of the SS massacre. He knew about the 'Hitler Youth'. They had already been involved in one massacre of their prisoners back at Caen in 1944, when they had allegedly butchered a number of Canadians taken prisoner during the battle for the French city. Indeed their commanding general at that time, dashing SS General Kurt Meyer, known to his men as 'Panzermeyer', was currently in Allied custody waiting trial for war crimes. The pressman's name was Captain Brian de Grineau of the *Illustrated London News*.

Now in all good faith he started sketching an account of what a shocked, pale-faced Parry told him, which would become the centre-fold of the old-fashioned paper for its 21 April 1945 issue. On the left of the picture there was a large, double-roofed barn, and at the foot of it some British soldiers standing with their backs to the wall. Above the drawing there was the inscription: 'Defiant Welshmen being mown down in sweeps of gun.' In the centre a burly SS man with a gun at his hip was carrying out the dastardly deed and the caption read: 'SS Executioner with Captured Bren gun.' To summarise it all, Captain de Grineau entitled the study 'Lest We Forget: The Massacre of Welsh Prisoners at Rethem . . . An Episode Which Shocked the World'.

In fact, Private Parry's tale was a complete fabrication. Yet again one of those rumours had arisen, such as that which had occasioned the men of the Argyll and Sutherland Highlanders of Canada to set fire to Friesoythe on that same terrible Sunday. For reasons known only to himself Private Parry had invented the 'massacre at Rethem'. When on this day the lead battalions of the 53rd Division 1/5th Welch and 7th Royal Welch Fusiliers pressed towards Rethem, fighting against desperate resistance to the last, they found their 'massacred comrades'. The Germans of the 'Hitler Youth' had sent their prisoners to hospital and as the history of the Manchester Regiment noted, 'had scrupulously observed the laws of war'.

But Private Parry's tale had its effect. The news of the 'Rethem Massacre' spread among the troops via that amazing grapevine which existed, despite the lack of communications among the various formations of Montgomery's armies: 'The SS are still the killers they have always been . . . Don't get taken prisoner by the SS . . . And don't take an SS man prisoner even if the murderous young swine is prepared to surrender . . .' The seeds of what was soon to come had been sown.

III

While the men of the 53rd Division were entering Rethem for the second time to discover that Private Parry's story was a complete fabrication, to their east men of another British division – the 11th Armoured Division – were coming into first contact with the grim reality, the true face of Nazi Germany.

That Sunday afternoon the advance units of the Division's 159th Brigade, commanded by no-nonsense Brigadier Churcher, were surprised to find two German officers approaching them bearing white flags. Thinking this was the start of the surrender which the fighting men had been expecting for days now, firing was ordered to cease and the two Germans were hurriedly escorted to Brigadier Churcher.

The Germans told Churcher that they were asking only for a local ceasefire. They reported that immediately to the 11th Division's front there was some kind of large camp, filled with seriously ill civilians who should not be allowed to leave the camp in case they spread typhus. Now the Germans were prepared to withdraw from the whole area so that there would be no fighting around the camp.

Puzzled a little, and eager to get on with the war, Divisional Commander 'Pip' Roberts, the youngest head of a division in the British Army, contacted his boss, Corps Commander 'Bubbles' Barker, who during the great evacuation from Dunkirk five years before had gained some kind of reputation for himself by slitting the windpipe of a grievously wounded soldier with a razorblade and saving his life. Barker agreed to the 48-hour truce and thus the guns of the 11th Armoured Division fell silent for the first time in weeks, as the first British units started to approach this strange camp. Its name was – *Belsen*.

Up front with the tanks of the 23rd Hussars, Captain Derrick Sington, a former journalist and linguist, was in command of Loudspeaker Unit One: two men and a van equipped with a battery of enormous loudspeakers. It would be the job of the three German-speaking soldiers to make the first announcements to the inmates of this strange camp, which seemed to present a danger to everyone, friend and foe.

Driving with the tanks through the dark masses of dripping pines along the dead-straight road which led through the Lueneberg Heath, a popular pre-war holiday resort for the dwellers of the north's great cities, Sington's nostrils were assailed by a strange, pungent, nauseating smell, which he couldn't then identify. Later he found it was the stench of death: the stench of the charnel house which the great isolated camp had become. Later Sington would write: 'It reminded me of the entrance to a zoo. We came into a smell of ordure – like the smell of a monkey house.'

Now the young officer was primarily concerned with the reception awaiting him at the red and white striped pole which barred the entrance to the first concentration camp that the British had come across so far in the Second World War. There stood a group of immaculately uniformed Hungarian and German officers, led by a powerfully built SS *Hauptsturmführer* with a scar across one cheek. His name, Sington learned later, was Josef Kramer, and he was the camp commandant.

The enemy officers saluted when Sington got down from his van and stated in German, 'I propose to go in and make a loudspeaker announcement.'

Kramer frowned warningly. 'They're calm now,' he said. 'It would be unwise to risk a tumult.'

Sington ignored the comment. He snapped that Kramer should open the gate to the horrors beyond. The latter was taken aback. He said, 'I can't do that without authority from the *Wehrmacht* commandant.'

Again Sington ignored the SS officer. 'Stand on the running board,' he commanded. 'You have to guide us round the camp, stopping at suitable points to make loudspeaker announcements.'

Desperately Sington fought back his tears when he saw the condition of the starving, dying prisoners in their ragged pyjamas: men and women – and children too – from over half of Europe, dragged from their homes by force and transported to this terrible place to die. 'Now the tumult is beginning, ' Kramer said in apprehension.

In that moment a panicked German soldier started firing over the heads of the crowd surging forward to the loudspeaker van. Sington drew his own revolver and yelled at the German to stop firing – or else. He stopped, but as Sington wrote afterwards:

Suddenly a dozen striped figures jumped into the crowd, hitting again and again with sticks and packing case strips. No leaps in a ballet could have astonished me as did those kangaroo jumps. They were like prancing zebras, these creatures in broad-striped garments careering here and there, smiting to left and right, bending double with the impetus of the blows they struck . . . Half way across the road, I saw a thin creature on his back trying to ward off blow after blow from a thick stick.

These were the dreaded *capos*, those who, although prisoners themselves, kept order for the SS guards through brutality and blackmail. One word and a prisoner would be selected for immediate death instead of reaching the same end by slow starvation.

But their days and those of Kramer and his guards were now over. Standing up in his van, Sington announced, 'The Germans have nothing more to do with this camp. The camp is now under the control of the British Army.' As if to emphasise his point, Sington pointed to an inmate dying in agony on a pallet of straw and snapped to Kramer, 'Pick up that man and take him to the hospital!'

Kramer flushed. He stepped back a pace and seemed about to refuse. Sington covered the SS officer with his revolver. '*Pick up that man!*' he ordered once again.

Face crimson with fury, Kramer, the camp commandant for whom human life meant nothing, bent and picked up the dying man. By the time the camp was finally burned to the ground, Kramer would be begging to die himself.

But on that day, the Sunday of the liberation, eight hundred human beings died in Belsen . . .

Now Montgomery's front was news again. The correspondents who had abandoned the Field Marshal's troops over the last seven days because there was more 'copy' elsewhere on the American front returned to describe this first major Nazi death camp liberated by the Allies.[3] Leonard Mosley reported the scenes thus:

The British soldiers who took over Belsen looked around and what they saw made them mad with rage. They beat the SS guards and set them to collecting the bodies of the dead, keeping them always at the double; back and forth they went all day long, always running, men and women alike, from the death pile to the death pit with the stringy remains of their victims over their shoulders. When one of them dropped to the ground with exhaustion, he was beaten with a rifle butt. When another stopped for a break, she was kicked until she ran again, or prodded with a bayonet to the accompaniment of lewd shouts and laughs. When one tried to escape or disobeyed an order, he was shot.'

When another correspondent, David Woodward, arrived at the death camp and was being briefed by a senior officer, a sergeant came up and saluted smartly. 'Excuse me, sir,' he said, 'but Dr Klein wishes to be shot, sir.'

The doctor in question, a member of the SS, had been saved from lynching by the British but had been pushed down into the tangled mass of mortality in one of the death pits, where, as Leonard Mosley wrote, 'He waded round and round, mad hysteria upon his face, thigh-deep in bodies and sinking, as if in a quicksand.'

No wonder he requested he might be shot. But his request was refused and he lived to be interviewed by the veteran Australian correspondent, Alan Moorehead. 'You had better see the doctor,' his accompanying officer told the journalist. 'He's a nice specimen. He invented some of the tortures here. He had one trick of injecting creosote and petrol into the prisoners' veins. He used to go round the huts and say, 'Too many people in here. Far too many.' Then he used to loose off his revolver round the hut. The doctor has just finished interrogation.'

Moorehead was led into the doctor's cell. 'Come on, get up,' the sergeant in charge yelled. Moorehead saw a man lying in his own

---

3 The concentration camp at Nordhausen had been liberated by the Americans a few days before; it was small in comparison with Belsen, which held an estimated seventy thousand prisoners.

blood on the dirty floor of the cell. Somehow he managed to raise himself on the back of a wooden chair. Then he flung his arms wide apart and whispered, 'Why don't you kill me? Why don't you kill me? I can't stand any more.'

The sergeant was not impressed. 'He's been saying that all morning, the dirty bastard,' he commented sourly . . .

Montgomery, the professional soldier who had seen much of horror and death in his time – had he not been abandoned himself as dead in 1914 during the last battles in France? – was above resentment and revenge. He reported the capture of Belsen to the War Office and went to see the camp himself. Later he wrote to one of his correspondents, 'The concentration camp at Belsen is only a few miles from my present HQ. You have actually to see the camp to realise fully the things that went on: the photographs (enclosed) were all taken by a photographer from my HQ . . . The SS Commandant is a nice looking specimen,' he added sardonically.

Petty as he could be about his personal repuation, Montgomery lacked vindictiveness. Unlike Eisenhower, who after seeing his first concentration camp, rounded upon a nearby GI, 'Now you know what we're fighting for!', Montgomery was prepared to let lesser authorities deal with those responsible for perpetrating such terrible atrocities. His concern was fighting – and winning – the war.

For now, on this terrible Sunday, he had finally received his orders and directive for the rest of the campaign in North-West Europe from Eisenhower. Berlin was again 'off'. As Eisenhower wrote in his directive, 'Present bridgeheads over the Elbe will be secured but offensive operations beyond the Elbe will be undertaken only on later orders.' Bradley's entire front on the Elbe would become a holding front, tying up nearly a score of US divisions uselessly, while Patton would attack into Bavaria and Austria, where Intelligence believed (wrongly) that the Nazis would make a last-ditch stand in the mountains in something called 'the National Redoubt'. Meanwhile Montgomery's own 21st Army Group was to attack alone across the Elbe, seize Hamburg and Kiel, cut off the Danish peninsula and 'be prepared to conduct operations to liberate Denmark' as well as 'clearing western Holland, north-east Holland and the coastal belt and enemy naval bases and fortifications [Emden – Wilhelmshaven – the Friesian Islands] which threaten the approaches to Hamburg'.

It was a very tall order for the British 2nd and the Canadian 1st Armies which were under his command. Already both armies were desperately short of fighting men, especially infantry. In the ten-month-long campaign there had been a 100 per cent (and more in some divisions) turnover due to casualties in all the rifle platoons. Reinforcements were terribly scarce. Already Montgomery had been forced to break up two infantry divisons to supply the rest with men to fill the gaps in their ranks. Now Churchill had just called up 45-year-old men to serve in the Armed Forces and the desperate expedient had been taken of withdrawing divisions from the Italian front to bolster up the Canadian and British strength in Europe. Where was he going to find the strength to carry out Eisenhower's orders? Already he had signalled the War Office the previous day that 'The general picture in the Bremen area and on the Weser front is of very determined resistance to keep us away from Bremen and stop us crossing the Weser and Aller.' Now, with the Canadians diverted to seize northern Holland, he would be left with three British corps – three armoured divisions and seven infantry divisions – to capture Germany's two major ports, Bremen and Hamburg, the whole of North Germany beyond the Elbe, and Denmark: territory currently held by at least one and a half million German troops of various categories.

By now, of course, his fighting formations were very professional, easily an equal match for the Germans, behind whom they had lagged for years as soldiers. The majority of his battalion commanders were just over 30, with company commanders as young as 21, commanding 'men' still in their teens. But they were all expert in night fighting, infiltration, combat in woods, etc. – skills which up to now had been dominated by the Germans. Yet they were all tired, too, their ranks depleted by losses. For the most part they had been in constant action ever since the beginning of February 1945, a month in which the 1st Canadian Army alone had suffered nearly sixteen thousand dead.[4]

As Montgomery warned the War Office after he received Eisenhower's directive, 'Formations in 21 Army Group are nearly all of them getting very tired. They have been fighting continuously since 8th February and operations across the Elbe to the area Lübeck-Kiel will probably go very slowly'. He added, 'It may well be that we shall have difficulty between the Ems and Bremen.'

So the little Field Marshal, with the beaky nose and brilliant blue eyes, brooded this Sunday night over his cup of hot milk and biscuits in the solitude of his caravan, which had once belonged to an Italian

4 Of these over ten thousand were British, from the British formations coming under Canadian command.

general in the desert.[5] How was he going to carry out Eisenhower's orders with the scant forces at his command? And even if he succeeded, what would be the purpose? Wasn't the greatest prize of them all – Berlin – going to be left to the Red Army? And weren't political and strategic considerations being thrown out of the window simply because American generals were too concerned with their own vanity and prestige, pandering to the Great American Public? As his friend Colonel 'Simbo' Simpson had written to him recently from the War Office, 'I had hoped SHAEF (Supreme Allied Headquarters) had seen sense as regards plans. It really is frightful to think of all the lives being wasted to satisfy American public opinion. If the American public only knew the truth!'

An exasperated Montgomery knew they didn't, and they would never find out either if the American generals had their way. After the war – and victory in Europe – they would close ranks and keep the real reason for Eisenhower's drastic change of strategy to themselves. The Great American Public would be told that all had gone according to plan and, because their generals had given them a victory, they would be satisfied with that. They would question no further.

So he pondered and brooded out there in his caravan in the middle of nowhere, while less than a score of miles away from his tactical HQ, thousands of desperate young Englishmen, languishing behind barbed wire at the great *Stalag*, some of them having spent years in German captivity, willed him to push forward and finally release them from their long servitude.

At Fallingsborstel prisoner-of-war camp there was an RAF sergeant who had been shot down on 4 September 1939 on a bombing raid over Wilhelmshaven and had thus become Britain's number-one prisoner of war. There were men who had been captured at Dunkirk, Crete, Tobruk and half a dozen other places that had been the sites of British defeats until Montgomery had turned the tide at El Alamein. Some of them had starved in the winter of 1940, laboured in Silesian coalmines in 1942 and 1943, and undergone the death marches before the advancing Russians in 1944, marching through blizzards for weeks on end. In one group of sixty-eight men only thirty survived. Those who could march no longer were dropped at the roadside where they were left to die. Now the seven thousand of

---

5 Like most of Monty's possessions, it, too was 'organised'. Even the chamberpot beneath his bunk had been 'organised' in a French château right at the beginning of the campaign. But then Montgomery had lost virtually all his personal possessions in the 1941 blitz on Portsmouth.

them, many not much more than walking skeletons, waited for the final liberation; and it had to come *soon* before death overtook them.

IV

But there were others, too, about whom the brooding Field Marshal could have known nothing that Sunday night, who waited their liberation with tense expectancy. For while the British POWs at Fallingsborstel knew that death might come to them through starvation, but not through deliberate, swift violence, the men and women – and children – of Neuengamme concentration camp just outside Hamburg knew that their days were numbered. The German authorities could not afford another Belsen. At this stage of the war, virtually already lost, Berlin wanted no further concentration camp scandals; and there was only one way to prevent that. It was simple in its brutality. The inmates of Neuengamme KZ [6] would have to be 'liquidated' before the British arrived on the scene.

On 31 March 1945 the cousin of the Swedish king, Count Folke Bernadotte, had come to visit the secluded camp hidden away in the rural plains which supplied Hamburg with its vegetables and fruit. He was escorted through the buildings and huts which housed prisoners from a dozen different countries by the camp commandant, Max Pauly, who couldn't prevent the middle-aged Swede from stopping to talk with Danish and Norwegian prisoners, both Gentile and Jew.

From that day onwards Neuengamme and area became a central collecting point for all Norwegian and Danish prisoners in German hands. At a price, the Swedish Red Cross had obtained a kind of controlled freedom for their fellow Scandinavians (ironically enough Folke Bernadotte, who had negotiated that freedom for both Gentile and Jew, would be assassinated by a Jewish terrorist three years later in Palestine). But if the Danes and Norwegians were now almost free and being fed by the Swedish Red Cross, the remaining prisoners knew their fate was virtually sealed.

Now as the thunder of the British guns could be heard at Neuengamme, the Swedes brought up convoys of white-painted buses to evacuate the Danes and Norwegians, leaving the rest to what was to come. For those who still had the strength to think, there remained two alternatives. They could allow themselves to be put to death by

---

6 *Konzentrationsslagen.e.* concentration camp.

the SS or they could seize and hold the camp until the English came.

The remaining Jewish children, mostly French and German, were taken away to be the last of forty thousand men, women and children murdered in the camp's seven-year existence. Now the remaining ten thousand prisoners had to make a decision; it was already clear that Pauly had a plan worked out for them.

It was time for them to take their fate into their own hands. Over the last few months, the fit men in the camp had been organised into three secret battalions. There were twenty-one illegal weapons hidden about the place, plus three pistols. And the plan to overcome the 800-strong guard billetted in the SS barracks had been worked out to the last detail by a five-man 'military committee' headed by Red Army Major Vassili Bukreyev.

Bukreyev, shaven-headed and hard, an officer who had been captured during the great battles of Central Russia, was for immediate, armed action. He told the others that there was no time to lose, even if the English were virtually on the threshold of Hamburg and liberation was almost there. He was supported in his arguments by his fellow Russian committee members, who were now fearful that even if they were rescued from the Nazis they would suffer punishment at the hands of their own people for having allowed themselves to be taken prisoner by the 'Fritzes' in the first place. They would have to show the feared green-hatted officers of the Party's secret police – the NKVD – that they had actively worked towards freeing themselves.

But the other committee members, although realising the imminent danger, still thought the time for an armed rising had not yet come. As one of them noted in his diary, 'The meeting was very hectic. The Russians insisted that we should act as soon as possible. We had to take advantage of the current lack of purpose of the Camp Commandant and his staff. If we didn't then we were condemning the whole camp to death.' The diarist, however, the Czech doctor Bogumil Doclik – who had been forced by the Nazis to carry out illegal operations on the imprisoned Jewish children, such as cutting out their glands – agreed with the majority that they should wait a day or so longer before they did anything drastic.

Perhaps the British might make a surprise attack around the flanks of the great part of Hamburg and rescue them? Or perhaps the Germans might simply surrender. The camp was already flooded with wild rumours that the Nazi prominenz were holding secret talks with the Allies' representatives in Sweden and Switzerland. Hadn't Bernadotte managed to talk the Germans into releasing the Danes and the

Norwegians? Why should they risk their lives now when liberation was in sight and they had survived so many hardships for so long?

So, to the chagrin of Major Bukreyev, nothing was done. The arms remained hidden and the camp's ten thousand surviving inmates slumped in their bunks, listening to the rumble of the barrage in the distance and waiting for the British on the other side of the River Elbe to come and free them.

What they didn't know was that it would be another two weeks before Montgomery's weakened forces could cross the river which divided them from freedom, and that, in the end, they would never be liberated by the British. Instead, in the greatest disaster of German maritime history, the British would unwittingly slaughter them. They would die as prisoners – violently. A great tragedy was in the making . . .

3

'Holy catfish ... What a mess!

I

On Monday 16 April 1945 the 'Nijmegen Home Guard' finally reached its objective. For six dreary, cold months the British 49th Infantry Division had been fighting a static war just short of the ruined Dutch city of Arnhem. There back in September 1944, a confident Montgomery, overruling all objections, had hope to end the war by 'bouncing the Rhine' in – for him – a tremendously bold airborne operation. That operation had failed miserably and the British 1st Airborne Division which had attempted to capture the bridge across the Rhine at Arnhem had been virtually wiped out. Now, this Monday, the men of the 49th Division, which had been in Holland ever since that failure (so long that they had been nicknamed 'the Nijmegen Home Guard' by the rest of the Army), finally settled the score and captured the site of that historic débâcle.

At the beginning of April, when the attack into Holland had first been mooted, there had been objections. These came not from the Dutch Government in exile in London, which wanted to return to the Hague as soon as possible, but from the Occupied Dutch themselves and the military, who were not quite sure how they were going to mount the operation. As Colonel C.P. Stacey, the official Canadian Army historian, expressed it after the war, 'It was questionable if it would be a kindness to the folk of western Holland to turn their country into a battlegound . . . and the Germans were likely to flood still more land as measure of defence or spite.'

The military were already worried, too, by the strength of the German defence. The depleted 1st Canadian Army to which the 49th Division belonged was an all-volunteer force and there were few volunteers coming from Canada now.[1] Indeed Montgomery had

---

1   In Canada itself there had been riots when an attempt had been made to introduce conscription In particular, the French Canadians opposed any form of call-up.

been forced to bolster up the Canadians' strength by withdrawing a whole Canadian corps – General Foulkes' 1st – from Italy, where it had been fighting since 1943 and was hard-pressed for riflemen to fill the gaps in its own ranks. Yet opposing these Canadian troops, some two corps, perhaps 100,000 men, there were 120,000 enemy troops under the command of the highly skilled German commander *Generaloberst* Johannes Blaskowitz, a hardliner prepared to fight to the end.

He was not alone either. Some fifty thousand of his troops were Dutchmen, including a whole Dutch SS division – the 34th SS Division (*Landsturm Nederland*). These Dutchmen, who had volunteered for the German Army out of conviction, opportunism or merely for adventure, knew there would be no future for them in a liberated Holland. Green as they were, they knew intimately the country over which they would fight and they would make the Allies pay dearly for any gains they might make. Understandably, therefore, Montgomery, worried about numbers and the strength of the German-Dutch opposition, hesitated at launching a major operation.

Finally, on 12 April, he gave the green light and the men of the 'Nijmegen Home Guard' started crossing the Rhine in force, heading for the industrial suburbs of Arnhem in brigade strength. Aided by tanks from the Canadian 5th Armoured Division and an assorted collection of 'funnies' from the British 79th Armoured Division, tanks which could throw bridges across ditches, clear minefields, blow up pillboxes, lay tracks,etc. (many of them the brainchild of no less a person than Prime Minister Churchill himself), the Yorkshire infantrymen made steady progress into the ruined city.

Fighting was severe. The Yorkshiremen fell heavily on all sides, but with fixed bayonets they pressed home their attack, while above them Typhoon fighter-bombers – 'Tiffies' the grateful infantry called them – zoomed in at 300 hundred miles an hour, firing salvo after salvo of their deadly rockets at the German defences, which had been built up steadily since the fiasco of the previous September.

Hand-to-hand fighting broke out. The Germans counter-attacked with a company of infantry supported by three French-built tanks. The Canadians reacted by bringing up their own armour. For the first time the Canadians, who had felt themselves second-class citizens in Italy, deprived of the most recent equipment, were armed with Shermans bearing 17-pounder cannon which, as one of them boasted, 'could thread needles . . . at 3,000 yards'.

Canadian Captain MacDonald of the 5th Armoured Division's 11th

Armoured Regiment, trundling into battle in one of the new Shermans, the upper deck packed with British infantry, found, however, that the huge monster gun was little use against the last-ditch defenders. They were prepared to die, for the future held no hope for them.

After clearing away a bunch of Dutchmen barring his progress with a few well-aimed rounds, he found that 'one had the guts to stay behind his bazooka near a railway embankment'. The lone SS man, still fighting when by now most Germans had surrendered, waited with his one-shot *Panzerfaust*; waited until the Sherman filled the primitive sight of this cheap German missile-launcher. Then he fired. The hollow shot slammed into the side of the tank. The 30-ton monster rocked as if it had been struck by a gale. It reeled to a halt. But, fortunately for MacDonald and his crew, the British infantry of the 49th Division had taken the full impact of the shot. When he opened his turret the bloody sticky carnage of what was left of the infantry section, a mess of shattered, red limbs and twisted weapons, appalled and sickened him. 'Holy catfish,' he recalled many years later, '*what a mess!*'

Despite the casualties which the leading infantry battalions – the Lincolns, the Duke of Wellingtons, the York and Lancs – were suffering, they fought on doggedly into Arnhem, that city which the previous year had held the attention of the whole western world for that terrible third week of September. The Duke of Wellingtons captured what was left of the city's zoo, and its C Company became the 'involuntary custodians' of the place. In vain, they looked for a polar bear to present to the division's commanding officer (for the divisional insignia featured just such an animal). But most of the zoo's animals had died of starvation or during the battle, including 'an elephant [which] had succumbed to shell-shock as a result of the heavy bombardment of the immediate area of the zoo'.

But although the fighting for Arnhem was almost over now, the war still claimed its victims from these young men in their moment of victory. Private Reg Dunkley, one of the few 'veterans' of Normandy (he was exactly 19), was chosen with six others to recce the wood to the battalion's immediate front.

'So off we went, seven of us in line abreast,' he recalled afterwards. When the enemy spotted the seven Normandy veterans shells started to rain down upon them. They turned and ran back the way they had come. The sergeant in charge was hit and killed. Next instant Dunkley was hit himself. 'I knew I was wounded. There was a singing and ringing in my ears. I knew my right kneecap had gone. You know, at

the dentist's you can feel the grating of the instrument on the bone –
so I could feel my kneecap grating; and it wouldn't go where I wanted
it to. I couldn't speak.' Later the doctors were forced to amputate his
right leg above the knee. But the young veteran's suffering did not end
there. Twenty years later he suddenly suffered two epileptic fits. 'My
wife was terrified the first time. I just went mad in bed.' The shrapnel
which had struck him that April day so long before had affected his
brain. Now, nearly a half a century later, the one-legged veteran, a man
in his sixties, still takes three tablets a day to control his fits.

Not far from where Private Dunkley lay paralysed, unable to speak
that day, listening to the stretcher-bearers remarking callously 'the
sergeant's gone for the chop', men of the 1st Leicesters were suffering
similarly. Private Bob Day, a veteran of the Salerno landings in Italy
who had already been wounded there, felt he had never experienced
anything like it during his combat career as he cowered, hugging the
ground, with the rest of his section:

Great jagged bits of metal were flying all over the place. When mercifully the firing
ceased, I looked up in a daze, scarcely believing I was alive. Then I heard screams
coming from the other side of the dell and I could see a young officer with one of his
arms nearly torn off . . . I turned to have a word with the Bren gunner and saw that he
was still leaning against the bank with his head bent forward. He appeared to be
sleeping. So I nudged him. But he was dead. There was a tiny hole in his back and he
must have been killed instantly. The irony of it was that the barrage hadn't come from
the Jerry guns but from our own. I can't remember his name, but he was a quiet
pleasant fellow who had told me only the day before that his wife had just had a baby.

Yet another young man had died violently, never to see the child he
had sired . . .

Matthew Halton of the Canadian Broadcasting Company followed the
troops that Monday through a town which was 'a deserted burning
shell'. Fires were blazing and the British were burying their dead. 'The
whole thing was a dreary disheartening sight – another of the destroyed
towns of a beautiful continent.'

Engineer soldiers were blowing up obstructions. Bulldozers roared.
Motor cycles bounced back and forth. Tanks and Bren-gun carriers
rattled forward to the motor highway which linked the newly captured
town with Rotterdam. 'All was the noisy clanking machines and
paraphernalia of war,' the reporter thought.

Then 'a lone Dutchman, the first civilian we had encountered' came

slowly down the long street towards the little group of Canadians. 'He
shook hands. "You have come back," he said quietly. Just that.' What
more could he say? Arnhem was ruined. The war was over for him. In
due course the British would feed him and the rest of the civilians
who had survived two major battles in the last six months. But
'butcher's bill', paid both by soldier and civilian, had been high.

Further north that day, at the newly liberated Dutch town of
Zwolle, there was the same mood of relief and resentment in the air as
Robert Dunnett of the BBC entered with the Canadian liberators.
Dunnett watched as the Dutch rounded up the small town's three
hundred collaborators, marching them down the main street towards
the former Gestapo HQ, the girls who had been 'too kind' to the
German soldiers with their heads shaven and their blouses ripped
open to show the bare flesh below. Some even had swastikas crudely
painted on their chests.

Then, when the crowd spotted the British correspondent and his
driver in their jeep, they surged forward and bombarded them with
questions. 'A young man wanted to know if potatoes, bread and
beans were rationed in England. Another if London had been badly
damaged by bomb or rockets . . . A girl chipped in to ask, "Is Deanna
Durbin still alive – and Shirley Temple?" . . .'

That Monday the mood everywhere in newly liberated South
Holland did not seem to be one of mere triumph that the Germans
had been beaten at last. There was a sombre undertone to victory.
Everyone had suffered too much and too long. As for the Dutch, too
many of them had succumbed to the heady blandishments of National
Socialism and Hitler's vaunted '1,000 Year Reich'. Soon there would
have to be a bitter reckoning between Dutchman and Dutchman. The
British and the Canadians, for their part, had fought for this piece of
wet, soggy, empty terrain for seven long months and they felt no great
sense of elation now that it was theirs at last.

Nosing round the ruins in the growing darkness that evening, as the
battle still continued in the distance, future writer Alexander McKee
blundered into a mined Dutch hamlet, now inhabited solely by the
dead: Germans, British and Canadians, some who had died this day
and others who had fallen six months before at the First Battle of
Arnhem. He came across a dead German from that battle, 'small and
like a mummy, all huddled up'. It was 'just a mess. It has no head – the
bones of the spine protrude from its mildewed collar; the thigh bones
are visible and bare of flesh; but his legs where the trousers are torn
away or ripped by rats, have a cold, mummy-like sickly covering that

was once human flesh.' Attached to the dead German was a 'black metal object, obviously a booby-trap, once cunningly concealed by the cloth. Now the rats have revealed the ghastly device.' Outside were two Canadians, similarly dead, one a 'great bloated thing, so unhuman that it's hard to distinguish him from the earth and wreckage on which he lies'.

Viewing these 'decaying putrid things', as the light finally faded and the noise of the battle grew muted, McKee thought bitterly of the cost of victory. 'These are the glorious dead,' he concluded, 'the politicians' speeches.' Then he set off for his billet from that haunted place, his rifle at the ready.

II

'There is only one thing worse than fighting with allies, and that is – *fighting without them!*' Thus Churchill was wont to speak in the spring of 1945 when it had become quite clear to him that America had now become the senior partner in the Allied coalition which was presently defeating Germany. On that unseasonally warm April Tuesday, the day after Arnhem had been taken, he had given to the House his personal tribute to the lately dead President Roosevelt. 'Sail on, O ship of state,' he had quoted passionately from Longfellow. Now he was ready to receive the most important American in Europe, General Eisenhower, the head of the Allied armies in Europe.

Across the Atlantic, the new president of four days' standing – Harry Truman – might well have placed a notice in his office announcing that '*The buck stops here*'. But real power as yet did not rest in his hands. The man who really controlled American affairs overseas was that stern, austere general, Chief of Staff George Marshall, whom even Eisenhower called 'sir'; and in the spring of 1945 Marshall was not very interested in politics, especially those of Europe. His main concern was winning the war militarily. Besides, opinion in America, created by liberal writers, journalists and movie producers, was that the future lay in the hands of the 'democratic' American and Russian peoples. The days of the European colonial powers, especially Britain, were numbered. Why concern oneself, then, with the desires and plans of the arch-imperialist, Churchill?

Eisenhower, Marshall's chief representative in Europe, arrived in London on that sunny Tuesday to be greeted with a pomp and ceremony which contrasted strongly with his first reception in the

British capital two and a half years before. Then an obscure brigadier-general, he arrived to find that even his driver, the pretty redhead Kay Summersby who was going to become his lover, was missing and he had to go looking for her before she could whisk him off to Claridge's. Now he was received at 10 Downing Street by a beaming, happy Churchill as he were a royal visitor.

Churchill's beam hid his dissatisfaction with the American General. As soon as the pleasantries were over – Eisenhower had brought some bottles of precious vintage bubbly from his HQ at France's champagne capital Rheims, so that Churchill might celebrate the victory soon to come in appropriate style – Churchill took the Supreme Commander to task for his lack of propriety the previous month. Then Eisenhower had communicated his plan not to drive to Berlin directly to the Soviet dictator, Stalin. He, Churchill, would never had tolerated a breach of protocol of that kind, even from the 'insufferable Monty'.

Boldly, a sure indication of Eisenhower's stature – for every division the British could field in Europe he could field three – and the comforting knowledge that back in Washington Marshall was backing him up to the hilt, the Supreme Commander stood his ground. He agreed that a better communications system ought to be established with their remote Russian ally, but on military matters such as the 28 March decision not to take Berlin, which Eisenhower regarded as a purely military affair without any political significance, he reserved the right to communicate directly with Stalin.

Churchill persisted in the importance of Berlin. Eisenhower side-tracked him. He said that it was vital he should clear his flanks in north and south first before he could concern himself with the matter of the German capital. He told Churchill that he had fewer than fifty thousand men on the Elbe (which wasn't strictly true), armed with little in the way of artillery. The Russians, for their part, who had commenced a huge offensive the day before, had at their disposal for the capture of Berlin 1,250,000 men and 12,000 pieces of artillery.

Churchill lapsed into silence and Eisenhower, who had a genuine affection for the 'Old Man', with his 'romantic' nineteenth-century ideas about war and the importance of one single decisive battle for a nation's future, changed the subject. As policially naïve as he himself later confessed that he was at that time, Eisenhower knew enough to realise that the whole of Central Europe was now falling into Russian hands to be used as Stalin wished.

Budapest had fallen to them and they had entered Warsaw and

Vienna. Soon Berlin would be theirs because he had declined to take it for reasons of pride and national and personal prestige. Now his only active American Army, Patton's Third, was about to start the last campaign of the war which could take them to Prague, the last remaining Central European capital not yet under Soviet influence or in its sphere of operations. And Eisenhower knew his Churchill. The 'Old Man' would want him to take Prague for any future political advantages it might offer in the post-war world.

Again, however, the American capture of Prague might well lead to difficulties with 'Uncle Joe' – as Eisenhower was wont to call the pock-marked Soviet dictator who was anything but avuncular – just as the Supreme Commander thought that the capture of Berlin would have done. Eisenhower was very much concerned that there should be no clash between the two armies, Allied and Russian, when they finally met. Hence he was prepared to lean over backwards to meet Russian wishes in this sphere. Besides, just as the area east of the River Elbe would become the Soviet Zone of Occupation after victory – why, therefore, waste American lives trying to take it? – so Prague and Czechoslovakia would become independent once again immediately they were liberated. There was no question of zones of occupation. Again, why suffer casualties trying to beat the Russians to the Czech capital?

But Eisenhower knew Churchill would object to this, as he had done, together with the British chiefs of staff, to his March decision not to take Berlin. Churchill had to be given something that would appeal to his sense of *Realpolitik* vis-à-vis Soviet Russia. Now, therefore, Eisenhower suggested it was vital that the British Army under Montgomery seal off the Schleswig-Holstein/Danish peninsula by reaching the Baltic before the Russians did.

At first it seemed to Churchill, sitting there like a pink Buddha, that Denmark was of little importance in comparison to Berlin or Prague. But Eisenhower warmed to his theme. Eisenhower worked on the idea. He told the British Prime Minister that, by reaching the shores of the Baltic before the Russians, the West could ensure that the exit to that vital sea would be denied to Stalin. This would ensure the future security of the Scandinavian countries and, of course, the British Isles themselves.

Somewhat appeased, feeling that Montgomery had not only a military role now but also a much more significant political one after all, Churchill walked Eisenhower to his staff car. Waiting in it was Captain Butcher, the Supreme Commander's PR man and poker-playing crony. To 'Butch' the two of them looked as 'homey as neighbours on adjoining Iowa farms'.

Now, as the staff car sped them through London's bombed, sordid streets – where it had only been a matter of three weeks since the last V-2 had fallen out of the stratosphere with such deadly effect – on their way to Eisenhower's 'weekend retreat', Telegraph Cottage, the Supreme Commander relaxed. He told 'Butch' that the 'PM' always walked to the car with him – sometimes 'even in his bathrobe'. He concluded that he had 'grown very fond of Churchill' and that, although they occasionally differed on military matters, they were the 'best of friends'.

Then he closed his eyes and ran through the message he would send to his mentor Marshall a little later. It would read, in part, 'I do not quite understand why the Prime Minister has been so determined to intermingle political and military considerations.'

That was the way the fate of Central Europe was decided in the spring of 1945 . . .

III

On that Tuesday, while Eisenhower discussed the new role for Montgomery with Churchill in the hope that the 'Old Man' would keep off his back about Central Europe and let him get on with the job of winning the war, Bradley had flown to join the 9th Army Commander at his headquarters near the Elbe. That afternoon Simpson's 2nd Armored Division and his 30th Infantry Division were attacking the major German city of Magdeburg on that same river. Again and again the German commander there had refused to surrender to the frustrated Americans. Now Simpson had had enough. He had called in the heavy bombers, which had levelled more than one-third of the city. Now he was sending in his combat troops.

Half an hour after Bradley had arrived at the HQ, the phone rang. The immensely tall Army Commander with the bald, shaven, glistening head picked up the receiver and listened for a few moments. Then, placing his hand over the mouthpiece, he said to Bradley, 'It looks as if we may get a bridge in Magdeburg after all. What'll we do then, Brad?'

The Army Goup Commander, with his GI glasses and lantern jaw, knew exactly what Simpson wanted him to say. 'Big Simp' wanted him to agree that the Magdeburg autobahn bridge would be the fastest and quickest route for a 9th Army to drive straight to Berlin. He shook his head, however. 'Hell's bells,' he snorted, 'we don't want any more bridgeheads on the Elbe! If you get it, you'll have to throw a battalion across it, I guess. But let's hope the other fellows blow it up before you're stuck with it.'

Minutes later Simpson's phone rang again. Again Simpson listened and then, putting down the instrument, said, 'No need to worry any longer. The Krauts just blew it up.'

On the other side of the Elbe, General Wenck – 'the other fellow', as Bradley liked to call the German enemy – was frankly puzzled by the Americans. The furious initial attacks by the Amis between 12 and 15 April had led him to believe that he was going to have to fight a bloody defensive battle on the river with his newly created army. 'Frankly I'm astonished,' he told his Chief of Staff, Colonel Reichhelm. 'Maybe they've outrun their supplies.' Whatever their reasons were, Wenck was glad of the respite. He now had time to whip his 12th Army into shape. Not that he was very sanguine about its chances in all-out battle with the Amis. His men were too spread out and in essence they provided a very thin screen along the Elbe before Berlin. 'If the Americans launch a major attack,' he told his Chief of Staff, 'they'll crack our positions with ease. There's nothing between here and Berlin.' *But why didn't they attack?*

Even General Kurt Dittmar, the German Army's radio spokesman, known throughout the Third Reich as 'the voice of the German High Command' and a broadcaster who had a large following in Allied intelligence circles, was also puzzled. As Simpson's 30th Infantry Division consolidated its position on the Elbe, he crossed the river with his 16-year-old son and tamely surrendered to the surprised infantry just after dawn. Immediately he was identified, he was taken to 30th Division's HQ and interrogated.

He told his interrogators that the Führer was definitely in Berlin and intended to remain there. Dittmar believed that 'Hitler will either be killed there or commit suicide.' This was news to the Allies. They had always believed that Hitler had already fled to the National Redoubt in the Alps, where he and the élite troops supposedly gathering there might well hold out for years to come.

'Tell us about the National Redoubt' someone asked.

The handsome General, who had broadcast the German High Command's daily communiqué from Berlin and was as well-informed as anyone at the top in Hitler's Third Reich, looked puzzled. The only thing he knew about the 'supposed National Redoubt', he told his interrogators, was something he had read about it in a Swiss news-paper the previous January. He agreed that there were pockets of resistance in Norway and Denmark and perhaps in the Alps. But they were there 'less by intention than by force of circumstances'.

His interrogators, who had been stopped on the Elbe because, according to General Bradley, the Army Group's main effort was to be made by Patton's Third Army against this fearful 'National Redoubt', were accordingly shocked. Pressed for more information, Dittmar shook his head and declared confidently, 'The National Redoubt? It is a romantic dream . . . *It's a myth* . . .'

But that autobahn bridge at Magdeburg was not the last surviving bridge across the Elbe. On the morning of 19 April, General 'Pip' Roberts, commanding Montgomery's 11th Armoured Division, was electrified by a report from his forward units that the railway bridge across the river at the little town of Lauenburg was still intact. Roberts, the undersized divisional commander who had risen from captain to general in four short years and who had seen much of battle, made a snap decision. He felt that the 'increasing proximity of the Russians mught induce the Germans [defending the bridge] to lay down their arms and allow us free passage'. Then he was sure be could have his 'leading troops 25 miles east [of the bridge] before Eisenhower was aware of the fact'. Could the Supreme Commander then keep the British from going for the Geman capital itself? He thought not. Hastily he ordered that an attempt should be made to capture the bridge at Lauenburg.

The attackers' plan was simple and direct. Three companies of the 4th Battalion of the King's Shropshire Light Infantry, supported by the tanks of the 3rd Royal Tanks, would attempt to rush the bridge. Once they had captured it by a *coup de main*, such as that which had surprised the German defenders of the Remagen railway bridge the previous month, they would form a small bridgehead on the far bank. In reserve the 1st Battalion the Cheshire Regiment would be waiting to give them any support they needed, while rocket-firing Typhoon fighter-bombers strafed the defenders of the cliffs on the far bank at Lauenburg.

The stream at Bullendorf which marked the frontline was hurriedly bridged and by 8.30 that morning the two leading companies, B and D, had set off on their daring mission, each supported by a troop of tanks and with the Typhoons clearing the way with their deadly rockets. General Roberts' hopes of no German opposition soon faded; German resistance thickened all the morning. But there was no stopping the British infantry. By 11.30 they were in sight of the bridge itself.

It was a long metallic structure disappearing into the town of Lauenburg itself and merging into a small boatyard, crowded now with barges unable to sail this hotly disputed river. Now the two companies took up their positions on both sides of the bridge's entrance, sheltering in the cover of the dyke which ran the length of the riverbank. From across the Elbe several 20mm flak guns, formerly used in the defence of Hamburg, spat fire at them. What appeared to be a solid white whirling wall of shells hissed flatly across the water at them. With deadly effect. Men started to go down everywhere.

Since it had landed in Normandy, the 4th KSLI had lost a quarter of its strength killed in action, with twice that number being wounded. Only the previous month they had suffered the loss of three of the battalion's four company commanders. Understandably the men didn't want to be killed now with victory just round the corner. Still the prospect of the bridge and the road which led to Berlin beyond spurred them on to take the kind of risks few of them had been prepared to take since they had crossed the Rhine.

While, in full view of the enemy gunners, Sergeant-Major Adams rattled out in his half-track ambulance to collect their wounded (he won his country's second highest bravery award for doing so), the British infantry pressed home their attack against some two hundred Germans and a Tiger tank defending the southern end of the bridge.

An artillery duel developed across the river. One British shell screeched into the cliff-top town of Lauenburg itself, penetrated the wall of the local folk museum and came to rest in the heart of a generously bewigged nobleman whose faded oil portrait graced its inside. The nobleman was, ironically enough, George II of England and Hanover, who had once ruled this part of Germany too.

But on this frenzied, embattled afternoon, neither side had time for such historical considerations. The Tiger tank, afraid it was too exposed to British fire, scuttled back across the bridge for the safety of the other side. Its departure heartened the attackers. They began to advance more quickly. They killed twenty of the defenders and captured another fifty more. As the afternoon gave way to the evening, the infantry had virtual control of the one end of the bridge, with the Shermans of the 3rd Tanks blasting away with their 75mm cannon at the far bank.

Then, surprisingly enough, orders came down from their Brigade HQ that the bridge wasn't to be crossed after all. In any case, so it was stated afterwards, the bridge had a gap in it and a captured enemy officer reported that there were four sea mines attached to the piers which could be exploded whenever the bridge commandant wished. While these orders were pondered, the enemy acted.

Abruptly there was a thick asthmatic crump. The bridge shivered. A series of vivid blue sparks ran its length. A violent crack. A sheet of purple flame split the darkening sky over the Elbe. The infantry ducked. The blast hit them across their faces like a slap from a flabby damp fist. Opening their mouths instinctively so their eardrums would not be burst by the explosion, the British watched aghast as the railway bridge at Lauenburg disintegrated before their eyes.

They had failed, too. Now, not one single bridge existed across the Elbe anywhere on the whole length of the Anglo-American front in Germany. General Roberts' scheme to trick Eisenhower into allowing the British to drive for Berlin after all had failed miserably.

IV

'The front was so close that not only could we hear the thunder of the guns, but we could see the shellbursts in the Hamburg area,' one of the few survivors of the tragedy of Neuengamme concentration camp, the Danish Dr Roesdahl, related long after the war. But the British failure to capture the bridge at Lauenburg that Thursday meant now that their liberators were as far away as if they were on the moon. Now the SS guards could deal with their burdensome, unwanted prisoners as they wished. It would be another two weeks before Neuengamme camp was taken.

First to be executed were the twenty-odd Jewish children and the four men, two Dutch and two French, who looked after them. Secretly that night they were taken to part of Hamburg's 'death zone'. This was in the suburb of Rothenburgsort, which had been so badly damaged during the week-long American and British raids on the port in summer 1943 that the whole area of ruins had been evacuated and declared out of bounds.

Here in a three-storey, damaged school in the Bullenhuser Damm, the SS had set up a small concentration camp, which had housed workers forced to clear up the bomb damage and perform other such tasks. Now, with the Tommies on their doorstep, the SS were in the process of turning the school into an extermination camp for those whom Berlin wanted to be 'liquidated' immediately.[2]

In this lonely, half-ruined school, the children were told by the camp doctor, Trzebinski, to take off their clothes. They were going to be given an injection against typhus. They undressed obediently while in another room six Russians were murdered silently.

At the door Trzebinski waited, chatting softly with a guard, SS Sergeant Frahm. The doctor, according to his own statement at his trial after the war, asked Frahm how the children were going to be 'dealt with'.

Frahm, his face pale, answered that the doctor was supposed to hang the children. Trzebinski turned pale himself now. In his own statement he said, 'I know I could have played the hero and saved them with my pistol, but they would have died anyway, only later. Now that I knew what terrible end faced them, I tried at least to lighten their last few hours.' So the SS Doctor filled a hypodermic with morphium and ordered the first little boy to lean over a stool. Thereupon he injected him with a lethal dose of the drug and told him he should now lie down and go to sleep. One by one the children received the fatal dose and settled down on the floor to 'sleep', covering themselves with their ragged clothes, while Trzebinski waited.

One of the older children, a 12-year-old French boy, couldn't sleep, however, and Frahm took him by the arm and led him away. The Doctor watched in open-mouthed amazement as, in another room, Frahm placed a noose round the neck of the dozy, half-asleep child and hanged him from the ceiling. 'In my time in the camps,' Trzebinski confessed after the war, 'I have seen a lot of human misery and I am pretty hardened to suffering, but I had never seen children hanged before.' The doctor, sick and trembling, went outside to swallow in great gulps of the night air, while Frahm continued with his devilish, self-imposed task, dragging on the children's feet with his full weight so that they died more quickly.

In the meantime truckloads of Russian prisoners were being driven into the wired-off courtyard to be executed in the school's cellars. One truckload seemed, like animals being led to the slaughter, to know what was going to happen to them. As the doors of the truck were opened, they jumped out with a great 'Hurrah', just as Russian infantry always did when they attacked, flung some salt into the nearest guard's eyes and made a run for it.

---

2 For those interested in such matters the buildings are still there and are again being used as a school.

Wild, confused firing broke out in the darkness. Russians dropped moaning to the ground. Here and there a few of the desperate prisioners, sunken, starved faces set in wolfish rage, grappled with their guards. Some managed to flee. But in the end the survivors were led away, shoulders sunk in defeat, to be executed.

Dr Trzebinski threw away his cigarette and re-entered that house of death. The room where he had left the children was empty, save for their bits and pieces of clothing. He tried the door of the other room, the one in which Frahm had hanged the first boy. It was locked. He found Frahm and asked the SS man to open the door.

Frahm did so. The dead lay in a neat row on the floor, All of them were naked and around each child's neck Trzebinski could see the red, scarred line left by the noose. Frahm had hanged every last one of them. The doctor asked for a strong cup of black coffee. Then he ordered Frahm to burn the children's clothes in the bathroom. That done, he and the rest of the murderers set off through the night back to Neuengamme. There was still a lot more work to be done before the Allies captured Hamburg . . .

In Berlin the monster who had instigated all this heartless savagery celebrated his fifty-sixth birthday surrounded by his paladins. Fortunately for the future of the world, it would be his last. Never again would these pompous, cruel, self-satisfied men and women in their black and grey uniforms assemble on 20 April to wish the man who had ruled the destiny of Germany for the last twelve years 'Die besten Glückwünsche zum Geburtstag, mein Führer'[3] and drink the German champagne and terribly sweet cakes that he favoured. This was the last time and even the monster knew. He told Keitel, head of the German High Command, who would live to stand trial at Nuremburg, 'I know what I want. I will die fighting in or outside Berlin.'

But there were many there that Friday, while in the distance the Russian guns thundered, heralding the final assault on Berlin soon to come, who had no wish to die: who were determined to save their hides come what may. Heinrich Himmler, the chinless, bespectacled head of the SS – 'loyal Heinrich', as Hitler had been wont to call him – was one of those. For years he had relentlessly pursued the Jews and the enemies of the Reich, torturing and slaughtering them by their thousands and their hundred of thousands in his concentration

---

3 'Best wishes on your birthday.'

camps. Now, on the very same day that his henchmen murdered those twenty Jewish children in the basement of the bomb-damaged school in far away Hamburg, Himmler – 'loyal Heinrich' – was prepared to think the unthinkable and act upon it. At the very hour that Frahm was so cruelly hanging the children, Himmler left the birthday reception to meet Norbert Masur, the Swedish representative of the World Jewish Congress!

'Der treue Heinrich'[4] was putting out the first Nazi peace feeler.

4   'Loyal Heinrich'.

4

'You have twenty-four hours in which to decide.'

I

The destruction of the bridge across the Elbe at Lauenburg and the consequent halting of 'Bubbles' Barker's 8th Corps, which had made that desperate dash to capture the last bridge across the river, seemed to herald the halting of Montgomery's whole army as this third terrible week of April came to an end. After a tremendous four-week advance from the Rhine, in which some of his armoured divisions had covered up to 60 miles a day, with his infantry divisions trying desperately to keep up, the drive north had virtually come to a stop.

Not only was the advance halted by that formidable water barrier, the Elbe, but the leading formations were running into the industrial suburbs of the great ports of Bremen on the Weser and Hamburg on the Elbe: built-up areas in which whole infantry divisions could be swallowed up easily. And all along the line, the German resistance – stiffened by U-boat crews, *Luftwaffe* air crews turned into infantry, and the teenage SS men from their training battalions in the north – was hardening.

While 'Pip' Roberts' 11th Armoured Division ground to a halt on the Elbe, on its left flank the most famous British armoured formation of all, the celebrated 'Desert Rats' of the 7th Armoured Division, belonging to General Ritchie's 12th Corps, tried to reach the Elbe. In the lead was the Division's 8th Irish Hussars, which had seen much bitter action in these last four years. The day before they had liberated twenty thousand Allied POWs at the great *Stalag* at Fallingsborstel and had been astonished to find it 'guarded' by spick-and-span ex-prisoners of the 1st Airborne captured at Arnhem the previous year, under the command of a formidable guardsman, RSM Lord.

That had been a good day and it had warmed the Hussars' hearts to free comrades, many of whom had been behind barbed wire since

Dunkirk and even earlier. Now the Hussars had been given a less welcome task: to work their way along the autobahn and try to penetrate the great industrial suburb of Hamburg-Harburg which lay on the southern bank of the Elbe.

The *Sunday Times* correspondent R.W. Thompson, who was with them, felt:

It is a difficult kind of war to explain – a very uneven war. Nothing can be taken for granted. The 8th Hussars have suffered terrible casualties . . . and their estimate of what they are up against is a sober one. I have never known troops more touchy than they are at this moment about the descriptions of enemy resistance. They don't like this 'swanning against slight resistance' stuff because they see their friends die each day.

Attached to the Hussars, Captain Robert Maxwell, MC of the 1/5th Queens, felt pretty much the same, as he wrote in a letter that day to his French wife:

This last week we have been fighting or advancing continuously and we are now very close to Hamburg and the going is harder the closer we get to the darned place . . . At the moment I am sitting in a farmyard and writing this letter on my knees, the sun is out and it is nice and warm. A few hundred yards from here a wood is on fire, a little way over to my left you can see our tanks and artillery knocking down another German village and so it goes on until the last Boche has either been killed or laid down his arms.

Despite their sombre mood and feeling of apprehension, the Hussars and their attached infantry of the Queens advanced steadily, if very slowly, towards the wooded heights beyond which lay Harburg. After an unsuccessful attempt by the 1st Royal Tanks to pass through the forest two days before, the task force now tried to by-pass it through the village of Tostedt.

At first they were stopped by German mobile assault guns and the feared German *panzerfaust*, the enemy missile-launcher with which any half-trained Hitler Youth could stop a tank worth many thousand pounds at the cost of pennies. Finally they captured the village and the advance continued. But the retreating Germans didn't make it easy for them. All along the roads leading to Harburg they had felled the trees, making a series of anti-tank barriers. In one case a bold 88mm crew placed their formidable weapon in the middle of the autobahn right behind a large tree. When the Hussars' tank rattled forward to clear what the crew assumed was yet another obstacle, the German gunners let go with one round at point-blank range. The Hussars' tank disintegrated and the gunners fled for their lives.

Indeed the German 88mm cannon which had been used in the aerial defence of the great port were proving to be a major headache. Used in a ground role now they could knock out any known allied tank easily at a thousand yards. That day the weary Hussars started to suffer from a kind of 88mm cannon phobia, as they encountered gun after gun. By the evening the Hussars had knocked out eight 88mm guns on the autobahn but they had covered barely six miles. The steam had gone out of their advance.

Indeed the 'Desert Rats' in general had had enough. Here and there the infantry had local successes. The 1/5th Queens assaulted and captured the hamlet of Hollenstedt on the autobahn. The 1st Rifle Brigade was engaged in hand-to-hand fighting in places and was forced to use the dreaded flame-throwers to clear a route through the forest. But as the leading troops reached the heights overlooking the valley of the Elbe and Harburg, their advance ground to a halt. The infantry of the 7th Division started to dig in and the weary tank crews pulled back to the rear. Two weeks later, when Hamburg finally surrendered, the 'Desert Rats' would be occupying these same positions, the Elbe still uncrossed.

The situation was a little different on the front of Ritchie's neighbour to the left, General Horrocks' 30th Corps. When on 20 April his two leading infantry divisions – the 3rd and the 51st Highland – reached the outskirts of Germany's second major port, Bremen, the Commanding General had to make a decision.

'Jorrocks', as he was known to his men behind his back, tall, lean, his ascetic, almost ecclesiastic face dominated by a great beak of a nose, did not like the idea of attacking a built-up area one bit, although he had four infantry divisions at his disposal. At this stage of the war he did not want to be involved in some kind of mini-Stalingrad, in which he might well suffer heavy casualties and inflict yet greater misery on the German civilians. Manpower in the British Army was short, and in his infantry companies most of his rank-and-file were teenagers; he did not want to kill those boys before their lives had really started

So because the Commanding General – who had himself been wounded and taken prisoner in the First World War and severely wounded again in the Second – did not want the fight for Bremen to become a blood bath, he attempted a subterfuge. That Friday he ordered his gunners to fire four hundred shells containing leaflets addressed to the local population into the beleagured city. They read, in German:

The choice is yours! The British Army is lying outside Bremen, supported by the RAF, amd is about to capture the city. There are two ways this can take place. Either by the employment of all means at the disposal of the Army and the RAF, or by the occupation of the town after unconditional surrender. Yours is the responsibility for the unnecessary bloodshed which will result if you choose the first way. Otherwise you must send an envoy under the protection of a white flag over the British lines. You have twenty-four hours in which to decide . . .

So Horrocks waited, as did his fellow corps commanders Ritchie and Barker, and indeed the whole of the army which Montgomery had assembled along the banks of the Weser and Elbe for the last stage of this long and bloody journey which had begun the year before on the Normandy beaches. For some, in fact, it had commenced long years before when the British Army had been flung ignominiously out of France at Dunkirk in 1940. Over the bitter years that had intervened they had suffered defeat after defeat, fought in desert and mountains in two continents and in half a dozen foreign lands. It had been a hard slog, along a long, cruel road back that had led from Dunkirk to this near-victory in the heart of the Third Reich. Now the question uppermost in the minds of even the less sensitive of them as the offensive ground to a halt was: how was the war going to end for the British Army – *with a bang or a whimper?*

II

'Monty, denied the glory of taking Berlin, had lost all heart for the fight . . . I believe he viewed his primary mission of sealing off the Danish border as demeaning.' This was Bradley's opinion of Montgomery's mood in that third week of April, as the latter's troops came to a halt. 'Monty . . . no longer seemed to have a sense of urgency about his mission.'

Possibly Bradley, gloating as he did so many years later about Montgomery's relegation, at last, to the role of junior partner in the great Anglo-American military coalition, was partially right. As that fateful weekend of 21/22 April 1945 commenced, Montgomery did seem hesitant, unable to make a decision about what to do next.

On Friday 20 April, Eisenhower had flown directly from London, after visiting Churchill, to meet his subordinate Montgomery at the little German town of Diepholz. Here, after Montgomery had 'belly-ached' (Monty's favourite phrase) about his lack of manpower for his new task, Eisenhower had promised him General Ridgway's US 18th Airborne Corps to help him in his drive to the Baltic. He agreed that, of course, Montgomery should be allowed to 'tidy up' his battlefield and capture Bremen before he assaulted the Elbe. But at the same time Eisenhower warned him that the Russian commander of the 2nd Belorussian Army, Marshal Konstantin Rokossovsky, was making rapid progress through Mecklenburg heading for the Elbe and the Baltic beyond.

Rokossovsky, a rough, tough, handsome soldier whom Stalin had had imprisoned in the Gulag between 1937 and 1940 before he had been released just in time to stop the German drive on Moscow, drove his men hard. He had taken the German surrender at Stalingrad and he now wanted the glory of reaching the Baltic before the Western Allies. Moreover, the Russian Marshal, who had a weakness for wine and women and who, according to Montgomery's Intelligence staff, seemed possessed of the same paranoid suspicions of Allied motives as his master Stalin, was keeping his cards held tight to his chest. So far he had revealed nothing of his intentions to the opposite numbers in the Anglo-American campaign.

What were the Russian's strategic intentions, Montgomery asked himself. Would he stop on the Elbe? Or would he attempt to push on into the Schleswig-Holstein peninsula and Denmark beyond? Undoubtedly the Red Navy was making its presence increasingly felt in the Baltic. Its submarines and, to some extent, its surface ships were busily engaged in sinking German vessels which were desperately trying to escape with the cargoes of human misery from the trapped German armies in West Prussia. Unconfirmed rumours coming in from neutral Sweden and occupied Denmark stated that the Russians were already landing parachute agents in Norway and Denmark to make contact with the communist resistance there, and there had been reports from the German-occupied Danish island of Bornholm that Russian agents were already in place.

Pondering the situation that weekend, Montgomery came to the conclusion that the Russians would not stop on the Elbe, unlike the Americans who were now stalled on the river waiting for the Russians to link up with them. Rokossovsky, a true servant of the dictator – 'Old Leather Face', as the Red Army generals called Stalin behind his back on account of his swarthy, pock-marked face – would attempt to grab as much German and Danish territory as he could, unless he, Montgomery, stopped him doing so.

But there was an imponderable in what would become a secret race between the two erstwhile Allies, Britain and Russia, for the Baltic coast: the Germans. Officially, the Allies were still fighting a war against the Germans. What role would the estimated one and a half million armed Germans facing him in the north-west play in this last campaign of the war?

Montgomery knew that the German generals, inspired – and deceived – by the propaganda put out by Dr Josef Goebbels, Minister of Propaganda and Public Enlightenment, believed that at any day an armed conflict might break out between the Anglo-Americans and the Russians. Then, if they played their cards right, Germany would be saved at the eleventh hour by joining the West in its fight against the Bolshevik hordes, as the 'Poison Dwarf' routinely called them.

Within the last six months Churchill, the only Allied politician in the West who seemed concerned with the new threat looming large on the horizon, had been forced to face up to a communist threat within his own camp. In the previous December, when the Belgian communist resistance movement had refused to be disarmed and it seemed that the communists might attempt to take over the government, Churchill had ordered Montgomery to move one of his divisions to surround the Belgian capital. One month later Churchill had sent British paratroopers into action against the Greek communists of the resistance who had tried to do the same thing in Athens. Even as Montgomery mulled over his own problems, down in Italy that elegant guardee Field Marshal Alexander was preparing to meet the threat of Tito's Jugoslav communist resistance by the use of troops and the RAF.

The Germans knew all these things too, and to them they augured well for a breakdown of the Allied coalition against them. Yet at the same time Montgomery knew from his own Intelligence reports that the Germans seemed determined to hold the line of the River Elbe in order to allow the hundreds of thousands of German soldiers and civilians fleeing from the Russians by sea and by land to reach the comparative safety of the west. Wouldn't they, therefore, make a fight of it once the British attempted to cross the Elbe and race to the Baltic coast before the Red Army could reach it? In essence, with the limited resources at his disposal, wasn't he going to be involved in a strange, unreal battle, with both his *Russian ally* and the *German enemy*?

Sitting in the caravan which he had 'liberated' from an Italian general in the Western Desert whom the 8th Army had nicknamed 'Electric Whiskers', just outside the farmhouse of Farmer Knacke, whose property in the village of Odeme[3] had been requisitioned for Montgomery's new TAC HQ, Montgomery felt angry and frustrated as well as sad at the lost opportunity of Berlin. As far as he was concerned, 'the oncoming Russians were more dangerous than the stricken Germans . . . the German war was practically over'. 'The essential and immediate task was to push on with all speed and get to the Baltic and there to form a flank facing east' against the Russians.

Now Eisenhower, who had hitherto been totally apolitical, was suddenly urging him to achieve *political* instead of military objectives! How could one work under a supreme commander who changed his mind so often and was usually swayed by the last opinion he heard? And Eisenhower himself had taken the chance of a rapid assault crossing of the Elbe away from him when he had removed the US 9th Army from his command three weeks ago. Now, Montgomery felt, he hadn't the strength to carry out the tasks Eisenhower urged upon him in order to achieve these new political objectives. As he warned the War Office that Saturday night, 'The Elbe is a big river similar to the Rhine and to cross it in the face of stiff opposition is a major operation.'

But it was not only the military position which dismayed and disheartened the little Field Marshal this Saturday, alone in his caravan with his gloomy thoughts. Two of his favourite 'eyes and ears', his youthful liaison officers John Poston and Peter Earle, had suddenly gone missing. Montgomery hoped they had merely been captured, 'if so we shall recover them because they cannot be got away.'

Montgomery was wrong. That Saturday night, Major Peter Earle was lying in the straw in a German farmhouse, badly wounded and unconscious, and Major John Poston, the youngest of his liaison officers and his favourite – 'steely blue eyed' and with a 'furious hawk-like face' – was lying on the damp cobbles of one of the backroads through the *Heide*[4] – dead.

'He was a Harrow boy and had hardly left school when the war began,' Montgomery wrote long afterwards about their first meeting back in 1942:

---

3 It is still there.
4 That great area of heathland that stretches between the Elbe and Hamburg to the south of the port.

He could see that I was a lieut-general and he knew I wanted an ADC but he had never heard of me before and he did not know what I was doing in Egypt. I said to him: 'My name is Montgomery. I arrived this morning from England and I am going down to the desert to take command of the Eighth Army. I have not been in the desert before and I want an ADC who will go about with me and generally help me. Will you come to me as my ADC?'

Montgomery recalled of that first meeting between 'the Master' and his future 'eyes and ears':

He was clearly somewhat startled; this was highly secret news, known to very few.

He didn't answer at once; he just looked at me, straight in the face. He looked sad; he had just been with Gott, who was known all over the Middle East and was obviously a hero to all young officers. And now his master was dead. I said nothing, but just waited for his answer.

At last the young officer from the 'Cherrypickers' (the 11th Hussars), who would win the Military Cross twice, said, 'Yes sir, I would like to come with you.'[5]

For three years Major Poston served him faithfully, becoming chief of his 'eyes and ears', that select little corps of officers, British, Canadian and American, who would be dispatched daily to the front to find out what the situation was at first-hand. In the evening they would return – if they survived – to report directly to 'the Master' of their findings.

Now on this Saturday Major Earle had been ordered to drive to 'Bubbles' Barker's 8th Corps at Lueneburg. His route lay through 'outlaw country', territory held by some two thousand German troops, wandering bands of *Volkssturm*, Hitler Youth, marines and young SS men. Many of them were just waiting to be captured. But there were others among them, young fanatics for the most part, only too eager to die for 'People , fatherland and Führer', as the legend of the time had it.

Just before he was about to leave, Earle came across Poston in his cherry-coloured beret finishing digging his own caravan out of the earth. He told his friend Earle that he, too, had been ordered to proceed to the same area. He was to visit the headquarters of 'Pip' Roberts' 11th Armoured Division and report on the situation there. 'We both considered this a complete waste of time,' Earle recorded afterwards, 'as the 11th Armoured Division was known to be resting.'

---

5 Montgomery's account of his meeting with Poston takes up exactly the same amount of space in his memoires as that of his meeting with his Chief of Staff de Guingand. It is indictive of the importance he attached to the relationship he had with the 25-year-old major.

Earle suggested they should travel together, as he was destined for Corps HQ and there 'I would discover more about the future plans for the Division than John would discover from the Divisional Commander.' Poston agreed and the two young majors set off together in Earle's jeep without the driver. The two of them reached Barker's HQ quite safely, where they learned that Barker was planning to cross the Elbe with his 53rd Infantry Division. Now, as darkness began to fall, they set off again at 45 m.p.h., driving down one of those dead-straight, cobbled roads, through the firs which ran on endlessly like battalion after battalion of spike-helmeted Prussian grenadiers.

Just after six o'clock they ran into trouble. From both sides of the road angry red flame stabbed the growing darkness. Harsh cries rang out in German. A stick grenade tumbled slowly through the air. They had run into an ambush.

Both were battled-experienced soldiers. Instead of trying to turn on the narrow road, higher than the sandy banks on both sides, Earle, wounded in the arm as he was, drove straight at the nearest German machine-gunner. The German screamed in agony as he disappeared beneath the racing wheels. Next moment the jeep slammed to a stop. Both officers were flung to the ground. Hurriedly, as German infantry began to come out of the trees, weapons at the ready, the wounded Earle tried to clean the chinograph dispositions of the 8th Corps which he had marked on his map. They were top-secret. He dare not let them fall into German hands.

A rifle cracked. Earle yelped with pain as a slug entered his back. He fell to the ground. Lying there helplessly, wounded twice, Earle heard Poston some three yards to his right, his sten gun empty, cry 'in an urgent and desperate voice, "N-No – stop – stop!" '.

These were the 25-year-old officer's last words. For in that same instant a German soldier thrust home his bayonet as Poston lay there defenceless, arms already raised in surrender. The bayonet pierced his heart and Major John Poston, 11th Hussars, who had known only war, was dead instantly . . .

III

That day many hundreds of young men, British, Canadian, German, American, Russian, and half a dozen other nationalities, died in Central Europe. But perhaps none died as bravely as Eddie Charlton, a former pre-war worker in Manchester's main abattoir, not perhaps the ideal training place for outstanding bravery and ultimate sacrifice for the cause.

Eddie Charlton had volunteered for the Guards Brigade immediately war had broken out, although he was barely 18. But Eddie was both a patriot and a pragmatist. He wanted to fight for his country and at the same time he thought of his future. At that time Manchester Police Force accepted only guardsmen for the force and Eddie dearly wanted to become a policeman. But the Army had told Eddie that as a butcher he would have to go into the Royal Army Service Corps. So he waited until 1940 when he was called up. Then he opted for the Brigade of Guards on the strength of a vague Irish connection rooted in the dim past.

Proud as he was of the Irish Guards – one of his favourite slogans, especially after he had had a couple of pints, was '*Up the Micks!*' – Eddie chafed at the fact that first the months, then the years passed and he had still not seen any action. In the end, a few months after D-Day, Guardsman Charlton, eager for some desperate glory, was finally posted to the Guards Armoured Division, 'somewhere in Germany'.

Despite the fact that they had been in combat since Normandy, the Guards Armoured Division, commanded by General Adair who had lost his only son in Italy in 1943, was still very much an èlite formation, loyal to the Guards' 300-year-old tradition. The division, whose insignia was a single eye which supposedly winked when it saw a virgin – '*and it ain't winked yet*' – frowned on the matey attitude between officers and men which had been encouraged by wartime propaganda in other formations. Here the men still stood to attention and snapped at their officers before they reported, 'Permission to speak, *sir!*' When they went into action, they did so with their collars buttoned, their brasses polished and their ammunition pouches and packs squared off with cardboard, as if they were about to go on guard duty in front of Buckingham Palace – 'Buck House' as they called it – itself.

In the spring of 1945 the Guards Armoured Division seemed to be the last bastion of rank and privilege in an army which would vote overwhelmingly for Labour at the first-war election. One battalion alone of the division – the 3rd Scots Guards – would produce a future Archbishop of Canterbury, a Lord Chamberlain, a Home Secretary, a Chief Scout, a chairman of Rolls Royce, a Senior Steward of the Jockey Club, etc.. etc. But despite the constraints of the Guards and his working-class background, Guardsman Eddie Charlton was happy and excited in his new role as co-driver in a Sherman of the Irish Guards' No. 1 Squadron – and at the prospect of imminent action.

It came on the morning of 21 April, as the Guards Armoured Division probed northwards to the German town of Zeven, trying to sever the links between the two great ports of Bremen and Hamburg. The day before, the Irish Guards No. 1 Squadron, commanded by Major Mick O'Cock, had cut the road between Rotenburg and Zeven. Then they had waited until an unsuspecting German convoy rolled straight into the ambush they had set. The Irish gunners opened up at point-blank range. The Germans dropped over the sides of their vehicles in panic as the trucks skidded to a stop, the British shells already exploding among them with deadly effect. The road was littered with dead and the ill-fated German 2nd Marine Division, and forty of their trucks were destroyed or captured. Major O'Cock ordered the crews of four tanks, under the command of Lieutenant Barry Quinan, to occupy the tiny German village of Wistedt.

The village had already been visited by a Guards patrol and been found empty. Now, as the four Shermans rolled forward, their decks littered with the paraphernalia of war and the crews' kits, everyone thought it was going to be a routine job: a sort of standing patrol. An hour before dawn the four tanks, including Lieutenant Quinan's in which Eddie Charlton rode, were in possession of the southern edge of the village, together with a platoon of infantry from the Grenadier Guards.

Being British soldiers, they immediately set about 'brewing up', boiling their 'compo tea', a mixture of sugar, powdered milk and tea, over their 'Tommy cookers'. That was when they heard the rumble of tracks from the direction of Zeven. Lieutenant Quinan was not particularly alarmed. He said, 'I wonder if it's the Grenadiers?' – meaning the rest of the infantry company. Rising to his feet he began to focus his binoculars in the very same instant that an armour-piercing shell, an angry whirling white blob of solid metal, passed so close to his head that it blew his black beret off. It was the Grenadiers all right, but not the British ones. These were the grenadiers of the German 15th *Panzer-Grenadier-Regiment*, commanded by *Leutnant* Hans-Juergen von Buelow, who would win the Iron Cross this day. And their orders were – to throw the damned Tommies out of Wistedt.

Immediately all hell broke loose. The Germans came in from all sides through the thin grey drizzle which now started to fall, supported by mortar fire and the harsh crack and thud of the assault gun's heavy cannon.

For the British defenders things began to go disastrously wrong. The troops Firefly tank (a Sherman armed with a 17-pounder cannon), the only one of the four capable of tackling the German mobile gun, stalled. Its whole electrical system had failed! Hastily Quinan ordered the crew to bail out, telling Eddie Charlton to dismantle the turret machine-gun for defence. Another tank was hit. The infantry started to go down on all sides. Within an hour the defenders were down to half their original strength.

Desperately Quinan radioed Major O'Cock for permission to withdraw. They were virtually surrounded and there was only one way of escape open to them – across the fields and through some neighbouring woods. Finally the Squadron Leader gave his approval and those that Quinan could collect in the confused house-to-house fighting made a break for it. Behind them they left the dead and wounded and their four tanks, all overrun by the Germans, most of their crews either dead or bottled up in the houses.

By now Eddie Charlton, the former butcher, was alone. Corporal Dick Sawtell, who had fled for shelter with him, had been hit and killed. What should he do? Surrender? Charlton, who during the four years he had served with the Guards had become exceedingly proud of the traditions of the Brigade, refused to do that. Instead he settled down to fight a lone war against the advancing German grenadiers. Delighted with the success of his surprise attack, which had caught most of the Tommies out of their tanks making tea, von Buelow pressed home the assault, only to find 'One enemy machine-gun belabouring us with endless fire.'

It was Eddie Charlton. For ten long minutes Charlton held up the Panzergrenadiers' attack with his one-man stand. A shell exploded nearby and he felt a searing pain in his left arm. It flopped to his side uselessly. He had been badly hit.

Carried away by that unreasoning blood-lust of battle, Charlton, dripping blood, struggled to a nearby fence. Here he set up the machine-gun and opened fire once more. Again he was hit. Weakening rapidly he continued somehow, managing to load and fire with one hand. Finally he was hit a third time, and could fire no more. He collapsed and there he was found dying in the rain by the Germans, while a few houses away a victorious *Leutnant* von Buelow was eating captured British rations and playing a captured gramophone record over and over again.

The butcher lad from Lancashire, who had despaired that he would ever see action with his beloved Guards – 'already the guards out in North Africa are adding more honour and glory to our name . . . Why we have been kept back so long, I don't know' he had written home in 1942 – died to the tune of a saccharine-sweet German operetta, Im Rosengarten von Sanssouci.

But Eddie Charlton's sacrifice on that cold, wet Saturday in April 1945 would gain him the last Victoria Cross of the war in Europe. The medal would bear that simple epitaph to the brave: 'For Valour'.

IV

But Guardsman Charlton's bravery would not be known till after the war, when those of his comrades who had survived were released from the German POW camps to tell their stories. On that Saturday, as the Guards prepared to counter-attack and recapture Wistedt, their Intelligence officers were already realising that opposition on their front was stiffening considerably.

From the dead and prisoners, they had identified their attackers as belonging to the 15th Panzergrenadier Division, a first-class formation which only two days before had been identified to the west of Bremen. Now here it was appearing so startlingly to the east of the port, determinedly attempting to stop the British cutting the road and rail links between Bremen and Hamburg.

That could mean only one thing. The Germans were not going to surrender the port tamely after all, as the Corps Commander of 30th Corps, Horrocks, had hoped. They were going to make a fight for the port. As if to confirm that German resistance was stiffening, reports started to come into Divisional HQ from yet another of the Guards Division's hard-pressed units this Saturday that another future holder of the Victoria Cross was dying. Just like Eddie Charlton, he would succumb to his wounds before he learned that he had been awarded his country's highest honour for valour.[6]

As Saturday ended, a worried Horrocks knew that the German defenders of Bremen were not going to accept his earlier offer of surrender. Reluctantly, for he was a humane, sensitive man who at this late stage of war did not want to inflict unnecessary harm on either friend or foe, he decided the Germans in Bremen had to be taught a lesson. He called in that British officer the Germans feared the most, the one who had devastated fifty-eight of their major cities and who, although he had been ordered on 16 April 1945 no longer to

---

6 The dead officer, Captain L.O. Liddell of the Coldstream Guards, had been recommended for the VC earlier that month for his bravery in action at the town of Lingen. Today, the two Guards' heroes are buried quite close to each other at the British military cemetery near the north German township of Becklingen.

bomb German cities, was still eager to rain death and destruction from the sky on the 'Hun'. Horrocks started to compose a signal to that bluff, abrasive commander buried in his underground headquarters near the British furniture-manufacturing town of High Wycombe. Perhaps even now 'Bomber' Harris could cow the defenders of Bremen into surrender?

Air Marshall Harris, who had commanded the RAF's Bomber Command since 1942, had once been stopped for speeding in his large American car by a young policeman. The latter, not recognising whom he was dealing with, snapped, 'You could kill someone if you go on like this.' Tartly, Harris replied, 'Young man, I kill thousands of people every night!'

And that was exactly what this hard, unfeeling man did. Throughout the war he never once visited any of his active service stations to see his crews off before an 'op'. Forthright, sometimes downright rude, Harris had learned his handiwork in the relentless school of colonial warfare, where rebellious 'natives' had been bombed into submission. He had no time for tutting moralisers, the 'bleeding hearts' and 'parlour pinks' who took objection to what had become the virtually indiscriminate bombing of Germany's cities. 'Bert' he was called by his cronies. But to his crews, who would suffer the heaviest casualties of any arm of the British armed forces during the Second World War (fifty-six thousand dead), he was 'Butcher' Harris, and to the public at large 'Bomber'. He lived up to both nicknames.

At 5.30 on the afternoon of Sunday 22 April, the air-raid sirens in Bremen started to shrill their urgent warnings (after this day there would be no more electricity to sound the alarms). Everywhere the citizens of the port rushed to their stout cellars or into the great overhead bunkers, some of them several storeys high and with an anti-aircraft cannon on the roof.[7] Out in the suburb of Vegesack one civilian watched the bombers coming and recorded in his diary. 'They were flying so low that you could count their four engines and nothing seemed to be stopping them.'

There were four to five hundred of them, Halifaxes and Lancasters flying at four thousand feet, coming in from the east, their bomb doors already open, ready to drop their deadly eggs on the tense city below. At first, however, it seemed that the city was going to be lucky.

---

7 Most of them were so strongly built that they defied post-war attempts to blow them up. They survive to this day.

The RAF bomb-aimers were notoriously bad when they had no 'pathfinders' to guide them, and the first bombs began to fall on open pasture harmlessly. But that was just at the start.

Now the aimers became more accurate. Their 1,000-pound bombs started to strike Bremen's industrial district, hitting shipping and motor-car factories. And then the dam along the River Weser was hit. The military authorities had planned to release the waters it held as soon as the British attack commenced, thus flooding a large area of pasture land and making it impossible for the enemy armour to advance. Now, struck by twelve direct hits, the water started to seep away harmlessly.

But the terrified civilians, huddling in their cellars or in the wildly swaying above-ground bunkers, were not interested in the defence of Bremen. All they wanted was an end to the bombs and the surrender of their native city to the Tommies. But that wasn't to be.

This night 180 of them would be killed and six thousand rendered homeless. And that raid of 22 April was just the start. 'Bomber' Harris would send in his giant bombers and the fighter-bombers of the TAC Air Force day after day until Bremen – or the great smoking ruins that were left of it – surrendered.

General Horrocks of 30th Corps had no time to wait, however, for Harris to do the job for him. Just as Eisenhower was breathing down Montgomery's neck urging him to get moving, so Montgomery was doing the same to him. The nettle of Bremen had to be grasped.

Up front in the newly captured village of Achim, an enterprising young officer of the 52nd Lowland Division, finding that the railway telephone line to Bremen was still operative, managed to get the Bremen stationmaster on the line. Hearing the bombs whistling down on all sides, the frightened German official hastily offered to act as an intermediary between the young Englishman and the German command.

Eagerly, impatiently, the young officer, his mind perhaps filled with dreams of rapid promotion, waited for the German to come back to the phone. But before the stationmaster could return, the phone in his hand went dead. 'Bomber' Harris's boys had cut off Bremen's power supply for good. There would be no surrender.

Reluctantly Horrocks began to issue his orders. A large part of the city lay north of the River Weser and could be most easily attacked from the east. Since his strongest and largest division, the 52nd (which hadn't suffered the same sort of casualties as his other three infantry divisions, the 51st, 3rd and 43rd), was already positioned on the

Weser around the town of Verden, he decided that they should kick off the attack. They would assault the port along the eastern bank of the Weser. To the 52nd's rear, the veteran 43rd Division would be held in readiness to intervene if necessary, especially if any German counter-attack developed.

On the south side of the Weser, Horrocks ordered his 3rd Infantry Division to continue their advance north-east in the general direction of Bremen and Delmenhorst, together with the most experienced of all his infantry divisions, the 51st Highland Division, known throughout the Army as the 'Highway Decorators' from their custom of plastering every town, bridge or hamlet they captured with their divisional sign of the red 'HD'. Thus, as the corps' dispatch riders hurried into the darkness with Horrocks' orders to the various commands, and while on the far horizon Bremen burned, he had settled his mind on a two-divisional thrust on each side of the Weser.

At midnight the assault infantry of the 52nd Lowland Division, dressed in their camouflaged ski smocks[8] and laden down with weapons, shovels and equipment, started to move across the 'start lines' in the division's bridgehead at the villages of Achim and Uphusen, heading for the attack of the morrow. It was pouring with rain. It beat down on them, dripped from their helmets and soaked their packs. But as the long files of teenaged infantry trudged through the mud, with their own 'heavies' rumbling to the rear, the young soldiers were not concerned with the rain and mud. Each man was wrapped up in his own little cocoon of worry and apprehension. Would they survive what was soon to come?

Over Bremen the first red signal flares hissed into the sky. It was the warning. The Germans knew they were on their way . . .

---

8   The division had been trained for four years as a mountain division, only to land for their first action in Holland – the flattest part of Europe!

5

'I think how horrid my mother was to me.'

I

The assault on Bremen started quietly enough. At four o'clock on the morning of 23 April 1945, two companies of the 6th Battalion the King's Own Scottish Borderers started to advance up the road between the villages of Bierden and Uphusen. They were the van of the whole 52nd Division.

Neither of the two company commanders had seen the ground by daylight and all that Major Stewart, the tall, thin-faced commander of the KOSB's A Company had to guide him was an aerial photograph of the terrain, which was pretty useless in the glowing darkness. His task was to negotiate a long scrubby rise and take his first objective, an old flak site once used for the anti-aircraft defence of Bremen. What the aerial photo taken the week before didn't show was that since it had been taken the Germans had built a fairly strong defensive system in the area, complete with machine-gun nests. In the meantime the flak site had been reoccupied by German troops.

Despite the rain, the darkness and the lack of information, the young Major confidently led his strung-out files of young soldiers up the road, while behind them and slightly to their flank the KOSB's C Company advanced to the same objective. As yet there was no sound save the stamp of their own heavy boots on the glistening wet cobbles and the permanent rumble of the 'heavies' in the distance. Now and then an urgent flare rose hissing into the sky above the German lines, colouring their anxious, tense faces an unreal blood-red.

But already things were beginning to go wrong. The area was packed with gun batteries and various headquarters, all using more powerful radios than the '18 set' with which the infantry was equipped. As a result the KOSB's own HQ soon lost contact with the two companies advancing towards the German positions.

At the HQ this had been expected. Still the battalion commander and his staff worried. In the little, half-timbered farmhouse HQ, which stank of hard work and stale cabbage, the staff chain-smoked and drank 'sarnt-major's char', a thick, dark-brown brew enriched with evaporated milk, in which the spoon stood upright. Constantly they urged the frustrated radio operators, crouched sweating over their sets, faces hollowed by the glaring white light of the hissing petrol lanterns, to raise the missing companies.

Just after five o'clock, as the first ugly white light of dawn started to flush the sky to the east and weary batmen began to pull down the blackouts, the strained officers at HQ could hear the first high-pitched, almost hysterical scream of the German MG 42, which could fire an amazing 1,000 rounds per minute. The bursts were answered by the heavier, more ponderous, slower rattle of a British Bren gun. The officers looked at each other significantly. They knew what the firing meant. The two missing companies had run into trouble. The battle was on.

Thirty minutes later the HQ radio crackled in sudden life. A Company's signaller came on the air. His voice distorted metallically, jumping occasionally as another burst of enemy fire slammed into the building where he sheltered, he reported: '*Three hundred yards short of objective . . . Jerry still in occupation . . . taking heavy Spandau fire . . . Intercepted message from C Company . . . state they're cut off from the rear ¨. .*' C Company was in what the Battalion CO Colonel Davidson later called 'a sticky position'.

C Company had struck heavy opposition almost from the start. They had bumped head-on into the German 280th Infantry Battalion, which outnumbered the Jocks by four to one. The German unit was a 'stomach battalion', so-called because it contained a large number of combat-experienced but stomach-ill soldiers, grouped together because of their special dietary needs.[1]

But if their stomachs were not altogether right, the Germans possessed a lot of what the British Army called 'intestinal fortitude' – guts. During the hours of darkness they had sneaked within 10 yards of the collection of wooden huts in which the KOSBs had taken cover and had attempted to blast them out with their *Panzerfausts* at point-blank range. Now as daylight came, slow, grey and reluctant, as if God

---

1 There were also 'ear battalions' made up of soldiers with ear problems, etc.

hesitated to illuminate the scene of slaughter down below, they were dug in a stone's throw from the trapped infantry, systematically ripping apart the huts with their machine-guns.

In the hut that sheltered C Company's HQ, bullets ricocheted frighteningly around the room. Plaster fell like snow. Fist-sized wood splinters and pieces of brick spurted from the shattered walls as the Germans hosed the place with fire. Frantically the signallers dug up the floorboards with their jackknives in order to bury their '18 set', their only link with the outside world. Something had to be done – and done quickly.

Not realising that Battalion HQ knew of their position from A Company's signaller, Lieutenant Harry Atkinson, who had already won the Military Medal for bravery as a sergeant, volunteered to bring help. Slipping out of the back door, he vaulted into the yard. He had hardly started when the German machine-gunners spotted him.

Tracer bullets sped towards him like a swarm of glowing red hornets. Atkinson dropped to the debris-littered cobbles as if hit. For fifteen long minutes he lay out there completely in the open, hardly daring to breathe, as the vicious snap-and-crackle of a fire fight went on over his head. Then judging it was safer to move, he slipped off his pack. Taking a deep breath he sprang to his feet and commenced running, as if the Devil himself were after him . . .

By eight o'clock the rest of the KOSBs had moved up behind Major Stewart's A Company. Here the CO and Stewart decided they needed more muscle. They asked for a 'shoot'. Divisional HQ gave its approval.

At ten minutes to ten, the whole of the division's artillery opened fire. For ten long, earth-shaking minutes the shells rained down on the comparatively small area to the KOSBs' front. Great fountains of earth spurted upwards in flashes of ugly yellow and red flame. The blast struck the waiting infantry across the face. Their skin felt as if someone had thrown sharp, stinging pepper at it. Then, as startlingly and suddenly as it had commenced, that tremendous barrage ceased and the infantry were moving forward again, supported by a troop of tanks from the Royal Scots Greys and the British Army's most fearsome weapon – a troop of mobile, flame-throwing Crocodile tanks!

First the infantry secured the edge of the village of Uphusen. Then the Crocodiles rattled into action. Covered by the Shermans of the Royal Scots Greys, firing steadily into the village all the time, the flame-throwers raced up and down the cobbled main street. Their gunners didn't hesitate, although they had seen the dreadful results of their handiwork in the past. They pressed their triggers.

Long streams of purple flame, tinged black with oil, slapped out of the barrels and curled around the houses held by the Germans. The screams of the defenders were mercifully muffled by the rattle of the tracks and the boom of the Scots Greys' cannon. At that short range of impact of that searing blowtorch was horrific. In an instant the Germans' flesh was charred a deep black and through the burnt mess the bones revealed shone like polished ivory. In a flash men were shrunk to the size of pygmies, frozen into a frightening, hunched-up position, the weapons they had been holding glowing an ugly dull purple.

In that half-hour the 'stomach battalion' took terrible casualties. But the Jocks pressed home their attack, unmoved by the sufferings of their opponents. In the unfeeling prose of the time, an eyewitness recorded, 'The attack was one hundred per cent successful. The Jocks tore through the town, pitching the Huns out of their holes, while the Crocodiles roasted and the tanks blasted them out of the buildings. D Company followed, yelling and cheering for all they were worth.'

By midday that Monday it was all over. The 'stomach battalion' had ceased to exist as an effective fighting force. What was left of it – 150 terrified prisoners – were hustled to the rear towards the waiting cages. Still under heavy artillery fire from Bremen, Uphusen now firmly in British hands and the advance on the port could continue.

II

The 'Big Lion', as his 'lords'[2] called him, arrived punctually at the little North German station at ten o'clock. It had taken his train eight hours to travel from Berlin. As usual Allied air attacks had disrupted the German *Reichsbahn's*[3] schedules. All the same the 'Big Lion's' body-guard of ex-U-boat crews and his armoured Mercedes, presented to him by a grateful Führer, were waiting to whisk him off to his new headquarters at the pretty Holstein town of Ploen, not far from its celebrated lake. And the 'Big Lion', otherwise Grand Admiral Karl Doenitz, the officer whose U-boats had nearly brought Britain to its knees back in 1942, had no time to lose.

The situation in Germany, a country now virtually split in two by the enemy driving from east and west into the heart of the Reich, was

---

2 Nickname for the U-boat crewmen.
3 German state railway.

chaotic. In his new position as the Führer's Deputy for North Germany, Doenitz had a full day in front of him. Since the previous autumn he had been in virtual command in the north, and he knew well enough how bad things were and how much there was to be done. Not only must he keep the Baltic open so that German troops and civilians trapped in East Prussia and in the Danzig area could be evacuated by the German Navy to Schleswig-Holstein and Denmark, but he also had to maintain 'the door to the West', as he called it, between Lübeck and the Elbe beyond Hamburg, in order to allow as many German troops as possible to escape from the advancing Russians.

As the five-ton Mercedes hurried up the provincial town's cobbled street, the hard-eyed, cold-faced Grand Admiral ran his mind over his resources and the personalities under his command, those who would have to support him in the momentous task ahead.

He had some one and a half million soldiers under arms, commanded by Field Marshal Busch who, unlike so many other senior *Wehrmacht* officers, was prepared to fight on although Germany was visibly collapsing. One of Busch's staff officers had once protested in Russia, 'Herr *General*, they are shooting hostages outside!' to which Busch had snorted, 'Then pull the curtains to, man, so that you don't see them.' The episode was typical of Busch. He could rely on him.

In charge of the millions of civilians who were now his responsibility was *Gauleiter* Wegener, who headed his fellow *Gauleiters* and the Party apparatus. Wegener was an unknown quantity. In any case the real power in the Party in North Germany was the man in charge of Hamburg, *Gauleiter* Kaufmann.

The dark-haired Party boss, now in his early forties, had once been a fanatic who had crushed 'Red' Hamburg ruthlessly. But ever since that terrible week in July 1943 when Allied bombers had destroyed nearly 60 per cent of Hamburg and the Führer had refused to visit the sorely hurt city and cheer up its citizens, Kaufmann had begun to lose his faith in Hitler. Now if there were to be a Judas among his followers, Doenitz knew it would be Kaufmann.

Although as a young U-boat commander just returned from an English POW camp he had gone through that terrible mutiny of the German Navy at the end of the First World War, the 'Big Lion' had the utmost confidence in his own service. Besides he had always insisted upon the strictest discipline among his sailors. They might get drunk, they might whore, but they had to respect authority – or else. In the ports of the north – Kiel, Wilhelmshaven, Emden and the like – there were a hundred thousand of his sailors 'on the beach', many of them men of his old U-boat arm now without ships. They would fight to the end, come what may. He knew that. His 'lords' wouldn't let their 'Big Lion' down.

Almost as if to confirm his trust in the Navy, an excited aide rushed to meet him as he entered his new headquarters, followed by his personal adjutant, Lt Commander Luedde-Neurath, an elegant ex-U- boat officer. 'Herr Grossadmiral,' he exclaimed, 'Lieutenant-Commander Cremer and his battalion have successfully penetrated the Tommies' lines!'

For a moment the 'Big Lion' was puzzled. Then he remembered. 'Ali' Cremer, whose mother was English, was one of his ace U-boat skippers who had been beached due to the lack of a boat. He had formed an anti-tank battalion out of ex-submariners in a similar position. It had been 'Ali' Cramer's intention to carry out commando raids with his sailors behind Allied lines, primarily to go 'tank-hunting' with the primitive but powerful German *Panzerfaust*.[4] 'Excellent,' he barked. 'It's a start.' And with that he strode into his office to commence his new battle with the unknown Montgomery. The little Field Marshal had suddenly acquired a formidable opponent.

In some of their last discussions in the Berlin bunker before the Reich Minister for Armament Albert Speer also fled north to Ploen, Hitler had frequently remarked of Doenitz, 'There's a man whom I respect . . . With Doenitz I know where I am. He is a National Socialist through and through, and he keeps his Navy free of all bad influences, too. The Navy will never surrender. He has implanted the National Socialist concept of honour in it. If the Army generals had had that spirit, they would not have abandoned cities without a fight and pulled back frontlines that I had strictly ordered them to hold.'

That April Hitler's assessment of his new commander in the north seemed correct. Indeed all of Doenitz's background and career pointed in that direction. With his cold, pale, expressionless face and piercing gaze, he looked the very epitome of the fanatic, one who had been brought up in the strict Prussian tradition of self-sacrifice for the cause and submission to higher authority. In his youth, his father had told the young Karl that he should allow himself, if necessary, to be 'chopped to pieces' for the Kaiser, and young Karl had tamely agreed.

---

4 According to German sources, Cremer and his men succeeded in knocking out some twenty tanks of the 7th Armoured Division south of Harburg that day.

It was that kind of sentiment that made young Lieutenant Doenitz, after five years in the Kaiser's Navy, volunteer for the then most dangerous and adventurous branch of the service – the U-boat arm. There after two years of high-sea duty in command of the U-68, Doenitz had attacked a British convoy off Sicily. Out of nowhere a British destroyer suddenly appeared and took a direct, high-speed course towards the surfaced submarine. The Tommies were going to ram him! Doenitz just had time to yell 'Crash dive!' as the U-boat's klaxon shrieked its warning, then the boat slipped below the surface. The tremendous steepness of its descent affected its steering, and thus it was that at dawn the next day the U-68 abruptly popped up right in the middle of an Allied convoy. On all sides the ships concentrated their fire on the startled German submariners. Frantically Doenitz ordered his crew to abandon ship. Minutes later, Doenitz was a British prisoner of war.

Doenitz remained in the enemy POW cage for over a year. He tried once to escape and failed. Then with two comrades he pretended to go mad, running around in circles, in the hope of a medical discharge. The British doctors who examined him were singularly unimpressed. A spell of solitary confinement soon cured him of his madness. But in the end Doenitz pulled it off. He swallowed huge quantities of pipe tobacco and managed to produce the symptoms of blackwater fever. The British let him go.

In July 1919 he was back in the Weimar Republic's new Navy: a Navy which had just suffered a mutiny and one from which the victorious Allies had banned submarines. So he went into destroyers, working himself steadily up the slow ladder of promotion by sheer hard work and an inflexible devotion to duty.

By 1930 Doenitz had begun to interest himself in politics, an interest uncommon in the German Navy at that time. However, because the *Kriegsmarine*[5] had a horror of the repetition of the naval mutinies of 1918–19, Doenitz seemed a logical candidate for the staff post responsible for preparing measures to meet what were called 'internal disturbances'. It was thought that in the depressed thirties, with nearly six million German workers unemployed, there might be another revolution from the left, especially in the great 'red' ports of the north. It was during this time that Doenitz first started to be attracted to National Socialism and Hitler.

When Hitler came to power in 1933, Doenitz was one of the few

5 The German Navy.

naval officers who welcomed his appointment as Chancellor. As he was to say at his trial after the war, 'Naturally I admired and joyfully recognised the high authority of Adolf Hitler because he succeeded in realising his national and social aims without spilling blood.' When, however, in 1939 Hitler commenced 'spilling blood' in earnest, Doenitz supported him even more strongly. He spent long periods at Hitler's various headquarters, and as the Führer knew little of naval matters Doenitz enjoyed more freedom of speech – and action – than did the Führer's generals.

He was successful, too. His submarines played havoc with Allied shipping. While Germans ate well and heartily, Doenitz's submarines forced Britain to cut its rations drastically. In 1941 Britain's weekly butter ration was sufficient perhaps to generously cover two slices of bread and the weekly meat ration might suffice to make an under-nourished hamburger. Thus when Admiral Raeder of the German Navy finally resigned in 1943 after years of disagreeing with Hitler on naval policy, Doenitz was promoted to Grand Admiral and took the old man's place as head of the German Navy.

Now he was Hitler's favourite sailor. The Führer gave him a large sum of money, forbade him to use an aeroplane in case it crashed, and would not allow him to travel in the occupied territories because of the danger of assassination. During raids on towns where Doenitz was located, Hitler would often telephone and ask with great concern whether the Admiral had already gone to his shelter.

By the winter of 1944–5 Donitz was in charge not only of the German naval and merchant fleets, but also of the distribution of oil and solid fuels throughout northern Germany, thus controlling industrial production and the transport system in that region. In short, by the time he took up his new military duties, Grand Admiral Doenitz was the most powerful man in the future battlefield, and one who had not yet lost faith. For with the British already on the Elbe, only a matter of some 50 miles from his new HQ at Ploen, he could declare confidently, 'At the latest in one year – perhaps even this year – Europe will realise that Adolf Hitler is the only statesman of any stature in Europe'!

III

That same morning Major Earle reported John Poston's death to Montgomery's HQ. He had been rescued by advancing British troops from the German farmhouse where he had been left, and had been taken for treatment to a field ambulance station. There he signalled the Field Marshal's headquarters, 'Regret to report John Poston killed at 1800 hrs, Saturday 21 April . . .'

Montgomery was informed immediately. 'Tears came into his eyes,' it was reported later, and 'he remained alone in his caravan for a considerable time'. Then he roused himself sufficiently to ask his personal doctor, Robert Hunter, to bring in the body of his favourite liaison officer. Hunter knew the liaison officers were 'a wild bunch' but felt that Poston was the wildest of them all. 'There were often occasions when Monty could or should have hauled him over the coals, but he didn't.' Hunter reasoned that it was because 'John Poston represented something Monty couldn't himself be – because Monty was so disciplined and kept himself on such a tight rein.' Now the Field Marshal would mourn two long days for the dead officer, when for years now scores, hundreds, thousands of his men had been dying daily in battle. He did so, in Hunter's opinion, because 'Monty had a sort of paternal affection for him.'

Others have suggested a latent homosexual streak in his nature. Indeed he 'always liked boys', as one of his liaison officers turned schoolmaster T.E.B. Howarth remarked long afterwards, and after the war he took up with Swiss schoolboy Lucien F. Trueb, met on a skiing holiday, whom he dressed up in a mini-field marshal uniform and personally towelled dry after his nightly bath. Strange behaviour indeed in Britain's most important soldier of the twentieth century, then in his sixties and at the height of his fame!

Once when he lay dying Montgomery was visited by one of his former soldiers who would become a field marshal himself, Lord Carver. Montgomery told Carver that he was 'just lying there waiting to die.' Carver protested that he must think of something. Montgomery replied with the sad comment that he did: 'I think how horrid my mother was to me.'

Perhaps that was the explanation for Montgomery's attraction for these young men and younger boys. Like everyone else he longed to be loved, and his mother had never loved him. Indeed in his whole life he seemed to have enjoyed both physical and emotional love only once, during that brief spell of marriage before the war, before his wife was taken from him so cruelly. His mother's failure to give him love had reinforced his inclination to erect barriers between him and his fellow human beings, making him appear so strange and so remote. But with young men like Poston he could relax, even love.

Thus it was that when Hunter found the body of John Poston he wondered whether he dare report the truth. 'It wasn't buried. I found it still lying in the ditch where he'd died. There was no mark on it save where a bayonet had been plunged through the chest.' Could he upset Monty any more by giving him the full details of what had really happened to his favourite? 'For the first time I was tempted to tell Monty a lie – to say that he'd been killed by a bullet or something during the skirmish. I . . . I knew Monty would be upset.'

In the end Hunter knew he couldn't lie. Montgomery would want to know the truth, however much it upset him. 'When he returned that day and I told him he just nodded, turned on his heel and went into his caravan.' That day his staff would get nothing out of the little Field Marshal, who commanded the destinies of over a million men and who was now going to decide the future – for the rest of the twentieth century – of a sizeable portion of northern Europe. For now Montgomery sorrowed for a lost love. Soon, standing at the open grave of John Poston, he would weep openly.

Just before midnight that day, several German cars drove up to the secluded house near Lübeck's largest park, the Swedish consulate in North Germany. Out of them stepped 'the loyal Heinrich' – Himmler – followed by SS General Schellenberg, his young ambitious head of the SS's own secret service. Scar-faced and cunning-eyed, the former lawyer had been urging his chief to make peace overtures to the Allies since 1943. He had once even planned to kidnap Hitler himself and hand him over to the Americans in Spain. Now Schellenberg's aim was being realised. Himmler was seriously seeking peace.

At the entrance to the consulate they were met by Count Folke Bernadotte, the aristocrat who had been responsible for having the Scandinavian prisoners released. Though he did not know it, his actions had prompted Himmler to have the concentration camp at Neuengamme clear before the Allies took it – there would be no second Belsen. Now those same prisoners, ten thousand of them, were bottled up in the holds of three merchant ships not a dozen miles away, awaiting their terrible fate. It was a macabre situation.

Bernadotte ushered his guests into a small room lit by candles and, after their initial discussion had been disturbed by an air-raid on Lübeck, Himmler said, 'I've come to realise you're right. The war must end. I admit that Germany is defeated.' He added that he felt he was no longer bound by his personal oath of loyalty to the Führer. In the present situation,' he stated, sipping the only drink he would accept, soda water, 'my hands are free. To save as much of Germany as possible from a Russian invasion, I'm willing to capitulate on the western front . . . but not on the eastern front. I have always been, and I shall always remain, a sworn enemy of Bolshevism.' His face, with its weak receding chin, flushed. Thereupon he asked Bernadotte if he would put forward his offer of surrender to the Swedish Foreign Minister, who could then contact his opposite numbers in Washington and London.

Bernadotte didn't like the idea. He said it was unlikely that the Western Allies would make a separate peace with a Germany still fighting on the Eastern Front against their ally, Russia.

'I'm well aware of how extremely difficult this is,' Himmler replied. 'But all the same I want to make an attempt to save millions of Germans from Russian occupation.'

Bernadotte considered, while outside the Baltic port settled down for the night. Neutral Sweden's position during the war had been difficult. To some observers Sweden had seemed to support Germany when the Third Reich had been winning. She had supplied her with goods and had even allowed German troops to use the Swedish railway system. Since 1944, however, with the change in the Allies' fortune and the ever-increasing Russian danger on the Baltic, Sweden had been attempting to prove that she had always been a firm believer in the Allied cause. Thus Bernadotte knew he had to pass on Himmler's proposition. He told Himmler he would do so and asked casually what the head of Germany's police *apparat* would do if he were turned down.

'In that event,' Himmler replied, 'I shall take over command on the eastern front and be killed.' But 'the loyal Heinrich' had no intention of dying in battle. He added hastily that he wished to meet Eisenhower, to whom he would surrender unconditionally and without delay. Leaning forward across the table, he asked in confidence, 'Between men of the world, should I offer my hand to Eisenhower?'

Glibly the Swedish Count answered that he thought Eisenhower *would* be prepared to take the hand of the man whom the West thought responsible for the atrocities of Belsen and Buchenwald.

Pleased, his mood restored by Bernadotte's willingness to help, Himmler left and personally took the wheel of his Mercedes. He put his foot down on the accelerator. Awkward and clumsy as he always was, the big car shot forward and went right through the nearest hedge to become entangled in the barbed wire which now surrounded the consulate!

101

Together the Swedes and the German conspirators managed to free the car and Himmler and his entourage lurched off into the blackout. But there was, Bernadotte remarked to his aides as they returned inside once more, something very symbolic about the departure of one who had once been the most feared man in Europe.

Bernadotte was right. Himmler still grandly thought he was in charge, ready to deal with top politicians and soldiers as he had been doing throughout the war. In reality he was on the run. Events had overtaken him, but he was still completely unaware of the repulsion and loathing that the mere mention of his name occasioned in civilised society. No one in his right mind was going to do a deal with 'the loyal Heinrich' this spring.

Yet although Himmler's peace feelers would have no real influence on the events of the next week, they were noted in both London and Washington. The peace feelers meant that the Germans were finished. If Himmler, who was regarded as Germany's number-three man after Hitler and Goering, was prepared to surrender then there was no fight left in Third Reich. Why was it, then, that Montgomery was sitting on his thumbs on the Elbe when it should have been a walkover for him to reach the Baltic? Already Churchill had cabled his Foreign Minister, Eden, in Washington:

It is thought most important that Montgomery should take Lübeck as soon as possible and he has an additional American Army Corps to strengthen his movements if he requires it. Our arrival in Lübeck before our Russian friends from Stettin would save a lot of argument later on. There is no reason why the Russians should occupy Denmark, which is a country to be liberated and have its sovereignty restored. Our position at Lübeck, if we get it, would be decisive in the matter!'

Suddenly Eisenhower, who had up to now been seemingly unaware that war also involved political aims, started to worry about the Russians. For nearly a week he had tried to obtain from the Russians some idea of where they might meet up with the Americans in central Germany – without any result. The Russians were playing the game with their cards held tightly to their chests and Eisenhower had already admitted to General Marshall, his mentor, that he would be 'badly embarrassed' if the Russians pushed to the limit of their future zone of occupation, which would involve American troops having to move back (they had already taken some of the future Russian Zone of Occupation).

Now with Montgomery seemingly stalling and refusing to make a dash for the Baltic, what might happen if the Russians got there before him? Would they claim the territory as their own, despite the previous agreements reached by the politicians on the future division of conquered Germany? Might not clashes with the Russians be the result? Might Eisenhower not be accused of pandering to the Russians on Berlin and Prague when they did just what they liked?

With Himmler himself ready to surrender, Montgomery had to be forced into moving. Accordingly the Supreme Commander cabled Field Marshal Brooke, the British Chief of Staff, and told that cold, bird-watching Ulsterman that he had done everything in his power to get Montgomery to move. He signalled that [I have] done everything that is humanly possible for me to do and that I have not been merely giving lip service to an idea without doing anything to implement it.' Eisenhower concluded the cable by telling Brooke that he had formed a reserve for Montgomery's use and that, in effect, he now washed his hands of responsibility for any further delay.

Eisenhower's crony, General Bradley, agreed that Montgomery needed a push. 'I expressed strong doubt that Monty could carry out his Lübeck mission without our virtually forcing US troops on him.' He and Eisenhower decided they would place General Matt Ridgway's 18th Airborne Corps, consisting of three American divisions and one British, at Montgomery's disposal whether he liked it or not. As Bradley concluded maliciously, 'No one could build a fire under Monty better than Ridgway!' As Bradley would write in his memoirs, 'Had we not primed Ridgway in advance and then rushed him to help Monty, the Russians would surely have reached the Danish border first and perhaps gone on to Copenhagen with possibly damaging consequences in the postwar world.'

In August 1944 General Marshall, that austere American who had filled the ranks of the US Army in Europe with his own protegés in a kind of American 'old boy network', had decreed that there should be fewer written records of the decisions made by his generals during the campaign in Europe. Some documents should be preserved, he maintained, but only under lock and key. 'For example,' he wrote, 'references in historical writings to the bitter discussions which have arisen from time to time over various plans of campaign, allocations of material etc. will be highly inadvisable in the future.'

Marshall, who was rightly concerned with the prestige of the US Army and its regular officers, was fond of pointing out that his old

chief in the First World War, 'Black Jack'[6] Pershing still held records
pertaining to that war and refused to release them to historians. He
knew, too, that his subordinate commanders – Bradley, Eisenhower,
Patton and all the rest of them – wanted to go down favourably in the
history books. All generals did. Only a handful of them would ever
admit later that they had made a single mistake during the whole
course of the Second World War (Patton, in fact, grandly admitted to
two).

Thus it was that when they came to write their memoirs in a
changed climate of opinion, when Russia was the new enemy of the
cold war, Bradley especially was eager to pass on to Montgomery any
blame for having failed to recognise the threat posed by the Russians.
As he would interpret the history of those last few days of the war in
Europe, it was he, Bradley, with the aid of General Ridgway, who
finally got Montgomery going. As Montgomery would remark when
the Americans now began to importune him to move north before
the Russians got to the Baltic, 'This is adding insult to injury . . .'

Just one month before, General 'Gentleman Jim' Gavin, the slim,
athletic commander of the US 82nd Airborne Division, a veteran
formation which had once been commanded by Bradley himself and
which had fought in North Africa, Sicily, Italy, France, Belgium and
Holland, had assembled his staff close to midnight on Palm Sunday at
his headquarters in Sissonne in France.

After checking security and telling his hand-picked officers in their
highly polished jump boots that 'nothing you hear tonight is to go
beyond this room', he had pulled back the wall curtain covering a
large map. 'Gentlemen,' he had announced dramatically, 'we're going
in for the kill. This is the Sunday punch!'

His officers had stared wide-eyed at what the map revealed. Their
objective was going to be the enemy's capital. They were being
prepared for an airborne attack on Berlin!

Gavin, who in twenty years had risen from private to general, had
touched the map with his pointer. 'Our piece of real estate is right in
Berlin,' he had said. 'Tempelhof Airport.' Then after adding some
further details he had dismissed his officers, leaving them to wander
off into the March night, chatting excitedly among themselves.

But since that Palm Sunday, the hours, the days, the weeks had

6 Because he had once commanded black US soldiers.

passed without further instructions from Supreme Headquarters about the bold operation to drop three airborne divisions, two American and one British, on Berlin's airfields. General Ridgway, commander of the 18th US Airborne Corps to which Gavin's 82nd Airborne belonged, had admittedly written to Gavin, sending him a copy of the letter he had sent to Supreme HQ, which stated, 'it is believed the reaction of the German mind will be tremendously influenced by the personal appearance of individual soldiers who participate in "Operation Eclipse".[7] It is the intention of this head-quarters to take into "Eclipse", "A" dress as well as field uniform.' But that had been all.

By the third week of April 1945 a thoroughly bored and impatient General Gavin and his élite division found themselves carrying out what amounted to garrison duties along the Rhine in the area of Cologne. Although Gavin's paras could hear the sound of battle on the other side of the Rhine, they were forbidden to participate.

Here Gavin's main problems were the 'DPs' and 'fraternisation'. The 'DPs' were the many thousands of former slave labourers from the East who did not want to return home in case they were sent to the Gulag as turncoats; they lived on what they could loot and steal from the terrified German civilians. 'Fraternisation' was the problem occasioned by Eisenhower's new ruling that no Allied soldier would associate with a German save in the line of duty – the 'non-fraternisation ban' as it was called.

But as a realistic Gavin saw it, knowing well the basic needs of the fighting soldier for food, drink and sex, 'After the long trek all the way from North Africa, some of the frauleins looked quite attractive . . . The GIs reasoned that as long as they kept on their airborne caps and their jump boots, as tokens of their patriotism, they should be allowed to do anything, or almost anything.'[8]

But Gavin was bored with DPs and fraternisation. He wanted to be at the kill. As a regular army officer, he didn't want to spend the last weeks of the war, while his fellow generals were still making the headlines, sitting 'on my butt' on the Rhine. He craved action. On Monday 23 April, Gavin decided he would lay it on the line to the Supreme Commander himself. Completely disregarding official channels and regulations on how one should approach a superior officer, the tall, handsome commander started to draft an angry signal

---

7 Codename for the top-secret Allied plan to come into effect when it appeared that Nazi Germany's defences were about to collapse.

8 General Patton, who believed a man who 'wouldn't fuck won't fight', summed it up more succinctly. 'It's not fraternization,' he declared, 'it's fornication!'

to Eisenhower. Exasperated by the long delay, he wrote that he was 'assuming' the airborne operation against Berlin would not be required. He ended the signal with a request for 'confirmation or clarification!'

In fact, Eisenhower was saving the veteran 82nd Airborne Division, for it had been secretly earmarked for an assault landing on one of Tokyo's airports. Now, however, with Monty obviously not prepared to assult the Elbe unless he had more troops, Eisenhower 'released' the 82nd Airborne. On 24 April he sent Gavin an equally terse signal, stating that 'Airborne operations to Berlin under Eclipse conditions' were not required. Instead Gavin was directed to assemble his division, once it had been withdrawn from the Rhine front, on the bank of the Elbe south of Hamburg, near the small river town of Bleckede.

Puzzled by this sudden, urgent transition from the relatively soft life and tempting fleshpots of a ruined Cologne to what seemed to be another mission, the airborne troopers started to pile into the waiting trucks which would take them 200 miles northwards to the Elbe, though as yet they did not know their destination.

Climbing aboard the 'deuce and a half',[9] one of them, Private 'Dutch' Schultz of the 505th Parachute Regiment, summed up the feelings of the rest of his comrades when he called to his pal, Private Joe Tallett. Cynically he commented to the 'kid', 'So I lead 'em into Normandy, yes? Into Holland, yes? Look at me, kid, I'm a blue-blooded American and the country's got only one of me.'

The other man, who had not dropped in Normandy and Holland as Schultz had, grinned and waited for the punchline, as all around them the drivers gunned their engines, as if impatient to be off.

'Yeah, they want to get their money's worth,' Schultz sneered. 'They ain't gonna waste *me* on Berlin. Hell no! They're saving me up. *They're gonna drop me on Tokyo!*'

But Private 'Dutch' Schultz would drop on neither Berlin nor Tokyo. Eisenhower was dispatching him and the rest of his comrades of Ridgway Corps to 'build a fire under Monty'. In due course, the US 82nd Airborne would achieve the most tremendous victory of its two-year-long fighting career: it would accept the surrender of a whole German Army Group. But it would be a hollow victory: one without any political significance whatsoever.

---

9   A 2½-ton truck.

BOOK TWO: GOETTERDAEMMERUNG

MONDAY 23 APRIL – MONDAY 30 APRIL 1945

'Come on, you lucky buggers – I've got a lovely battle for you!'

30th Corps Brigadier to his staff, April 1945

1

'Come out and bloody well fight!'

I

General Horrocks, commander of the British 30th Corps, called him 'von Thoma'[1] of the 'wicked Wyvern', and was apt to make fun of him in a gentle, teasing way. The officer he referred to was Major-General Thomas, commanding the 43rd Division, which had the Wessex Wyvern as its divisional patch.

Indeed Thomas, a tall, horsey-looking man who invariably wore riding breeches and polished riding boots although he was an infantry commander, was wide open to ridicule. Yet his division was a tough, seasoned fighting force, which had suffered a tremendous twelve thousand casualties during the course of the campaign, a complete turnover in personnel in fact. In some of his battalions, battalion commanders had been killed and wounded with frightening regularity. In his 7th Hampshires, for example, two of the three colonels had been killed in action. His Duke of Cornwalls had also lost two of their three colonels in battle, while his 179 Field Artillery Regiment had suffered the loss of three out of four of their COs. In the unlucky, but plucky 43rd Infantry Division, even brigadier-generals got killed in action.

But despite their horrendous casualties, the division, which felt it had been squeezed out of the ever-increasing battle for Bremen, was now ordered by Horrocks to develop an attack on the Hamburg-Bremen autobahn north-east of the village of Achim. After that attack was successful, Thomas was to lead his division to support the 52nd Lowland Division in its attack on the port itself.

The going was tough. Not only were advancing troops fighting the enemy, they were also battling the terrain, sandy in patches but boggy

---

1 The real von Thoma had been a German General captured by Montgomery in the desert.

in others, which made it very difficult for vehicles of the 43rd Reconnaissance Regiment which was in the van. Time and time again the lone
armoured cars which crawled down the cobbled roads of the area,
both sides fringed with the thick, sinister firs, were bogged down,
easy victims for some crazy Hitler Youth armed with a *Panzerfaust*. And
at this stage of the war, the 43rd Reconnaissance Regiment, which had
lost a third of its men on its very first day in Normandy,[2] had become
very cautious. No one wanted to die now that the war was virtually
over.

But the long-haired, 16-year-old fanatics in their camouflaged
capes which reached down to their ankles, cycling from ambush
to ambush with their *Panzerfausts* strapped to the handlebars as if
they were homebound from school, seemed eager to do just that:
to die themselves and take a couple of the hated Tommies with
them.

Formerly the area had been marshland reclaimed for farming, and
water was rarely far from the surface. Now the drivers of the armoured
cars and tanks either risked getting bogged down in the fields on both
sides of the road or had to chance the road itself. The boys of the
Hitler Youth seemed always there when some lone tank was stuck in
the mire or a solitary armoured car ventured up a road. Then the
Panzerfaust would blaze fire, the rocket trailing behind it a stream of
angry red sparks as it slammed home against the side of the vehicle.
Within minutes the unfortunate tank or armoured car would be a
blazing coffin and the long-haired boys would be running for their
lives once more, dirty childish faces wreathed in grins like cheeky
schoolboys who had got away with placing a drawing pin on the chair
of some unpopular teacher.

Of the thousand tanks that Montgomery employed for the attacks
along the front between Bremen and Hamburg, some 150 were
destroyed that week and another 500 were damaged sufficiently to be
withdrawn for repairs. But despite the terrain and the losses, which
according to eyewitnesses 'bordered on insanity' in some places, the
43rd Division pressed on, heading steadily for the autobahn, losing as
always the boldest and the bravest among its ranks. That day the 4th
Dorsets lost its third CO, wounded in a short, sharp exchange of fire in
a fight against German sailors.

But in the midst of the fighting and tragedy there were moments of
light relief that day. First there were the German marines who,

2 They had been aboard the troopship *Derry Cunihy*, which was either torpedoed or ran into a mine.

although they were prepared to fight to the death, were taken prisoner easily. The reason? Their infantry training was so scanty and bad (some of them had merely one day's instruction in ground warfare) that they had positioned themselves facing the wrong direction. Then there were the six *Luftwaffe-helferinnen* – the German equivalent of the Women's Royal Air Force – captured together with the flak guns they had been 'manning' by the 5th Duke of Cornwall's Light Infantry.

The day before, the 43rd had received a carefully worded and deadly serious pamphlet from Army HQ which had warned:

Your attitude towards women is wrong in Germany. Do you know that German women have been trained to seduce you? Is it worth a knife in the back? A weapon can be concealed on the chest between the breasts, on the abdomen, on the upper leg, under the buttocks, in a muff, in a handbag, in a hood or a coat . . . How can you search a woman? The answer to that one is difficult. It may be your life at stake. You may find a weapon by forcing them to pull their dress tight against their bodies here and there. If it is a small object you are hunting for, you must have another woman to do the searching and do it thoroughly in a private room.

But as 'private rooms' were not too readily available on the battlefield, the infantry of the Duke of Cornwalls were at a loss what to do with the six heavy-jowled women in their grey uniforms. In the end nothing was done and they were treated with the utmost correctness. 'Besides,' as Brigadier Essame of the 43rd commented afterwards, 'they were very plain . . .'

While the 43rd worried about their female prisoners, the 3rd Division prepared for its attack from the south. The 'Iron Division', as it had been known in the First World War, had once been commanded by Montgomery himself back in 1939 and it, too, was a seasoned veteran formation that had landed on D-Day and suffered many casualties since. Now the division was confronted with a water assault across flooded fields towards the villages of Dreye and Arsten and then a drive into Bremen.

All day long the officers of the division with the red-and-black triangle divisional patch watched the flooded area for any sign of life. But apart from a few Holstein cows grazing on the higher ground 'it all seemed very harmless,' as one of them remarked afterwards.

In fact, that section of the Bremen front was defended by some two thousand men, one-quarter of them from the 18th SS Training Battalion, plus an estimated six thousand *Volkssturm* veterans. Many of the latter were inadequately armed and not prepared to fight. But what the old men lacked in fighting spirit, the SS made up for. They, for the main part, would fight to the end.

Now the equipment started to pile up as the men of Montgomery's old division prepared for the waterborne assault. Dozens of rubber boats were brought forward. Everywhere MPs – the redcaps – were busy nailing up unit and direction signs on wooden boards, indicating battalions and brigades, marshalling area and field dressing stations. Yards of bridging equipment were readied and miles of white tape to mark where minefields were. The piles of shells for the waiting 25-pounder guns grew into mini-mountains. Now all waited for the attack to start.

As the clumsy box-like ambulances rattled up, their sides and roofs decorated with large red crosses, each one bearing that sinister legend which would give them number-one priority on the way back from the front – 'ATTENTION – CARRYING CASUALTIES' – the Typhoons came zooming in. They came in low with an ear-splitting roar. One by one they peeled off from the formation. The pilot fired. The Typhoon seemed to stagger momentarily in mid-air. Next instant the rockets were hissing forward from under their white-striped wings like flights of angry hornets, straight for the silent village of Arsten, while the artillery bombardment that had been pounding the front all day grew to a deafening crescendo. It wouldn't be long now.

At ten to eleven the final artillery plan went into operation. In one last burst of wild fury the British gunners swept the German line. The Germans knew what was coming. Green and red signal flares hushed into the glowing darkness to hang there for a few moments before swooping down like fallen angels. Here and there came the first angry hiss of high-velocity German machine-gun fire. The battle had commenced.

At eleven o'clock three companies of the 7th Shropshire Light Infantry started to double down the road to Dreye. Captain Healey, commanding Y Company, was hit almost immediately. He fell and lay still. Captain Clapham rallied the leaderless men. They surged forward once more against intense small-arms fire.

Behind them came Major Read of Z Company, firing his carbine from the hip while his men roared their encouragement. Abruptly Read heard the click of his firing pin striking nothing. He had used up all his ammo! Undaunted he ran on. He stumbled into a German weapon pit, wielding the useless carbine like a club. The German occupants fled.

But the big Major's luck was running out fast. A German bullet shattered both his legs. He fell as if poleaxed, bleeding heavily. Some of his men doubled forward to help him. But he waved them away. The attack must go on. So he lay there where he had fallen on the road, cheering his company on, crying crazily in the Germans' direction, 'Come out and bloody well fight!'

Now a private soldier, Private Wood of the Intelligence Section, took over. He paused and yelled in German, chest heaving wildly, that the defenders' situation was hopeless. They were outnumbered. They had better surrender now, while they still had the chance. The trick worked. The Germans knew well enough that men crazed with battle often refused to accept surrender. They started to tumble out of their positions in droves, hands clasped above helmeted heads, crying their 'Kamerad . . . Kamerad . . . Nicht schiessen'[3] with desperate urgency.

An hour later Dreye was in British hands and two hundred Germans went into the bag.

The 3rd Division's Royal Ulster Rifles were luckier than the Shropshires. They crossed the flood area to their front in forty-seven armoured Buffaloes of the 4th Royal Tanks. Of course the roar of the amphibious tanks alerted the Germans and a wild fire fight broke. But in the darkness the Germans could inflict little damage on the infantry or on their carriers. Minutes later all forty-seven of the 'swimming tanks', as the infantry called them, reached the other side and discharged their cargoes.

The Ulstermen, tough, hard, profane young men for the most part, darted forward. They captured two German 88mm cannon and with typical Ulster cheek turned them on their former owner. German shells began to rain down on German-held Arsten.

Meanwhile the engineers behind them sprang into action. A Bailey bridge was flung across the water at the site of a ruined German bridge. The infantry pushed on. They spotted the next bridge and captured it before the German defenders could blow it up. A road-block loomed up out of the darkness. They destroyed it by mortar fire and pressed on. Still the German defenders held on to the houses on both sides of the destroyed road-block. Angry red flame stabbed back and forth. An officer shouted an order. The mortarmen, sweating

3 'Don't shoot.'

113

over their heavy 3-inch mortars, turned their attention on to the houses. Mortar bombs howled into the burning sky and came slamming down on to the houses, scattering tiles and bricks in a crazy cascade of noise and violence. That was it. The Germans started to stream out to surrender. By the time the steam had run out of the Ulstermen's attack, they had captured five German officers and 128 men.

How many civilians died in the attack is not known. In beleaguered Bremen, now without water, light or gas, bombed and shelled by day and night, all organisation had virtually broken down and the authorities had ceased counting the dead. But one survivor, an 8-year-old girl then, recalled many years later:

'A terrible artillery bombardment . . . set in. It was so bad that we couldn't run to the shelter and stuck it out in the cellar. Half an hour later the first British tanks started to roll through the streets. We ran upstairs. All our windows were broken. My uncle sat up in bed, covered in bits of glass, but unhurt. Outside there were dead everywhere. He said, 'You know that was the worst half-hour of the war for me' . . .

For some of the men of the 'Iron Division' it was their worst half-hour, too. Lieutenant Peter Lloyd, leading a platoon of the King's Own Scottish Borderers near the village of Habenhausen, had just cleared an enemy barracks when:

Suddenly we were sniped at from our right flank. We were completely exposed on this flank! I could hear bullets whining very close and hugged the ground frantically. The terrifying thing was that we could not locate this solitary sniper. A man lying close to me was hit in the head and died shortly afterwards. Each of us tried to crawl as best we could to safety. Then another man was hit in the arm. Try as I could, I could not locate the fire and the platoon behind us could not pin it down directly. By now I was afraid to raise myself an inch from the ground. Our Piat man had been hit, too. I wriggled as best I could to a small wall in order to get protection from this enemy who was picking us off one by one. I could hear the ping of the bullets all the time and the shots seemed very close indeed. However I managed to reach the wall all right. Then a cry from H, 'They've hit me.' He went lunging past, clasping his arm and making a run for it . . . I got to my feet and ran, ran as hard as I could.

Minutes later the Germans were counter-attacking. Bremen was not going to be taken that easily.

II

While in Bremen the battle still raged, on the western bank of the Elbe the soldiers of 'Bubbles' Barker's 8th Corps waited for the call to action. Before them stretched the fast-flowing waters of the river, in some spots half a mile wide, which they were going to assault. Beyond lay the wooded high cliffs held by the Germans, and on the heights the main road – Route Four – which ran between Berlin and Hamburg.

Together with the 1st Commando Brigade, the 15th Scottish Infantry Division, which had already carried out two assault river crossings of the Seine and Rhine, was to attack between the riverside villages of Artlenburg and Avonsdorf, famed before the war for their freshwater eels, and establish a bridgehead centred on the hamlet of Schnakenbek on the other side. This bridgehead would be held for a day at an extent of 2,500 yards and a depth of 1,500, while General 'Pip' Roberts' 11th Armoured Division passed through it on its drive for the Baltic and the key port of Lübeck. Then the infantry would fan out in the general direction of Hamburg.

Although the 15th Division had not faced much opposition in the last two weeks and the Germans seemed on the verge of collapse, the planners at Barker's Corps HQ were not sanguine. The assault would have to be worked out carefully and would not take place before Bremen had fallen, just in case reserves were needed. As Montgomery had already noted, 'the Elbe is a big river similar to the Rhine and to cross it in the face of stiff opposition is a major operation'. Some of the planners agreed with him, privately thinking that the crossing would be tougher than their Rhine assault the month before.

One of the problems was that there were only two approach roads – from Luneburg to Artlenburg and from Scharnebek to the Lauenburg bridge, which had now been blown up by the German defenders – to where the assault troops would cross. Between these roads there was sandy marsh and bog so that the heavy vehicles – tanks, trucks and the Buffaloes to be used in the crossing itself – would be limited to two single roads. That meant that the vehicle equipment for *twenty thousand soldiers* would be confined to two poor country roads.

But that wasn't the end of their difficulties. On the other bank the wooded heights rose to 100 feet in some places so that the enemy enjoyed a perfect view of the 8th Corps' lines to a depth of 6 miles. Accordingly the Germans would be able to spot any offensive move made by daylight. So the planners were forced to stop any vehicular movement to the proposed crossing sites by daylight and had decided that the actual assault would have to take place during the hours of darkness – an added complication.

And the planners' difficulties didn't end there. Not only were they faced on the German side by an enemy division of some eight or nine battalions, but they had also to contend with the hundred flak cannon of Hamburg's anti-aircraft defences now being used in a ground role. If the Germans were to spot the assault in time, the Buffaloes in mid-stream would be sitting ducks for the huge 88mm cannon.

In addition, there was only one exit from the bridgehead on the other side: a steep, cobbled, winding 20-foot-wide road that led from a lone waterside pub through Schnakenbek and on to Route Four. This solitary country lane, for it was little better than that, would have to bear the major part of the 15th Division's vehicular traffic and the tanks of 'Pip' Roberts' 11th Armoured Division, which would use it as a starting point for their race to the Baltic. The Schnakenbek road, the planners concluded, would be a major headache.

But there were further complications as well. Colonel Foster, the 8th Corps' chief engineer, would follow up the initial crossing by throwing a Bailey bridge and a raft-ferry across the river where it was 300 feet wide. These two installations would have to be ready in time for the 11th Armoured Division and the 5th Infantry Division, which was now being brought secretly from Italy to reinforce the 8th Corps, to begin their drive north. In fact, the whole race to the Baltic coast would stand or fall on the failure or success of Colonel Foster's bridging operations. Then over those two bridges would pass more than five thousand vehicles of the two divisions, ranging from 30-ton tanks to half-ton jeeps.

That day as he surveyed the scene, hidden from the view of the German defenders on the other side, Colonel Foster was plagued by several grave doubts. What would happen, he wondered, if the Germans counter-attacked from the heights? Or if their artillery, which had now risen to three hundred guns, zeroed in on his bridge? Or if they threw in their last reserves of jet-fighters and bombers which could outfly anything the RAF currently possessed? It was all very worrying.

But while the planners worried, the infantry in the main relaxed, save for small reconnaissance parties made up of officers. The latter visited the places where their battalions were going to attack, moving stealthily to the river at night, their boots and equipment muffled. For long hours they lay in the damp grass on top of the dyke, studying the ground as best they could. On the other side everything was quiet. Not a light showed, save very occasionally a dimmed car headlight moving along Route Four. It was as if the front had gone to sleep. As one of the unseen observers would write afterwards, 'It was so peaceful by the riverside in that perfect

116

spring that it was hard to associate the scene with the hard battle to come.'

Up to 1942 Churchill had despaired of his soldiers. Privately he remarked several times that they seemed to have lost their will to fight. Time and time again they had let themselves be routed and defeated. They had lost one battle after another – Narvik, Dunkirk, Crete, Singapore, Tobruk and all those other foreign names which spelled shame and defeat. 'Will they never fight?' he had once moaned in despair.

El Alamein and Montgomery had changed all that. 'If we can't stay here, then let us stay here dead!' Monty had ordered before that great battle in late 1942. Some thirteen thousand of them had stayed there, dead. But thereafter the Army's fighting spirit surged. There would be setbacks admittedly. There would still be men who laid down their arms and surrendered without a fight. In Normandy a whole battalion of infantry cracked and had to be disbanded. At Arnhem, while the 1st Airborne Division was fighting for its very existence, there were scores of men, supposed to be the nation's élite, who hid cravenly in the cellars and raised their arms in surrender when the Germans came without having fired a shot.

During the course of that battle General Bittrich, the one-legged commander of the II SS Panzer Corps told his officers, 'Remember that British soldiers do not act of their own initiative when they are fighting in a town and when it consequently becomes difficult for officers to exercise control. They are amazing in defence, but we need not be afraid of their capabilities in attack.' Of course there was a great deal of truth in the SS General's assessment, even now when the Army had been fighting over ten months on the continent. The average Tommy did move at a slow and deliberate pace, doing only what was ordered of him – no more, no less.

In part, the British Army's centuries' old tradition was to blame. Whereas the young recruits to the Hitler Youth Division of the SS could not even present arms in 1943, comparable British recruits to Montgomery's army were still spending two hours a day on the parade ground 'square bashing' and practising drills that went back, in some cases, to the eighteenth century.

The Army's class structure, too, helped to stifle initiative in the rank-and-file. There was too great a gap between the officers and men. In the Guards, the soldiers still used the old formula 'permission to speak' before daring to address an officer. Each officer, even the most junior, had his batman – 'my servant' – who produced his morning tea and shaving water, even during combat; and whereas German and American officers messed with their men, the British officer tried, wherever possible, to eat separately.

The officers didn't help, even though many of them were drawn from the lower middle classes themselves. They still cultivated upper-class attitudes, as if they had all attended public schools (which they hadn't), their speech replete with the casual sporting metaphors and analogies of such schools. They did not advance with their tanks, they had a 'gallop forward'. Their spells in the line were regarded as 'a jolly good – or bad – innings'. In some of the 'better regiments' 'game books' were kept of the officers' personal score in German dead, and certain sections of the front were known to possess 'excellent rough shooting'.

Even the Army's most dedicated and professional soldier, Montgomery, could not resist that upper-class sporting image. He was always about to 'knock the enemy for six' in his battles, and hated to fight them 'on a sticky wicket'. In his Order of the Day before crossing the Rhine, he spoke of 'cracking about . . . chasing the enemy from pillar to post', ending by wishing his troops 'good hunting to you all on the other side'.

By 1945 the rank-and-file of Montgomery's Army had been infected by the work of those earnest, bespectacled sergeants of the Royal Army Educational Corps with socialist leanings, who had lectured them regularly on current affairs before the Invasion, giving everything 'a Marxist gloss', as future Labour MP Harold Lever noted. Other future Labour MPs, Woodrow Wyatt, Christopher Mayhew, John Freeman, all members of Montgomery's Army, felt that the men were eager to learn about the Brave New World the left promised them. The men sensed themselves to be every bit as good as their 'toffee-nosed' officers with their 'cut-glass accents', and looked forward to a post-war world in which the old class structures would be overthrown.

As young Major Denis Healey, a former communist and at that time a convinced socialist serving in Italy, would state one month after the war was over, 'The upper classes in every country are selfish, depraved, dissolute and decadent . . . There is a very great danger, unless we are very careful, that we shall find ourselves running with the Red Flag in front of the armoured cars of Tory imperialism and counter-revolution!' That kind of windy rhetoric probably went above the heads of most of Montgomery's men. They wanted a better world, certainly, but they didn't want revolution or any more wars; they had seen enough of warfare. Still they had become, as their crustier officers often complained, 'bolshy'; their loyalties directed more to 'mates' and 'oppos' of their immediated company than to the battalion and the 'cause', whatever that was.

By now they had suffered 125,000 battle casualties in the campaign (in proportion to their numbers three times those suffered by the Americans), and they had become tough, hard, young men who often led short and brutal lives, terminated by sudden death. They were no great respecters of person or property. As the official combat historian F.S.V Donnison would state later, 'There was wanton slaughtering of livestock. Museums were pillaged, banks were rifled. Churches, monuments, works of art were desecrated, archives destroyed.' There was widespread looting too, and a few cases of rape. But though the authorities usually turned a blind-eye to petty looting – what could the ordinary infantryman carry with him on his back anyway? – rape was punished immediately and severely. Of all the armies engaged in the battle for North-West Germany, the British Army was still the best disciplined and most orderly.

So now they waited, these young soldiers who would fight the British Army's last action of what would probably be its last major campaign of the twentieth century. They ate their 'armoured pig' and 'armoured cow' (spam and corned beef), 'soya links',[4] and cheap bacon that came out of the compo ration tins in long rolls, wrapped in greaseproof paper, to be cooked on their petrol-powered 'Tommy cookers'. Invariably as the boxes were opened and the tins distributed, some 'wit' would ask, *'Hey corp, which tin has got the cunt in?'*

As always, when not in action, their routine was inflexible: the hard, boring, very simple life of the front soldier spent in a hole or a wrecked cottage, the only amenity being the 'thunderbox,' a pole spread over a pit, equipped with 'army form blank', khaki-coloured squares of lavatory paper. They refilled magazines, repaired their uniforms with their 'housewives' (the army-issue sewing equipment), strung wire, had 'a short back and sides' (their hair being cut by some amateur barber wielding his clippers round a tin bowl suspended on the head of his 'customer'), smoked their 'coffee nails', drank their 'char' and 'bullshitted', talking the long hours away till 'it' all started again.

For 'it' wouldn't be long now. Soon these hard, 'bolshy', brave

---

4 Triangular-shaped, skinless sausages made of soya beans.

young men would be going into action once more; and this time they would end up fighting not only the Germans but also those soldiers who were to be the harbingers of the 'new world' (or so those earnest sergeants of the Army Educational Corps had told them) – the Russians!

III

For a month now the German Army Group Vistula, made up of General von Manteuffel's Third Panzer Army and General Tippelskirch's First Panzer Army, had been retreating before Rokossovsky. Ever since the Red Army's breakthrough on the River Oder in East Germany, they had been fighting and withdrawing, fighting and withdrawing, for 150 long, bloody miles.

Both German commanders despaired. Both were veterans who had fought on the eastern and western fronts and had risen from generals at the outset of the war to army commanders. Now they were at the end of their tether. In particular von Manteuffel, the undersized aristocratic gentleman-jockey who had achieved great successes against the Americans the previous December, felt that the war was virtually lost. The time had come to sue for peace. All the same he was still reluctant to do so. Not only was the fate of his own men at stake, but also that of those thousands and hundreds of thousands of humble German peasants fleeing from the advancing from the Russians.

On the same day that Colonel Foster, the 8th Corps' chief engineer, made his last survey of the Elbe before the assault, von Manteuffel, a commander respected by friend and foe as a daring and brave soldier, was visited by his superior, the craggy-faced General Heinrici.

Heinrici, who affected the gaiters and fur-collar greatcoat of the First World War German officer, walked with the undersized Panzer General in the garden of his headquarters, with the boom of the Russian cannon in the distance reminding them that Rokossovsky was attacking yet again. The older General said that he had just come from Hitler's bunker in Berlin and that the Führer had insisted that none of his generals should retreat any further. They would have to hold their positions to the last. 'Is it possible for you to carry out this order?'

Von Manteuffel remembered SS General Steiner, one of his commanders, telling him the other day that he had not one single tank left but that he had received reinforcements: 'Five thousand Luftwaffe pilots, each with his little Iron Cross hanging around his neck. Tell me what do I do with them?' He had replied, 'I have no doubt that on Hitler's maps there is a little flag saying 7th Panzer Div., even though it got here without a single tank, truck, piece of artillery or even a machine-gun. We have an army of ghosts.' Now, with a cynical smile on his thin lips, he said quietly to Heinrici, 'Without Panzers, without anti-tank guns and with inexperienced troops already out on their feet how can anybody expect me to hold any longer?'

Heinrici persisted. 'How long can you hold?'

Von Manteuffel shrugged his skinny shoulders. 'We can probably hold where we are for the rest of the day. Then we'll have to move back.'

Heinrici pointed out that this meant mobile warfare.

'We don't have much choice,' Manteuffel countered. 'If we stay where we are, we'll be encircled like the Ninth Army.'[5]

Numbly Heinrici drove back to Berlin to inform the High Command that von Manteuffel would be forced to withdraw in the very near future and that even Steiner of the SS was about to throw in the towel. As he told one of his subordinates about Hitler's insane orders to stand and fight, 'I refuse to carry out these suicidal orders any longer. It is my responsibility on behalf of my troops to refuse these orders and I intend to do so. It is also my responsibility to account for my actions to the German people.'

Back at his command post Heinrici was greeted by the phone ringing. Without taking off his old-fashioned greatcoat, he picked up the receiver.

'Manteuffel, Herr General,' a clipped voice rapped. 'The Russians have penetrated into the marches,' he said without any further ado.

Heinrici knew what that meant. Von Manteuffel's second line of defence had been overrun already. It would now be impossible for the little tank General to maintain his present position without his troops being overrun by the Russians. He hesitated.

Von Manteuffel didn't. 'I request immediate permission to pull back into prepared positions. *It's now or never, Herr General!*'

Heinrici still hesitated. He knew Hitler never tolerated a large-scale retreat by his troops. Even now when everything was lost he still dreamed he was fighting the war with the *Wehrmacht* of that year of victories, 1940. But that army had long vanished into the snows of Russia. He frowned, his old face wrinkling about the steady grey eyes.

---

5 The 9th Army was another formation under Heinrici's command.

He made his decision, knowing as he did so that he was risking his own neck. It would not be the first time that the Führer had had a general hanged for having ordered the retreat. 'All right then,' he snapped to the waiting von Manteuffel, 'start the retreat.'

Now, with Bremen still not taken and with Ridgway's 18th Airborne Corps still not arrived on the Elbe to give Montgomery the strength that Eisenhower thought he needed before he would move, the Russian steamroller had commenced moving westwards once more . . .

2

'If only the British would hurry up and get across the Elbe.'

I

At ten o'clock on the morning of Wednesday 25 April, Doenitz received North German Party leaders. They were all there, fat for the most part and balding, and dressed in their decoration-laden brown uniform, heavy with the gold braid which had earned them the derisive name of the 'golden pheasants' among the populace. They were all there, that is, save *Gauleiter* Kaufmann of Hamburg. He dared not leave the safety of Hamburg, where he had surrounded himself with a bodyguard of armed university students. He feared that Doenitz, or the hard-liner Field Marshal Busch who had his HQ outside the great port, might arrest him as a potential traitor.

It was a warm morning at Ploen and because of the heat the windows of the hut in which the 'secret meeting' was being held were opened. Thus it was that Kaufmann's representative Dr Fischer, once a committed National Socialist yet like his boss now eager for surrender, was an unwitting listener to the proceedings as he lounged outside in the morning sun.

Doenitz was in good form. He was obviously convinced that the battle for North-West Germany should continue. Admittedly the news from beyond the Elbe to the east was bad, but he wanted to fight on. His voice, as Fischer listening outside the window described it later, was 'firm and soldierly'. He declared that he had received an order from the Führer – here his voice shook slightly with emotion at the mention of the holy name – 'to defend North Germany', and 'as a soldier' he intended to carry out that command.

After discussing transport problems and those occasioned by the inmates of prisons and concentration camps, including Neuengamme, Doenitz said he had made a decision. All German troops west of the Elbe in the area under his command would be withdrawn for the defence of the other bank of the great river.

Dr Fischer's face puckered up in disdain. He told himself bitterly that the three-day-long battle for Bremen, which still was not over, had been in vain. General Becker's determination not to surrender there, and the resultant cost in German lives, military and civilian, had been for nothing. Yet more Germans – perhaps hundreds, even thousands of them – had died for a lost cause.

Now Doenitz ended the conference with the words, 'The Führer's tactics are determined simply by the welfare of the German people. As capitulation must mean the end of the German nation, it is clear that they have to fight on.'

After the 'secret meeting', Dr Fischer accompanied *Gauleiter* Wegener, the head of the Party in North Germany, to meet Kaufmann in Hamburg. They drove in silence through the bombed-out streets, the old familiar places barely recognisable after that terrible week of raids in 1943. From over the Elbe they could hear the sound of the English guns; that was all. The city already seemed dead, as if it had been abandoned for good.

Kaufmann was 'a bundle of nerves', Fischer thought, as they were admitted to his HQ after close scrutiny by his student guards. Kaufmann was indeed at the end of his tether, torn by his desire to save Hamburg and his fear that Doenitz or Busch might have him arrested at any moment and shot against the nearest wall.

An icy conversation followed. Wegener laid down the law. He was all for fighting on as long as it suited the Party's purposes. He put forward Doenitz's point of view that they could only gain good terms from the Tommie if they made them pay for every metre of ground they gained. Kaufmann did not respond. He had already put out his own peace feelers through Denmark and Sweden to the Allies. He was already 100 per cent committed to surrender.

In disgust Wegener left to visit his highly pregnant wife who was living in the suburbs of the city. Soon she would give birth to their child while the guns of the 7th Armoured Division slammed their shells into the city: a child who wouldn't see his father for many years, for Wegener like all the rest of the 'golden pheasants' came under the category of open arrest. He would spend the next years of the middle forties in that same camp to which he had consigned many unfortunates – Neuengamme.

But 'bundle of nerves' or not, Kaufmann was not going to desert his own *Gau*, as Wegener had done Bremen. He was going to stick it out, despite the dangers to his own person. He would continue attempting to surrender Hamburg before it became a battlefield. That afternoon he moaned to one of his student bodyguard, 'If only the British would hurry up and get across the Elbe.'

But despite Doenitz's decision to withdraw the *Wehrmacht* across the Elbe and Kaufmann's urgent desire to surrender Hamburg, there were still those on the other side of the river who were making it difficult for the British.

Since 21 April the Desert Rats of the 7th Armoured Division had been stalled on the high ground overlooking the suburb of Hamburg-Harburg on the far bank of the Elbe. There they occupied a front of 7,000 yards, with the 2nd Devons dug in in the village of Vahrendorf, a street with a pub and a couple of shops nestling in wooded hills, while to the left the line was held by the 1/5th Queens.

All that third week of April, the Germans had been carrying out hit-and-run attacks on the two infantry battalions, coming from the heights, filtering in silently through the great ancient oaks, to drive for the British positions, firing from the hip as they came. Twice the defenders had driven off spirited counter-attacks. As Captain Maxwell of the 1/5th Queens wrote to his wife in Paris that week:

For the last three days, we haven't advanced an inch, we are in defence and the Boches on our front are very aggressive; they keep on jabbing at our lines, attacking here, attacking there, as if they didn't know that half of their country had been occupied already. Sometimes I begin to think that I should have joined another regiment because somehow or other the Queens always seems to attract all the Nazi fanatics on its front.

Even as he wrote that letter to his French doctor-wife, the future publisher was aware of the 'German plane overhead and our guns are firing at it and here come some shells; our own guns have opened up now and it is like Dante's Inferno . . . The air is filled with all sorts of noises, whines, cracks and booms . . .' What Maxwell was listening to was the last desperate attempt by the German defenders of Hamburg to break through the lines of the British defenders before the general withdrawal across the Elbe. It would end in a tragedy . . .

Vahrendorf, resting at the foot of the largest hill of the whole of the Elbe plain, known in the local dialect as the *Kiekeberg* (roughly 'look-out mountain'), from which an observer could look down right into Hamburg itself, had been a thorn in the side of Hamburg's Battle Commandant, fat, pudgy-faced General Wolz, for a week.

Two days before the Devons had carried out a highly successful attack on the Germans in that area, using flame-throwers. They had taken a mixed bag of prisoners from various formations and had killed thirty-six of Wolz's men. Now Wolz in his belligerent mood wanted revenge. He ordered the best men still under his command to teach the English a lesson.

They were the young fanatics of the Training Battalion of the 'Hitler Youth' Division , which had been set up in 1943, its 'men' mostly 17-year-old volunteers from the Nazi Youth Organisation. Known throughout the *Wehrmacht* as the 'Baby Division' on account of its teenage soldiers and officers, none of whom were over 30 save its first commander who was 34 (instead of the traditional German Army issue of beer, its members received milk and boiled sweets), it had stopped dead three British divisions and one Canadian at Caen. The cost had been terrible: some ten thousand casualties, including twenty-two commanders and the divisional commander.

Now its Training Battalion – originally at regimental strength before casualties had decimated it – made up of combat-experienced officers and NCOs leading young recruits, some of them only 16, prepared to carry out Wolz's orders. At dawn they started to creep through the woods in their camouflaged tunics towards the positions of the Queens and Devons, coming across the *Kiekeberg*, young hearts filled with hate. With Hamburg on the verge of surrender, these young fanatics were still prepared to throw their lives away for some desperate glory.

In the middle of writing that letter to his wife, Maxwell was forced to break just as he was explaining that 'it is exactly a month since I had my boots or clothes off . . . and I must have a bath tomorrow even if I have to get the water under sniper fire', for 'all shooting has just started. My platoon is being attacked. I must go . . .'

For some while heavy fighting raged in and outside the village of Vahrendorf. For a while it seemed the SS 'men' would overrun the Devons' HQ set up in the village's only pub, *Erhorns Gasthaus*. But that wasn't to be. Slowly the two British battalions started to drive the Germans back into the trees. Here and there the SS began to surrender, even the fanatics now losing heart. For everywhere the cobbles were littered with the bodies of their comrades, sprawled out in the wild, abandoned poses of those done violently to death. The heavy hammering of machine-guns and the snap and crackle of rifle fire died away to single shots and then altogether, leaving behind a loud echoing silence broken only by the curt angry shouts of the Devons rounding up their prisoners. 'Come on, yer Jerry buggers . . . over here . . . *Schnell . . . schnell . . .*'

What happened next can perhaps be explained only by reference to the events of the previous week: the discovery of the horror camp at Belsen and that strange story related by Private Parry of the 1/5th Welch Regiment. In that week the Desert Rats to which the Welch Regiment belonged had passed through the bridgehead at Rethem and they had all heard how the SS of the 18th SS Training Regiment had massacred their prisoners there. Now it was their turn to take their revenge on the young SS fanatics. In groups they started to lead away their seventy-odd crestfallen prisoners lined up there among the debris and dead.

It was about this time that one of the few civilians who still remained in the village emerged from the cellar in which she had been hiding during the battle to hear yet another angry burst of fire. Frau Witt was curious and surprisingly unafraid. With age and death imminent, fear disappears. So it was that when the second outburst of firing ended, she left her half-timbered cottage to investigate.

She didn't get far. A British corporal armed with sten-gun ordered her angrily to stop where she was. Then he saw that she was merely an old, inquisitive woman. He laughed and pointed to a shell crater, as if that was explanation enough.

She peered short-sightedly inside it and saw that it was filled with the bodies of dead SS men. 'Twenty of them,' Frau Witt thought she understood the corporal to say before she decided it was safer under the circumstances – she could see just how excited and angry the Tommies were – to go back to her cottage as swiftly as possible.

Later, when the battle had passed on and the few civilians were allowed to go about their business (for the British had imposed a 22-hour curfew on those they had given the right to stay in the area), they found a total of forty-two dead young SS men buried in a common grave, eighteen of whom were never identified. Many of those who were identified, such as Martin Muskowitz or Josef Seyewiz, were in their teens, as young as 16.

Sadly the villagers dug up the corpses and re-interred them on a lonely hill-top at the edge of the village not far from the Kiekeberg itself, but away from Vahrendorf's own civilian cemetery for by then no one wanted to be associated with the SS. So it is that forty-four years later ex-servicemen's organisations still make a pilgrimage to those lonely graves to pay tribute to the youths whom they maintain were 'shot in cold-blood after being taken prisoner at the orders of a crazed, blood-thirsty British NCO'. [1]

Whatever happened that day – for the truth of the 'massacre' will never be known now – it was still clear that those who ran the affairs of what was left of the Third Reich were prepared even now to throw away the lives of their young men when all was lost.

II

Youth was being sacrificed everywhere. On the last day of the German defence of Bremen, one hundred apprentices of the famed Focke-Wulf factory were ordered out of their hostel and told they were soldiers. The boys, aged between 15 and 17, were given rifles and a few *Panzerfausts* and 'ordered to the front'. They went eagerly, hungry for the great adventure of war. They were soon to have it.

In the early hours of 25 April they were given the task of defending the local carriage works in the suburb of Hemlingen, known to the outside world as the home of Beck's beer. Like soldiers of the Foreign Legion, defending a desert fort against the Arabs in some Hollywood B-movie, they lined themselves up along the walls of the carriage works and waited for the adventure to commence.

They didn't wait long. A short, sharp artillery barrage swept the ruined works, forcing the pale-faced boys in their blue overalls to keep their heads low, as razor-sharp, fist-sized chunks of gleaming, hot metal howled lethally through the air. Then, as the last mortar bomb screeched from the dawn sky, the Glasgowians came in, bayonets fixed and gripped to their hips.

For the most part they were teenagers themselves, products of the Gorbals and the hungry thirties. Stocky, bandy-legged youths who had filled out on the homely honest fare they had received in the Army, they had 'nae time to play games with yon frigging Jerries'. They swept in from the flank, catching the defenders by surprise. A brief fire fight broke out. Then the Glasgow Highlanders were among them, 'wee' bayonets flashing, butts smashing cruelly into the suddenly

---

1 In 1988 students from that same anniversary from which Kaufmann drew his bodyguard in 1945 prevented the annual pilgrimage from taking place. There were rowdy scenes and the police were called. 'The day afterwards a hundred veterans came, mostly ex-SS,' the part-time warden of the place told the author, 'and nobody minded.' ·

1. General Montgomery speaking to war correspondents at his H.Q. – his first press conference since the invasion started (Port en Bessin, June 1944).
   (Supplied by Robert Hunt Library)

2. The last defenders – Hitler decorating Hitler Youth who won the Iron Cross in battle, 30 March 1945.

3. The bomb-littered streets of Duisberg, the largest inland port in Europe.

4. The wreckage along the waterfront of Germany's second port, Bremen, which fell on 28 April 1945.

5. Hamburg on the day of its surrender – 3 May 1945 – devastated and apparently
   deserted.

6. Hamburg after its fall. Here submarines litter the dockyard at the great Blohm and
   Voss works.

7. The Hamburg-American Line's 27,000-ton *New York* after being bombed during an air attack on Kiel.

8. Bombed ruins in Kiel, photographed the day after the German surrender.

9. 1/7th Bn, Duke of Wellington's 16 Platoon of D Coy, attack with tanks at Arnhem, April 1945.

10. Even some Germans welcome the British as liberators.

11. Prisoners being interrogated after the capture of Zeven, among them youths of only 14 years old from the Volksturm.

12. Prisoners in Bremen.

13, 14. The British crossing sites.

15. Bleckede am See, where the Americans crossed.

16. In Bremen the fire brigade were captured, and are here seen lining up for checking.

17. On 27 April 1945 Westertimke POW Camp was freed by the British. Russian ex-POWs were loaded on to lorries in Sittensen, to go to a camp run by the British Army.

18. Two German Civil Police making way for a British soldier in the main street of Verden, after the capture of the town.

19. German labour camp workers retreating to Amiens to join the FFI forces.

20. At the Brandenburg Gate the Russian poet Dolmatovsky recites poems to the troops (Berlin, 2 May 1945).

21. A Russian girl 'slave-worker', liberated by the British advance, greeting her countrymen after the link-up at Wismar on 3 May 1945.

22. Meilsen, where the first secret surrender talks took place.

23. The German Commandant arriving at Cuxhaven at the mouth of the Elbe, in order to surrender the town.

24. British soldiers interrogating members of the staff of the German State Railway H.Q., who were captured near Lübeck while they were trying to leave the country.

25. A sergeant-major in the SS being taken from his home by men of the 9th Bn. Durham Light Infantry. He had hoped to flee in civilian clothes, but was denounced by the German officer in the rear.

26. The German cruiser *Koln* resting on the bottom of the dock at the German naval base of Wilhelmshaven.

27. German civilians crowding round British tanks on guard at the Dummthor Railway Station, Hamburg.

of

All German armed forces in HOLLAND, in

northwest Germany including all islands,

and in DENMARK.

1. The German Command agrees to the surrender of all German armed
   forces in HOLLAND, in northwest GERMANY including the FRISIAN
   ISLANDS and HELIGOLAND and all other islands, in SCHLESWIG-
   HOLSTEIN, and in DENMARK, to the C.-in-C. 21 Army Group.
   This to include all naval ships in these areas.
   These forces to lay down their arms and to surrender unconditionally.

2. All hostilities on land, on sea, or in the air by German forces
   in the above areas to cease at 0800 hrs. British Double Summer Time
   on Saturday 5 May 1945.

3. The German command to carry out at once, and without argument or
   comment, all further orders that will be issued by the Allied
   Powers on any subject.

4. Disobedience of orders, or failure to comply with them, will be
   regarded as a breach of these surrender terms and will be dealt
   with by the Allied Powers in accordance with the accepted laws
   and usages of war.

5. This instrument of surrender is independent of, without prejudice
   to, and will be superseded by any general instrument of surrender
   imposed by or on behalf of the Allied Powers and applicable to Germany
   and the German armed forces as a whole.

6. This instrument of surrender is written in English and in German.

   The English version is the authentic text.

7. The decision of the Allied Powers will be final if any doubt or
   dispute arises as to the meaning or interpretation of the surrender
   terms.

B. L. Montgomery
Field-Marshal

4 May. 1945
1830 hrs

28. The 'instrument of surrender', signed by Field Marshal Montgomery and the
German command – Friedeberg, Kinsel, Wagner, Polleck and Friedel – on 4 May
1945.   *(Supplied by John Frost)*

ballito STOCKINGS

RELY ON THE QUALITY..

Sunday Graphic

No. 1,570 (E) SUNDAY, MAY 6, 1945 A KEMSLEY NEWSPAPER TWOPENCE

The Name speaks for Itself!

CLAREE'S BLOOD MIXTURE

3 MORE GERMAN ARMIES MAKE TOTAL SURRENDER

Norway C.-in-C. Also Reported 'Ready To Capitulate'

FINAL GERMAN CAPITULATION WAS BROUGHT NEARER LAST NIGHT BY THE UNCONDITIONAL SURRENDER OF THREE MORE GERMAN ARMIES.

All three armies fell to the group commanded by General Devers—two to the Americans and one to the French—and with them probably another 400,000 men passed into Allied hands.

At the same time there were unconfirmed reports from Stockholm that General Boehme, Nazi Commander in Norway, had decided to capitulate; that a British military mission had arrived in Oslo; and that Terboven, Nazi Governor in Norway, had resigned.

The day's surrenders in the South—apparently ordered by Kesselring—meant almost an end to the fighting on the American fronts except in Czechoslovakia.

There Patton's Third Army captured the German 11th Panzer Division in a new offensive over a 110-mile front in which they took 12,000 prisoners.

Simultaneously the Russians attacked from the East, while Czech Patriots wirelessed for help, saying German tanks were advancing on Prague.

Despite the Cease Fire at 8 a.m. yesterday, fighting broke out in Denmark, and Copenhagen was shelled.

FULL STORY ON BACK PAGE

SURRENDER

'Sunday Graphic' cameraman Reginald Clough records Field-Marshal Montgomery's greatest triumph as General Kinsel, German plenipotentiary, signs unconditional surrender.—*Full Picture Story and Document on Middle Pages.*

29. The front page of the *Sunday Graphic* showing General Kinsel signing unconditional surrender. *(Supplied by John Frost Newspapers)*

30. The *Daily Mirror* of 8 May 1945, reporting on the VE-Day celebrations in London.

frightened, contorted faces of the German youths. In an instant the apprentices, no longer desiring to be heroes and to die for 'People, Fatherland and Führer', broke and started to flee up the street, followed by the Highlanders. Behind them they left five boys sprawled out dead and twenty badly wounded. In their first and only action the Focke-Wulf apprentices had suffered 25 per cent casualties.

But in the centre of the embattled city, in the depths of his concrete bunker which was secure against anything but a direct hit, General Becker, the driving force behind the defence of Bremen, cared nothing for the deaths of those young men. He was still cast in the heroic mould. He signalled Berlin: 'Infantry attacks beaten off. Have no more ammunition. Defending with all the forces remaining to me. *Long live the Führer!*'

It was the 'spirit of Stalingrad', his admiring staff officers told each other, a little awed. The General finished dictating his signal, then took out his pistol and laid it in front of him on his bottle-littered desk. It was very clear to all present that day that the Tommies wouldn't take General Becker alive.

While teenage boys died purposelessly and General Becker within the safety of his bunker posed and lived to die in *bed*, the fighting in Bremen continued. But already many of the 'old hares', as the veterans were called in the German Army, had had enough.

By the evening of the 25th, the Third Division's 2nd Lincolns had taken Bremen's airfield and were resting after the hard battle. Major Glyn Gilbert of the Lincolns' C Company was standing next to the control tower, together with one of Doenitz's beached U-boat officers who had fought as infantry. 'It had been an exceptionally bitter little action,' he recalled long afterwards, 'and the German survivors, mainly U-boat crews, were being fallen in to be taken to the POW cage.'

Now the defeated sailors marched past the senior U-boat officers, carrying their wounded with them, proud in defeat but glad it was over at last. The U-boat skipper called out, '*Gut gemacht, Jungs!*'[2] He received a 'spontaneous and tremendous' cheer from his seamen. The victors were moved. The two officers saluted each other and the U-boat captain followed his men into captivity.

Later Major Gilbert recalled, 'I have never forgotten that incident, as this German naval officer and his men provided a perfect example of leadership and high morale at a time when their country was in ruins and their future was quite unknown.'

2 'Well done, lads.'

But Gilbert's Company Sergeant-Major Sam Smalley brought the Major back to reality, the noble gestures of war forgotten suddenly. 'That's about it then,' he said a little wearily. He meant the end of the 2nd Lincolns' fighting days.

Suddenly Gilbert felt very low, 'very tired and sad about the casualties we had suffered in the last few hours'. He didn't realise it then but he was the only rifle company commander not killed or injured in the whole 3rd Division, a formation of some fourteen thousand men when it landed on D-Day.

Sam Smalley grinned up at the weary Major. 'Japan next, I suppose,' he said. But the 3rd Division wouldn't go to Japan, [3] nor would it fight another battle. Its fighting days in Europe were over, as the Company Sergeant-Major had correctly predicted.

At two o'clock on the morning of 26 April, while the weary Lincolns slept heavily, a lone British officer of the same division appeared at the police station located at No. 3 Hemelinger Street and demanded from the surprised elderly *Schupos*[4] that they should connect him with their senior political leaders. Yet another British officer was going to make the attempt to get the city to surrender.

After three days of bombing and shelling the lines were down virtually everywhere but the police did manage to raise Bremen's police HQ over an emergency line. There it was hastily agreed that a senior policeman would try to bring General Becker to the phone at three o'clock that last morning of the battle. While outside the occasional machine-gun still chattered like an irate woodpecker and there was the hard dry crack of a sniper's rifle, the lone British officer and his German hosts in their green-grey uniforms, their heavy-lined faces unshaven and dirty – there was no longer any running water – waited.

As agreed, at three o'clock precisely the phone rang. Hurriedly the police sergeant in charge picked it up. He listened for a moment or two. Then his face fell. Instinctively the British officer knew what had happened: Becker was still refusing to surrender. He was right. Becker had flatly refused to take part in any talks with the British attackers, although he knew Bremen was doomed and any further defence was futile. For already those *Wehrmacht* units around Bremen not actually

---

3 The 3rd got as far as Palestine, just in time to be involved in yet another bloody conflict between Jews and Arabs.
4 Literally 'bobbies'.

engaged in the defence of the city were withdrawing in accordance with Doenitz's new order. He would need every man he could lay his hands on for the defence of the new line on the Elbe.

The 3rd Division officer gave in. Becker had had his last chance. Now Horrocks' infantry would go in for the kill. Far away in the lines of the 4th KOBSs of the 52nd Lowland Division, he could hear the faint skirl of the pipes. It was Piper Jock Gray, leading the KOSBs into the shattered streets of Bremen's business district. Suddenly the night was full of the electric sounds of 'Hawick's Queen of a' the Borders' and 'Joddarts Here'. The Blue Bonnets, just like the Lincolns, were going into their final attack of the Second World War . . .

Not far away Brigadier Joe Vandeleur, commanding the 43rd Division's 129th Brigade, was also wide awake. He was putting the final touches to his plan of attack for this Thursday. He and his men had been given the doubtful honour of delivering the *coup de grâce* at the siege of Bremen. Just like the 3rd and the 52nd, the 43rd would be fighting its last major action of the war. Soon the fighting would be centred on Barker's 8th Corps on the Elbe.

Vandeleur's orders from General Thomas, the Divisional Commander, were to clear out Bremen east of the railway line which bissected the city. Where this line passed through the *Bürgerpark* – citizens' park – it threw off a branch to Utbremer Forst. Within the loop formed by two lines, hidden inside groves of trees inside the park, there was a series of bunkers. These bunkers housed Major-General Sibert, Becker's chief subordinate, and the Flak Artillery HQ. The guns under the command of the Flak Artillery were the basis of Becker's fire power. It was assumed that if the 129th could kill or capture Sibert and knock out Flak HQ, then Becker would be forced to give in at last.

But Vandeleur was not too sanguine. Intelligence from captured German prisoners indicated that German infantry had dug in in force in the streets leading to the loop. His young soldiers would undoubtedly have a fight on their hands before they could reach the bunkers. So he decided he would advance on a two-battalion front – some 1,600 men – as far as the *Bürgerpark*. Then with his reserve battalion, the 4th Somerset Light Infantry, rushing forward in their armoured troop carriers, the Kangaroos, he would strike the death blow.

In bright sunshine the 4th and 5th commenced their attack. Advancing by a complicated system of leap-frogging, the inevitable 'char' mugs bouncing up and down on their packs, the Wiltshires took their first, second, third, fourth and fifth objectives without too much trouble. Things were going to plan, Vandeleur thought happily.

At 7.30 that bright sunny morning, the two lead companies clattered forward in their little Bren-gun carriers to take their sixth objective. Abruptly their advance was brought to a halt by a hastily erected barricade of steel rails. 'Sixty-one-minute barricades' the infantry called them contemptuously – 'sixty minutes to put 'em up, one minute to pull the buggers down!'

Just the same the infantry vaulted over the steel sides of their little tracked vehicles and prepared for trouble. All they found defending the barricade were two scared, long-haired youths armed with a Spandau machine-gun. 'These two heroes', as one eyewitness put it, 'were given a kick in the pants and sent packing.' Hurriedly a gang of frightened civilians were ejected from the nearby ruins and told to clear the obstruction – or else!

The advance continued. A huge 7-storey-high concrete flak tower barred the Wiltshires' way. It was surrounded by high blast walls and looked a very tough nut to crack. But its completely demoralised garrison of 160 men surrendered without a shot being fired. Again the infantry pushed on. It was going to be a walk-over, they started to tell each other.

From a side street a German multiple flak connon burst into frenzied action. A stream of 20mm cannon shells streamed towards the infantry. They went to ground. Urgently the Company Commander radioed for help. The stalled infantry didn't have to wait long. A heavy Churchill tank armed with a strange stubby cannon rumbled up. It took up its position and fired one of its mortar bombs. It hurtled right into the air, a dark whirling object which seconds later came whizzing down right upon the cannon. The cannon disappeared in a flash of ugly yellow light, the crew flying in all directions in a welter of whirling, shattered limbs.

Road-block after road-block was taken. Here and there some lone hero tried to stop the advance. He was shot and the tracked vehicles rolled on, grinding the dead man into as bloody pulp on the cobbles. Nothing seemed able to stop the heady exciting advance of the two Wiltshire battalions. By late afternoon they were in sight of their final objective, the Bürgerpark.

Suddenly, startlingly, it happened. Just as the Wiltshires' A Company entered the northern end of the big park, heavy small-arms fire swept their ranks from a pillbox. They started taking casualties. Hurriedly they went to ground, doubling towards the nearest houses, as the bullets stitched ugly patterns at their flying heels.

Major Colverson of C Company came racing up in his carrier. He wanted to assess the situation. Unwittingly his driver took the Bren-gun carrier right by a hidden German machine-gun nest. The German gunner did not need a second invitation. He opened up at this tempting and unsuspecting target at point-blank range. The carrier skidded to a crazy stop, with Major Colverson dead before it did so.

Angrily, Colonel Corby of the 4th Wiltshires called down artillery support. Then he went forward personally to observe the effect of the gunners. But in that built-up area it was difficult for the division's gunners to assess the range correctly. A shell fell short. Corby dropped moaning to the ground, severely wounded by one of his own shells. He was the third colonel of the Wiltshires to be killed or wounded in the campaign.

For a while the Fourth's assault stalled while the 5th Wiltshires continued the advance. Then their advance slowed down as they came to the same barracks from which the firing was pinning down their comrades of the Fourth. Lieutenant Blackman ordered his Bren-gunners to cover all exits to the place, while he rolled forward slowly in his little Bren-gun carrier, the gunner's finger tensed on his light machine-gun as they came ever closer.

But there was no need for alarm. The first German soldier they came across promptly put up his arms and yelled fearfully, face trembling, 'Kamerad!' A minute later he was followed by ninety-seven of his companions, who at this late stage of the war had no desire to die for Führer, Admiral Doenitz, or anyone else for that matter.

Now civilians told the Wiltshires that other German soldiers ahead were also prepared to surrender. Again Lieutenant Blackman, commanding 13th Platoon, took the lead. He told himself they always seemed to get the dirty end of the stick, perhaps on account of that damned thirteen. Still he felt confident. He had no reason to suspect any treachery from the cowed, beaten German civilians.

His platoon moved forward towards the crossroads held by the Germans, only a few hundred yards from the park. But hardly had they started when machine-gun fire erupted viciously from houses to both sides. They had walked straight into a trap! Furious, the Wiltshires took cover and started returning the enemy fire, while a shaken Blackman whistled up the tanks of the Sherwood Rangers who were supporting the Wiltshires.

The Shermans rumbled up. Instantly their gunners, protected behind their 10-ton turrets, started to return the German fire, firing over open sights, slamming their shells straight at the enemy positions. Tracer flew back and forth. The walls of the ruins shivered under each

133

new impact like theatrical backdrops in a high wind. Masonry came slithering down in red streams. All was murder and confusion. For one long hour the uneven duel continued until finally all the German machine-gun nests were knocked out. But still the German snipers, hidden in the smoking, burning rubble continued their deadly handiwork. Even now, British and German soldiers died in this hopeless, purposeless battle for the ruins of what had once been a great city.

Wynford Vaughan Thomas of the BBC had followed the fighting troops into the city, now virtually under British control. Setting up his 40-pound 'portable' recording unit, the lightest in the world, and clipping his mike on to a shattered girder, he started to give his impressions of the dying city to his audience back home. Placed on a disk, it would be transmitted on the BBC's *War Report*, immediately after the 9 o'clock news.

In his fruity Welsh voice, the jolly, heavy-set correspondent said, as the continuing small-arms fire indicated that all resistance was not yet crushed:

I am in the centre of the city of Bremen if you can call this chaotic rubbish-heap in which our bulldozers are working as I speak . . . a city any more. There are walls standing, there are factory chimneys here and there, but there's no shape and no order and certainly no hope for this shell of a city that was once called Bremen. These endless vistas down small streets to the houses leaning at drunken angles and this inhuman landscape of great blocks of flats with their sides ripped open and the intimate household goods just blown out into the bomb craters . . .

The foreign workers – there must have been thousands here in Bremen – are already on their way out. They go tramping past our lads and waving to them in their jeeps and the lorries and the bulldozers coming into the city now in a steady stream.

In fact, though the BBC correspondent couldn't tell his home listeners this, the liberated foreign workers from the east were now going on one huge rampage, looting, raping, murdering, taking their revenge for the cruelties heaped upon them during the war. Soon the foreign workers would become more of a nuisance and headache for the victorious British soldiers than the Germans.

But that was, as Wynford Vaughan Thomas commented maliciously, the price of defeat: 'The inhabitants of Bremen have got to stay in the ruins of their city. And now they have ample time to walk around and see the results of total war.' Indeed they would. For years they would have to live in those grim, rat-infested ruins under which the dead of years of bombing were buried, as some of them are even today, half a century later. The citizens would assuredly have time enough to reflect upon 'total war'.

While the civilians made their adjustments, however, and the BBC man reflected upon the cost of defeat for the Germans, there was still some fighting to be done by the men who paid the final butcher's bill – the poor bloody infantry.

Leading the Wiltshires' attack, Captain Edwards did a personal reconnaisance of the five roads meeting at the south-east corner of the *Bürgerpark*, which the troops nicknamed with their usual lack of originality 'Hyde Park Corner'. He decided that it was the obvious core of the Germans' defence and planned a deliberate assault to be carried out by the Somerset Light Infantry, kept in reserve all that long day by Brigadier Vandeleur.

At ten o'clock that night, with the light long gone, the Somersets' C Company advanced on 'Hyde Park Corner'. On both sides the houses were large turn-of-the-century villas, their gardens surrounded by high walls. They made ideal defensive positions, each villa a small fortress in its own right. But this time the hard-pressed, long-suffering PBI had an ally – that most terrible weapon of all the flame-throwing Crocodile tank.

The Germans reacted at once. A mixed bunch of defenders – policemen, soldiers, sailors – opened up with machine-guns and *Panzerfausts*. Scarlet flame stabbed the glowing darkness. Tracer hissed back and forth in a kind of lethal Morse code.

Major Watts, the leading Company Commander, didn't hesitate. He summoned his 'big friend' and those feared Crocodiles waddled up to commence their deadly work. They rattled to within 60 or 70 yards of their targets, impervious to the bullets howling uselessly off their thick steel sides like ping-pong balls, and fired. There was a hush like some primeval monster taking a deep breath, and then the tongue of scarlet, oil-tinged flame shot out and wreathed the house, scorching and shrivelling everything in its path. In an instant the earth was black and steaming.

Screaming Germans, their uniforms burning fiercely, rushed into the gardens and rolled back and forth wildly in a vain attempt to put out those all-consuming blue flames. But they couldn't. Their struggles grew weaker and weaker and then they lay there, letting the flames consume them, their heads hideous and charred in pools of burning flame. One eyewitness recorded how:

The battle which ensued was almost appalling in its magnificence. When the enemy attempted to come out of the houses and fight in the open, he was caught by the fire of the infantry and the Besas [a machine-gun] of the Crocodiles. When he stayed inside the houses, he was roasted alive. Burning houses cast a lurid light over the flame throwers as they slowly waddled up the streets and by the infantry as they dashed from house to house.

Carried away by this terrible spectacle, Brigadier Vandeleur cried, 'I'm going in with the leading section!' For a moment the middle-aged General seemed about to dash after the young soldiers. Hastily his staff grabbed him and held on.

With the resistance at 'Hyde Park Corner' finally dealt with, the Somersets rested for a little while. During this time out of war, Major Beckhurst of the Somersets bumped into Major Pope of the 4th Wiltshires. The cheerful young Wiltshire Major, who affected a huge RAF-style handlebar moustache, was reconnoitring the area and he pointed out a large concrete bunker that rose over 30 feet above the park. It seemed to both of the young officers worth investigating.

Together with a section of infantry, the two majors advanced on the place and in the glowing darkness were just able to make out an eagle holding a swastika in its claws above the entrance. There to either side were two lines of dud British bombs which had been dropped on Bremen during the war and which had failed to explode. The officers looked at each other significantly. This might be the place after all!

Cautiously they entered the main door. The place was dimly lit and smelled of human sweat and cat's piss. Suddenly a German officer popped up out of nowhere. He recognised the uniform immediately. '*Die Tommies sind da!*' he cried. The soldiers lunged forward. He was disarmed at once and ordered gruffly to move in front of the intruders.

Fingers wet with sweat gripping their weapons, nerves tingling electrically, the little party of British soldiers penetrated ever deeper into the bunker. The place was a regular rabbit-warren. Small rooms and staircases ran off in every direction. All was utter confusion. There were discarded weapons, shells, belts of machine-gun ammunition, empty cans, bottles, many bottles, everywhere.

Slowly, cautiously, the little party worked their way from room to room. They came across fourteen German soldiers, all of them wounded and abandoned. There was little they could do for them. They continued down the smelly corridor, lit by faint yellow lights enclosed in wire cages, and then they opened a door to find thirty German officers seated around a long wooden table, piled high with empty champagne bottles. There were plenty of other 'dead soldiers' on the floor, too. The Germans had been celebrating their defeat.

One of the officers rose unsteadily to his feet. He was a big, fat man, with a broad, unintelligent, sour-looking face. 'Sibert,' he said with a stiff little bow. '*Generalmajor Sibert!*'

Beckhurst looked at Pope significantly. They had heard of Sibert. He was Becker's number two. This was the officer who had ordered his young fools to fight to the 'last round and the last drop of blood'. Indeed the rumour was then circulating among his remaining soldiers that their battle commandant had been 'killed in action, pistol in hand'. Instead he had gone, as his British captors put it crudely 'on the piss'. Tamely General Sibert, the advocate of resistance to the last, handed over his pistol to the British soldiers.

Thereafter he was whipped off to the Divisional Cage of the 43rd Division, complaining all the way, to join eight thousand of his men already behind barbed wire that night. The Battle of Bremen was over. Now there was nothing to stop Montgomery from making his dash for the Baltic.

3

'We British always win!'

I

On the evening of 27 April, Montgomery received yet another prod to get him moving. By now he had suffered a whole week, nursing his grief for poor dead John Poston and at the same time being constantly irritated by messages from Eisenhower and others, urging him to hurry up with his crossing of the Elbe. Now Eisenhower sent him yet another cable, reminding him of the importance of Lübeck and the Danish peninsula, and promising 'this HQ will do anything at all that is possible to help you insure the speed and success of the operation'.

It was too much for the little Field Marshal. He signalled back:

I have always realised the great importance of getting quickly up to the Elbe and crossing it without delay and it was for that purpose that I issued M563 dated 28 March. That plan could not be implemented quickly as you took the Ninth Army away from me on 3 April and left me very weak in the north. The whole tempo of operations in the north slowed down after that and I did the best I could with what I had left. We have had some very heavy fighting against fanatical resistance.

In this remark Montgomery was perhaps thinking of Bremen, where even little German boys of 8 had joined in the battle for the port. 'It is not easy to recover time,' he protested, but he ended by stating, 'You can rely on me and my troops to do everything that is possible to get Lübeck as quickly as we can'.

Montgomery had already made his decision on the date of the Elbe assault the day before, sure now Bremen had fallen that he had the necessary reserves. He had signalled the War Office:

I have examined the situation on the Elbe front about Lauenburg and it seems that the enemy is in some strength in that area. But the need for an early crossing is great and I have given orders to Second Army that we must not wait until 1 May. The assault crossing will now be made on night 28 /29 April, i.e. Saturday night.

Now there were twenty-eight hours to go . . .

On the Elbe itself, crowded in the barns and fishermen's cottages that lined the river behind the protection of the dyke, the infantry waited. On the other side there was little sign of the enemy, save for German staff cars which drove up and down the Lauenburg road, as if the Tommies were a hundred miles away and not one mile.

The Germans were in no way aggressive. Indeed the local boatmen in their black corduroy suits and peaked caps still plied their trade in mid-stream. For there the Elbe had become a kind of no-man's land for both sides, as long as the boatmen stayed in the middle of the river.

A ferryman once poled his little craft to the British side of the river and approached a group of Jocks on patrol there. He offered to take a group of them across to the German side for twenty pfennigs a head. The Jocks declined. They gave the 'old codger' a Woodbine and sent him politely on his way.

One of the Commando officers, belonging to the brigade which was going to lead the assault and scale the cliff at Lauenburg, decided to try and get the town of Lauenburg to surrender to him single-handed. He found a motor-boat tied up on the British side of the river and set off to carry out his task. He had almost reached the other bank when his engine stalled, leaving him drifting helplessly in full view of the Germans dug in there. Obligingly enough, they hauled the crest-fallen Commando officer to safety. But instead of putting the young officer in the bag as they should have done, they repaired his launch for him and sent him back the way he had come. It all looked too easy, much too easy . . .

In Bremen, while the man of Barker's Corps waited for the assault to come this Saturday, Horrocks' 30th Corps 'tidied up'. A thin rain had now commenced falling on the newly captured port. By the cold, grey light of that wet dawn, Bremen presented a picture of sordid horror. Its centre around the shattered *Hauptbahnhof*, the main station, and its famed Roland's Square was blocked with great piles of brick and stone rubble. Lamp standards twisted into impossible shapes by the artillery fire were silhouetted grotesquely against the leaden sky. Here and there shattered gas mains added their stench to the stink of open sewers. The air was still full, too, of the cloying smell of burning buildings.

Everywhere the thousands of slave labourers from the East, with the word 'OST' stencilled on the backs of their tattered jackets and blouses so that they could be easily recognised by the Nazi authorities, went on the rampage. Streaming out of their camps all over Bremen, they indulged in a wild orgy of looting, murder and rape. Brigadier Essame of the 43rd Division, watching it all, thought:

Their behaviour, especially that of the Russians, can only be described as abominable. Brutal treatment by the Germans had reduced them below the level of beasts, but it is doubtful whether they ever had far to fall. Some even drank themselves to death on commercial spirits in the docks. Fighting, rape and open murder broke out, and our troops had to intervene.

Here and there individual German civilians risked sudden death at the hands of this mob, when they ventured out of their cellars or bunkers to grab their first breath of fresh air in four days. Green in face, broken-spirited, they stared in helpless bewilderment at the lunar landscape which had once been their home.

The soldiers of the 52nd Division, which was now taking over the ruined city from the 43rd, were forced that day to search every surviving bunker for weapons and Germans on the Intelligence Corps' 'wanted list'. But the Nazi bosses of Bremen had all fled, leaving the city to its fate. The Gestapo, which had terrorised the place for years, had also gone, already equipped with the false papers that their HQ in Berlin was turning out by the thousand.

Indeed the only senior National Socialist leader left in Bremen was found shot that Friday morning, slumped over an empty bottle of Cognac. Opposite him lay sprawled his wife, a bullet through her temple, too. He had taken what the Germans called 'the officer's way out'.

General Becker, the most senior officer left in Bremen, had not, however, taken the 'officer's way out'. All night long, deep in his bunker, his officers had tried to convince him to surrender and thus stop the senseless slaughter. But he did not seem to hear. He appeared to be sunk in a state of apathy. In the end Colonel Mueller, an officer of 8th Flak Division, took matters into his own hands. He went in search of the English, accompanied by a captured British soldier bearing a white flag. He reached the Wiltshires just as Major Pope of the great moustache was about to give the orders for an attack on the bunker.

Tamely Becker, whom his British captors thought 'pleasant', went into captivity. There he would remain for two years behind barbed wire until he was released to retire to Harz mountains, where he died in 1967 – in bed, of course, unlike all those young men and boys he had sent purposelessly to their deaths through his indecision.

General Horrocks, a much more compassionate man, had seen much of war and always felt strongly for the men under his command.

He decided that now the war was ending his men would need recreation. That day he decided the sailing yachts of all sizes and shapes tucked away in the creeks along the River Weser near Bremen would come in handy in the days of peace to come. He ordered a couple of armed soldiers from his victorious divisions to be placed on each boat to make certain the vessels didn't disappear. To the victor belonged the spoils.

He hadn't reckoned with the Royal Navy.

A few days later he would receive a signal from the senior British admiral in charge of the Bremen port area, demanding that the boats be handed over to the Navy forthwith. Horrocks refused flatly. He signalled 'Who captured Bremen – the army or the navy?' Back came the terse message, 'Everything that floats belongs to the Navy.' To which Horrocks replied, 'Rather than hand them over, I'll sink the lot!' Horrocks won.[1]

On this day, though, Horrocks was still feeling benevolent towards the Royal Navy, for on this Saturday he did allow one of his divisions to engage the enemy for the Navy's benefit, even though Horrocks already knew that Himmler was attempting to sue for peace and he wanted no further unnecessary deaths. Instead of urging his commanders to 'get cracking' as he had done throughout the campaign, he had been going around inventing excuses to slow them down'. He could see them looking at him in astonishment and he told himself they were saying behind his back, 'The Old Man has lost his nerve at last.' But the needs of the Royal Navy could not be denied, although his decision to let the Guards Armoured Division continue fighting this day against the redoubtable 15th Panzergrenadier Division would probably cost his men's lives. He ordered them to attempt to liberate the great prisoner-of-war camp at Westertimke to the east of Bremen, which housed thousands of Navy and merchant navy prisoners.

The day before, General Roth, the Commander of the 15th Panzergrenadier Division, had asked the Guards for a truce of ten hours in which to remove the prisoners of war at present at Westertimke [eight thousand soldiers of the British Empire] out of the zone of danger and hand them over to your division'. But the Guards hadn't fallen for it. Roth, a cunning old fox who had fought the British ever since the Western Desert in 1941, was, they felt, just trying to buy time so that he could extract his division to fight on another day. So they had turned

---

1 That summer Horrocks, so concerned with the welfare of his soldiers, got into serious trouble by suggesting that one way to get round the non-fraternisation ban was to import French and Belgian prostitutes for them. Just like Montgomery's similar suggestion back in 1940, it nearly cost him his job.

down the truce. Now this Friday a mixed force of Scots and Welsh Guards set out to liberate the camp – by force if necessary.

It had rained all night. The ground to the Guards' front was a morass, criss-crossed with drainage ditches. It certainly was no place for a tank battle. But there were other dangers, too. Almost immediately, as the Guards advanced under mortar and shell fire, they found not only the main roads heavily mined but also every side road. Their HQ group stalled at once. The main road they had taken was so cunningly mined that there were mines on top of mines, some of them rigged with delayed-action charges. It was an engineer's nightmare.

The Guards had to abandon their vehicles and attack on foot across the sodden fields. Three German self-propelled guns scuttled out of the dripping trees to stop them. The guns were knocked out one by one. But casualties were mounting.

Now the leading squadron, plus a company of infantry, were ordered to push on and reach the camp by dark. The tanks, laden with infantry, hadn't gone far when the first one went over a mine and skidded to a stop, a track falling behind it like a severed limb. Fortunately there were no casualties this time.

A bunch of Germans attacked from the woods. A fierce battle ensued. Twenty Germans were killed and a further twenty taken prisoner. They pointed out where the camp lay. Just then another German self-propelled gun appeared. But seeing the British tanks, it scuttled for safety behind some huts marked with a red cross.

The Guards were taking no chances. Firing high explosive they soon had all the huts, red cross or no red cross, blazing and started to advance again. Now they began to make their first contact with the naval POWs. They came in all shapes and in all colours, for many of the merchant seamen were black, brown and yellow, and they seemed to be getting a little out of hand.

'Already around the camp chicken feathers in all directions testified to the fact that the looters had not wasted their time,' as one eyewitness recorded. 'The previous night when the German guards had fled, a few holes had been cut in the wire and some of the worst characters in the camp were now outside, looting, etc. in the neighbouring houses.'

The eyewitness skated delicately over their other activities with that 'etc.', but it was clear that order was breaking down in the camp. Soon the liberators came across the senior merchant navy officer, Captain Norman, who was now in tears at the breakdown of discipline in 'his' camp. Swiftly forty-odd guardsmen, including two who had been captured in 1940, were armed with German rifles and order was restored. Even now, though, they could not stop the prisoners streaming out through the wire, including one colourful personage dressed as a Russian Orthodox priest, complete with robes and beard. One wonders what the future Archbishop of Canterbury, the then Lieutenant Runcie MC of the Scots Guards, made of him?

But apart from the looters, the Guards were cheered by the spectacle of these thousands of Lascars, West Indians and Chinese, whom the Germans had tried and failed for years to persuade to change allegiance, especially the Indians.[2] One in particular seemed to exemplify their spirit. He was 'a very dark' West Indian fireman, wearing a looted bowler hat, smoking a cigar and obviously very drunk. Once he met an officer, raised his bowler and promptly fell off his bike. Not in the least disconcerted, he solemnly replaced his looted hat and cried, before continuing on his erratic and carefree way, 'We British always win!'

II

On 3 April, in front of loyal and trusted followers, *Gauleiter* Kaufmann of Hamburg had explained why his long-time loyalty to Hitler had been transformed into dislike, even hate:

As *Gauleiter*, I'm responsible for 200,000 men and children in Hamburg who couldn't be evacuated. We National Socialist leaders are responsible for the fact that things have gone this far. We cannot escape our responsibility by simply taking poison or letting ourselves be beaten to death. It's my duty to do everything I can for the people entrusted to me. The only solution I can see is capitulation. It's immaterial what happens to me.

Brave words under the circumstances. But Kaufmann knew they were only words as long as effective military power rested in the hands of Doenitz and Field Marshal Busch. Now, forgetting his personal danger, Kaufmann attempted to circumvent the other two by direct negotiation with the British by means of his contacts in Denmark and Sweden. In order to save Hamburg, he offered to attempt to ensure personally the surrender of Schleswig-Holstein and Denmark without a

2   The Germans had successfully raised and armed an Indian Brigade, made up of captured men from the British Indian Army. They had fought in Normandy but with little success.

143

fight. In return he wished for two things only: the immediate halting of aerial attacks on Hamburg, and the accelerated crossing of the Elbe and the occupation of Mecklenburg on the other side of that river by the Anglo-Americans.

His reasoning was this. Doenitz now maintained to his followers that the battle in the north-west must continue in order to save the many hundreds of thousands of German soldiers and civilians who were fleeing before Rossokovsky's Russians. He had to keep the 'door to the west' open – that area between the Elbe and the Baltic now threatened by Montgomery. But once that 'door' was closed by an Allied advance, he would have no further justification for continuing this wasteful and criminal battle against the Allies. It also meant that Kaufmann would be safe from any attempt at revenge by dyed-in-the-wool Nazis.

His message was sent by secret channels arranged by the 'secret ruler of Sweden', the banker Jakob Wallenberg, through Denmark and Sweden to the British Foreign Office in London. Kaufmann asked that, in return for his surrender to General Lyne (Commander of the 7th Armoured Division) and his efforts 'to weaken the defences on the Elbe in the area Hamburg, Lauenburg etc.', the British Army should immediately set in motion its drive for the Baltic. *Gauleiter* Kaufmann 'wanted' an answer by midday on Saturday 28 April. Otherwise he would not be 'responsible for any further blood-shed'. Now, it seemed, Montgomery was under pressure not only from the Americans, but from the Germans, too![3]

But while Kaufmann and Eisenhower both urged the little Field Marshal to get moving, because the Germans were virtually finished – hadn't Himmler himself sued for peace? – Doenitz, the commander in the North, still seemed to fight it out.

On that day General von Trotha, the representative of Heinrici's Vistula Army, was present at Doenitz's daily conference in Ploen. He told the meeting categorically that, in view of the masses of refugees fleeing westwards who were being savegely attacked by marauding bands of Russians, and in view of the general situation within the Reich, there was little hope. They would have to capitulate sooner or later.

Doenitz did not accept his reasoning. He said, 'No one has a right to deviate from the line laid down by the Führer!'

---

3 Kaufmann's role was almost played out. Soon he would be imprisoned in the same camp just vacated by the merchant navy prisoners – Westertimke. And there he would be joined – for a day at least – by no less a person than Heinrich Himmler.

This brought up the question of a successor to the Führer. They all knew that Hitler was determined now to remain in Berlin and presumably die there. Once Hitler was dead they would be released from their personal oath of loyalty to him and could act accordingly. Himmler, who at his meeting with Bernadotte had confided in his General Schellenberg 'I dread what is to come', was now optimistic once more.

It would be another twenty-four hours before Himmler's treachery was discovered by Hitler and his dismissal ordered. Meanwhile he felt he still had some role to play. He asked Doenitz if, were he to take over power in place of the Führer, the Grand Admiral would be prepared to work with him. Dutifully Doenitz replied that he would place his services at the disposal of any government appointed by the Führer or his successors.

Thus the discussions went on, blind to the catastrophe taking place all around. Von Trotha, who had once been a convinced Nazi himself, felt they were living in a dream world. Didn't they realise that the power to make decisions had now been taken out of their hands? It was the enemy who now called the tune. They were all living in cloud-cuckoo land! They weren't the only ones . . .

By the morning of Saturday 28 April, Heinrici's Vistula Army was breaking down on all sides before Rokossovsky's attacks, and his senior generals were in open revolt. Still Hitler's minions tried to stave off the inevitable. Field Marshal Keitel – Hitler's ramrod-stiff, wooden-jawed (some people said 'wooden-headed') senior military adviser – personally phoned von Manteuffel that day and accused him of 'sheer defeatism'. He added that he was coming to the little Commander's HQ to find out exactly what the 3rd Panzer Army, retreating before Rokossovsky, was up to.

Manteuffel informed Heinrici and together they drove to meet Keitel, coming from Berlin, in a wood near a small lake. Here von Manteuffel took the precaution of hiding three of his staff officers, armed with machine pistols, behind some trees. If Keitel tried to have him arrested, the three officers would intervene.

Keitel, known behind his back as 'Lackeitel' (a compound of his name and the German words for 'lackey' and 'vain') waded straight into the two officers. 'The Army Group is only moving backwards,' he bellowed contemptuously. 'The Group and Army leadership is too soft! If you'd follow the example of other people and have the nerve to take rigorous steps and shoot a thousand deserters, Army Group would hold its ground.'

Stiffly Heinrici, in his old-fashioned uniform which marked him clearly as a 'front swine' from the trenches of the First World War, retorted that he didn't 'operate that way'.

Keitel turned on von Manteuffel, towering above the diminutive 3rd Army Commander. He accused him of withdrawing without orders. Heinrici spoke up in the defence of his subordinate. Impatiently Keitel cut him off with the statement that he, Heinrici, wasn't 'tough enough'.

Suddenly Heinrici lost his temper. He grabbed the Field Marshal's arm. Spluttering with rage, he forced him down the road by the lake to another main road. It was jammed with soldiers of his Army Group Vistula, obviously in full retreat towards the west. Finger shaking, he pointed at a horse-drawn cart, obviously looted from some farm or other, now abandoned by its owners. The cart was filled with combat-weary airmen, a mess of sprawling limbs and equipment, covered with dust. Like so many of the rest they were culls from the *Luftwaffe*, forced to serve as infantry. 'Why don't you set an example for me *yourself?*' he cried, angered by this wooden-jawed, vain officer who had never heard a shot fired in anger throughout the war.

Keitel tore himself free. He advanced on the cart, wielding the field-marshall's baton of which he was so proud, and ordered the airmen to dismount: a German field marshal giving orders to a bunch of war-weary, shabby private soldiers. 'Take them back to Third Panzer Headquarters,' he commanded, 'and have them court-martialled!' Angrily he set off back to his staff car. Then he paused and wagged his forefinger threateningly at Heinrici. 'From now on, strictly follow the orders of the High Command!' he shouted, face flushed with rage.

'How can I possibly follow those orders when the High Command isn't even properly informed about present conditions!' Heinrici cried back, ignoring the bewildered stares of the fleeing soldiers.

Keitel poised at the open door of his Mercedes. 'You'll hear the result of this conversation!' he yelled.

Von Manteuffel, as defiant as his chief, stepped forward and said firmly, 'The 3rd Army will follow only orders given by General von Manteuffel.' He prodded his skinny little chest with his thumb to make his point perfectly clear.

Keitel glared at the two of them. Again he stated they should obey orders and said, 'You will be responsible for the verdict of history.'

'I'm responsible for all the orders I give,' Manteuffel maintained, defiant even in the face of the 'verdict of history'. 'And I won't blame anyone else for them.'

Behind him his three staff officers came out of the trees, machine pistols at the ready, prepared for trouble. But Keitel had had enough. Without another word, he spun round and dropped into the seat of his car. The driver didn't hesitate. He shot off down the road back to Berlin, as if the Devil were after him.

For the time being this public slanging match between Germany's most senior soldier and the country's most experienced generals had ended. But it was significant. Army Group Vistula was going to run its own affairs from now and Rokossovsky was facing a foe who was about at the end of his tether.

Now Rokossovsky's army, heading for the Elbe, was sweeping all before it. The tall, handsome General, who had been born a Pole, had not been given the honour of capturing Berlin. But he did know, now that Berlin was surrounded and almost finished, that it was vital for Stalin to penentrate as far west as possible. Once 'old leather face' had laid his hands on something, he'd keep it regardless of whatever treaties he might have made with the Western Allies. Stalin wanted to control the whole of Central Europe and even further west if he could manage it. Possession of the mouth to the Baltic meant Germany and Scandinavia would come under Russian domination.

Already this day, Russian planes were circling over the German-occupied Danish island of Bornholm in the Baltic, as well as most of the eastern Danish coast. Denmark was supposed to be liberated as an ally, not occupied. But it seemed Rokossovsky had other ideas.

Bornholm's position at the western mouth of the Baltic, 57 miles from Denmark proper and 22 miles from neutral Sweden, gave it a special importance as a naval base and it had been occupied by the Kriegsmarine, the German Navy, since 1940. Now the senior naval officer on Bornholm, Commander Kamptz, decided he must start building up the island's defences with the Russians almost at the door.

That Saturday the Chief Danish Administrative Officer on Bornholm, Peter Stemann, [4] visited Kamptz and said jokingly, 'For the sake of Bornholm and its inhabitants, you don't need to go to any great trouble to defend the island against attack.' Sternly the German naval officer insisted he had to pursue a rigorous defence against the Russians. The Dane went away very worried. Kamptz had told him he

---

4 The German occupation of Denmark was the most easy-going of all their occupations of conquered territories. They even let the king remain on his throne. For them Denmark was 'the butter, milk and eggs' land, and they were content to leave it like that.

would surrender to 'one single British officer'. But there was no hope of the British reaching the island before the Russians.

Later Stemann would come up with the idea of forming a 'Danish Army' on the island, by arming a few of the local civilians. Then the Germans could surrender to them before the Russians. As a result there would be no need for the Russians to invade the place. The German naval officer considered the suggestion for a while, but in the end he turned the proposal down. There would be no surrender to this 'instant' Danish Army. Kamptz would take his chance with the Russians. It was to be a decision he would regret.

One week later Rokossovsky's Russians of the 2nd Belorussian Front would land on Bornholm after a 'softening up' attack by Russsian dive-bombers which killed both Germans and Danes alike. Next day the victors would have a message printed in the local Bornholm newspaper stating that 'The island will be occupied *temporarily* by the troops of the Red Army until those questions about Germany in connection with the war have been solved.'

The islanders heaved a sigh of relief, their fears allayed. The Russians were there 'temporarily'. In fact, Rokossovsky's men would stay on this, the first piece of Danish territory they had taken from the Germans, for eleven long months – right into 1946. The capture of Bornholm would confirm Churchill's worst fears. What the Red Army took, it kept!

But, as yet, Doenitz was keeping a firm grip on the Baltic, though the Red Air Force and Russian submarines were becoming ever more of a problem. Night after night ships packed with soldiers and refugees were sailing from the eastern Baltic ports threatened by the Russians, bound for Schleswig-Holstein and Denmark. Terrified of the advancing Russians, for tales of their barbarity and cruelty had preceded them, the fugitives were prepared to brave the dangers of the Baltic. Out there lurked Soviet submarines which sank any craft they encountered, even if they were packed with civilians and bore the red flag of hospital ships.

Some of the fugitives harboured the fond hope that the British and Americans would join in their battle against the Red Army. That day a Captain Breuninger who would remain behind handed a letter to a sergeant who was leaving that night as soon as the fog set in over the water. It was the last one he would ever write to his father. In it he wrote:

Some officers claim to know that the British will send ships to pick us up. It is even said the English troops will land here and attack the Russians on the flank together with us . . . If we have fought the English and Americans it is only because they did not want to understand the meaning of our fight in the east . . . We only know that to this day we have fought Bolshevism, the enemy not of us alone but of all Europe. We have seen Bolshevism in action as no one else has. We have seen the Bolshevist paradise. We know what we fought for.

Now, as Captain Breuninger remained behind in a vain attempt to stop the Russians, Germany's civilians began to learn about the enemy from the East, too. Everywhere Rokossovsky's men were beginning to overrun the slow-moving German treks fleeing westwards. Their long lines of horse-drawn carts, with stove pipes sticking through roofs on which were perched mattresses as a primitive kind of protection from dive-bombers, were constantly being attacked by marauding Cossacks.

Suddenly, startlingly, they would come racing across the flat countryside, sabres flashing, uttering hoarse, wolfish cries, just like their half-savage ancestors had done for centuries when they had guarded the Tsars' frontiers. Swiftly the few elderly guards with the trek would be rendered helpless. Then the merciless killing, looting and rape would commence. Behind them as they galloped away, more often drunk than not on looted schnapps, they would leave a scene reminiscent of some pioneer caravan in the American West which had been attacked by wild Red Indians.

Those who stayed behind, thinking flight from the Russians useless, fared little better. Claus Fuhrmann, a clerk, recorded the arrival of the first Red Army men in his village:

There were no young men left in the place, only a dozen old cripples and women and children remained. Like all of us, Ellen [a woman friend] had disbelieved the atrocity stories about the Russians. She had gone up to a pair of Russians in the street in all friendliness. She was immediately seized and raped. When they released her, she ran away into the woods and stayed there until nightfall.

The cold drove her back to the village where she hid in a barn. Her Russian 'friend' and his comrades had already been looking for her and finally discovered her hiding place. They took off their belts and beat her. Then they dragged her into a house where more than a dozen of them were billetted. All of them used her the whole night for their enjoyment.

As Ivan Krylov, a staff officer with Rokossovsky, commented afterwards, 'Cossacks have been waging war for generations and the customs and habits are well established.' He was told by one Cossack *sotnik*, or captain, arrested for wild behaviour towards German civilians:

According to our custom when a town is taken by storm the men have a right to do their own individual commandeering. Long-established custom allows a Cossack to carry off as much as he can load on his horse. But you see my men are motorised and they interpret the custom in their own way by loading up their lorries.

Krylov thought the Cossack captain 'was a good fellow and he had been twice decorated' for bravery. Still he was forced to send him off for a court martial, one of the few Russians to be disciplined for what was now amounting to wholesale looting and mass rape.

By nightfall that Saturday, while the British and Americans massed on the Elbe, the Russians had completely broken through the line which was shielding the withdrawl of Manteuffel's 3rd Panzer Army. Despite their recent row, Heinrici felt he had to telephone Keitel personally and tell him what had happened.

Keitel's reaction was predictable: rage and accusations. 'That's what happens when you take it upon yourself to abandon positions!' he snapped.

'I have never taken it upon myself to abandon any position,' Heinrici answered coldly. 'The situation has always warranted it.' Then suddenly he asked for permission to abandon the Baltic port of Swinemünde. At the moment it was defended solely by raw recruits, most of whom had never even fired a rifle.

'Do you think I could possibly tell the Führer that the last strong-hold is going to be abandoned?' Keitel thundered over the phone.

'And why should I sacrifice those recruits for a lost cause?' Heinrici objected, beginning to lose his temper again. 'I'm responsible for my men. And I have been so in two wars.'

'You have no responsibility at all!' Keitel cried. 'The person who issues the orders in the first place' – he meant the Führer – 'has the responsibility.'

'I've always felt responsible to my conscience and the people of Germany. I simply cannot squander lives.' Again Heinrici asked for permission to withdraw.

'You must hold Swinemünde!' Keitel insisted.

'If you insist, you'll have to get someone else to carry out your orders,' Heinrici shot back.

'I warn you,' Keitel yelled at him. 'You're old enough to know what it means to disobey an order.'

'*Jawohl, Herr Generalfeldmarschall*,' Heinrici said, weary now of the whole damned business. 'I repeat if you want this order carried out, find someone else.'

Keitel's voice was icy and menacing when he spoke. 'I warn you a second time,' he said. 'Disobeying an order means courtmartial.'

Heinrici threw caution to the wind. Like Doenitz, he too was the son of a pastor. But unlike the Grand Admiral, he had never subscribed to the National Socialist call. For years his promotion had been delayed because he had refused to allow the Party and especially the Gestapo into his area of operations. Now he cried, 'This is an impossible situation – the way I'm being treated! I've done my duty to the best of my ability and with the complete approval of my fellow officers. I'd lose my self-respect if I allowed myself to be forced to do something that I felt was wrong. I will inform Swinemünde that Field Marshal Keitel insists it be defended. But since I can't concur with this order, I place my command at your disposal.'

Keitel didn't even think. He bellowed back over the phone, 'With the authority vested in me by the Führer I herewith relieve you of your command. Turn over all your official business to General von Manteuffel!'

But von Manteuffel was in no mood to stab his old chief in the back at this, the eleventh hour. He signalled Keitel that he refused to accept either the new appointment or the promotion that went with it. He finished his signal to Berlin with a defiant 'Here orders are given by Manteuffel!'

In essence that was the end of Army Group Vistula. After forty years in the army, serving the Kaiser, the new Republic and then Hitler, Heinrici was in disgrace, dismissed in the very last days of the war. As for von Manteuffel and his fellow commander von Tippelskirch, both of them had virtually lost control of their fleeing units. Both of them, too, had one thought uppermost in their minds now: they would attempt to surrender to the Anglo-Americans before the Russians caught up with them . . .

And back in Hamburg, with the rumble of the British guns on the other side of the Elbe growing in intensity as the British were going to move at last, a desperate *Gauleiter Kaufmann* asked Albert Speer, a friend and Hitlers' Minister of Armaments who had achieved great power in these last two years, if he could now broadcast the speech which Speer had secretly recorded a few days before.

Speer had written the speech on a tree stump out in the woods where he couldn't be observed. Then, under Kaufmann's personal supervision, it had been recorded in the studios of Radio Hamburg, which now housed Germany's most notorious propagandist William Joyce, known to the British public as 'Lord Haw-Haw'.

But the speech was so explosive that Speer had insisted that Kaufmann could not use it without his express permission. Now Kaufmann thought the speech by such an intimate of the Führer as Speer might bring about instant surrender. What else could be the effect, he considered, of such a statement as 'the war is lost ... In order to avoid unnecessary reprisals and to survive the catastrophe, the German people must turn over to the Allies all such factories and industrial plants as have not yet been destroyed.' Surely that would have the desired result and Hamburg would be spared the terrible fate of its neighbour, Bremen?

Speer refused.

Later Speer, who could – and did – justify everything, felt that 'once more Hitler had succeeded in paralysing me psychically. To myself and perhaps to others, I justified my change of mind on the grounds that it would be wrong and pointless to try to intervene now in the course of the tragedy.'

Probably Speer was just plain scared. Not wishing to argue with Kaufmann, he excused himself and set off to join Doenitz and Himmler at Ploen. Perhaps he, like Himmler, thought they might still rescue something from the sinking ship, tragedy or no tragedy.

But Kaufmann was not 'paralysed'. Like Heinrici and von Manteuffel, he knew he had to do something. There were still 600,000 civilians living in Hamburg and if it came to a battle their suffering would be immense.

Field Marshal Busch, whose HQ was just outside Hamburg, would fight to the end, he knew that. Kaufmann would get no help from that direction. But he did have one ally among the military. He was General Alwin Wolz, the commander of the 3rd Anti-Aircraft Division, who had been made 'Hamburg Battle Commandant' at the beginning of April.

At that time he had conducted several talks with the pudgy Air Force General and sounded him out. Wolz agreed that the only way to defend Hamburg was to evacuate the civilians first, but that was impossible. There was only one answer, he told Kaufmann, and that was to surrender the city.

But by now Wolz was suspect. On 23 April, Busch had visited the Air Force General's HQ in Hamburg's *Rothenbaumchaussee*, a large flak bunker. He had told Wolz that he expected absolute obedience from him. Wolz replied that he was considering suicide. He couldn't stand the thought of any more innocent civilians being killed in the city.

Busch was unimpressed. He snapped, 'Then take a *Panzerfaust* and go and knock out an English tank rather than talk about killing yourself!'

In the end Wolz had agreed to continue in his post and, as he himself said, he behaved like '*den wilden Mann*' – a crazy person. He ordered barricades to be erected and machine-gun nests to be set up, and formed a regiment from sailors, policemen and flak gunners which attacked the British 7th Armoured Division and knocked out forty tanks.

But Busch had seen through his activities. He had already ordered Wolz to be replaced by another *Luftwaffe* general, Koehler, who was known to be a tough hard-liner. Koehler was expected to take over the post of Hamburg's Battle Commandant on 2 May.

Now Kaufmann waited to hear the results of his approach to the British through the Swedish banker Wallenberg. He had asked the Swede to get the British Embassy in Stockholm to give an answer to his note by midday on Saturday 28 April. But as midday approached there was no call from Sweden. The British remained obstinately silent. Of course, Kaufmann did not realise that his request for a meeting with a British representative was, at this moment, out of the question. For this night, Montgomery would attack over the Elbe and no British representative was going to risk his life at the time of the assault. The British reply to his memo would come *after* the Elbe had been successfully crossed.

Kaufmann, however, did not know that. Now he agonised. Sooner or later his 'treachery' would come out and he had no illusions about what would happen to him if he fell into the hands of the 'flying tribunals', made up of fanatical Army or SS officers, which were now roaming the countryside administering rough justice to soldiers and civilians alike whom they thought weren't prepared to die for 'People Fatherland and Führer'. They would string him up at the nearest tree or lamp-post with the usual crude sign dangling from his neck, 'I am a craven defeatist!'[5]

Four days before, he had refused an invitation to Doenitz's HQ in Ploen because he feared the former would have him arrested as soon as he arrived there. His luck would not last for ever; time was running out. At last he made a decision, perhaps spurred on by the ever-increasing rumble of the British guns on the other side of the Elbe. There was now only one way to save Hamburg – and naturally himself – he would contact the Tommies directly.

---

5 These *Standgerichte* were an old tradition in a German Army in times of crisis. Usually composed of three officers, they were prosecution, defence and judge in one, who could order the maximum sentence carried out without reference to a higher authority.

4

'Herr Leutnant, this is what we are fighting against!'

I

Back in Britain the Saturday afternoon had been spoiled here and there by rain. Fortunately the Cup Final had taken place in good weather the previous weekend, with the royal family watching, including the 19-year-old Princess Elizabeth in her new ATS uniform. Chelsea had won.

Still the streets had been thronged with men and women with plenty of money in their pockets. Most of them were working sixty hours a week and there was overtime enough for those who wanted it. Not that there was much to buy, though for ten days now Union Jacks had been on sale on the streets of London and other large cities. For peace was just round the corner after a war which had already lasted five years and eight months; and everyone wanted to be ready for the big 'shindig' soon to come. Already the papers were reporting that 'thousands' were pouring into London 'to be in on V-E Day'. Police were bringing in reinforcements. But the 'Bobbies' had been instructed to allow 'considerable latitude'. There was only one fly in the ointment – London Transport had just gone on strike over the manning of the new summer timetable!

Already the politicians were gearing up for the first election in ten years. The *Daily Mirror* that week had headlined 'Labour's Programme For The Peace – Nationalise Bank of England, fuel, steel and transport'. 'In addition Labour pledges itself to carry out the social security plans, to ensure work for all and to see that money is no longer the passport to the best health treatment.' All the facts, the unknown journalist recorded, were in a booklet entitled *Let's Face the Future*, to be published on Saturday 28 April.

That Saturday the pubs were full and although the beer was weak – 'gnat's piss', as it was invariably called these days – there was enough of it. There were fish and chips back in the shops after a winter when there'd been no fish, just chips and potato scallops and now that the blackout had been lifted there would be no danger walking home, even if you had had a little too much of the 'gnat's piss'. As for the flying bombs and V-2s, it had been two weeks now since the last one had struck home with such terrifying effect. The war was virtually over, wasn't it? The new Labour booklet, priced twopence, *Let's Face the Future*, hit the nail right on the head.

Three hundred miles away on the Elbe, the post-war leader of the Liberal Party, Jo Grimond, currently on the staff of General Ross's 53rd Infantry Division, which would be soon crossing that river under fire, was not so sanguine about that future. General Ross, who was not cast in the Montgomery mould and whose chief pleasures apart from soldiering were 'poker and good food', took what was to come in his stride. But the craggy-faced Scottish politician felt the division had had enough. Since Normandy only one CO survived; all the rest had been killed or wounded. It seemed to Grimond that 'most of the fighting' had been done 'by the same three or four infantry divisions', including his own. This night there would be no future for yet another group of young men who would die violently in battle.

Some knew it. As they dropped to the ground from the backs of their 3-ton lorries and filed into their marshalling area west of the Elbe, the assault infantry of the 15th Scottish Division and the 1st Commando were given their last hot meal and told to get a couple of hours' sleep.

But most of them were too nervous to sleep. Some of them had taken part in the assault crossings of the Seine and the Rhine, and even the Normandy landings themselves. Yet even they were as nervous as the teenage replacements who now filled their ranks.

So they squatted on the grass and smoked and chatted. Here and there the more experienced changed into clean underwear – 'vests, cellular, for the use of' – and the knee-length army underpants. If they were hit, the clean fabric forced into the wound was less likely to result in gas gangrene than if their underwear was dirty. Others methodically stripped their rifles or the magazines of their Bren light machine-guns, rubbing the brass cartridges one by one and checking that every third slug was tracer as the drill prescribed. Some tucked their metal shaving mirrors into the pockets of their khaki blouses, next to the 'French letters', as a frail means of protection for their heart. They had all heard the wonderful story of the soldier in some other battalion – it was always in another battalion – who had been saved this way from a 'Jerry bullet with his number on it'. Some prayed, but not many.

At eleven o'clock that night the men of the Royal Scots and the Royal Scots Fusiliers, known as 'Pontius Pilate's Bodyguard' because the regiment had such a long history, filed on board the Buffaloes of the Royal Tanks which were going to take them across. Again they were told by staff officers, fussing about with their clipboards and orders, to 'get your heads down'. But now sleep was out of the question, even for the most hardened 'old sweat' among the assault infantry.

For exactly one hour later the whole of 8th Corps' artillery opened up with a tremendous roar to blast the German positions across the Elbe in a typical Montgomery 'Alamein Barrage'. For the last time in the Second World War, British infantry in Europe, their faces glistening as if with sweat in the ruddy reflected light, were awed and deafened by the sights and sounds of this great bombardment and the dramatic crimson spurts of fire that had begun to erupt everywhere on the other side of the river. The softening up had commenced.

At Artlenburg now, the Fifteenth's crossing point, the sky was as bright as day. Scores of searchlights aimed their icy white beams at the low cloud, artificially creating what was known as 'Monty's Moonlight.' It would light the way for the attackers soon. Now the infantry could stand unharmed at their side of the river in the deep shadows and stare at the sides.

Over the Elbe a fantastic pattern of myriad purple stabs and flashes of deep-orange flame took shape and died like man-made forked lighting. Here and there a maverick shell exploded close to the far bank and tossed up a sudden spurt of cherry-red flame, like a Roman candle of monstrous size. And all the while, white tracer shells from the British 3.7-inch Bofors anti-aircraft guns, which were being used to mark a path, hissed across in diagonal streams, drawing a racing bright light behind them.

But the waiting infantry had little time now for the terrible beauty of that scene. Their moment of truth had arrived. At two o'clock precisely the air was filled with a droning ominous roar, like a squadron of heavy bombers coming in low. One by one, the 20-ton Buffaloes swung along Artlenburg's main street which led to the Elbe. Up the dyke they went, swinging to left and right along the dyke. Beyond lay the water, 'shorts' sending up great whirling fountains of wild white water. There they waited momentarily, each in its exactly allocated place. A signal. And they were off.

Hurriedly they scrambled and roared and slithered down the dyke, their tracks showering everyone watching with mud and pebbles. Like a school of ponderous hippos they slid into the water. Slowly they began to advance against the current. It was three knots and hard to fight. But they were making progress. The infantry, ducked low, tensed. They were getting near mid-stream.

Almost immediately the gunners of the 8th Corps' artillery lifted their fire from the opposite bank and moved further inland. In the darkness and confusion of the river crossing they didn't want to fire on their own men. Now the men in the Buffaloes were on their own.

The Germans were not slow to take advantage of the respite. Bursts of vicious tracer skimmed across the river. Light cannon joined in. Like glowing ping-pong balls, gaining speed by the instant, the streams of shells hurtled towards the craft. Mortars broke into obscene throaty life.

Spurts of boiling water erupted on both sides of the little fleet. The crouching infantry could hear the bullets patter down on the metal sides of the Buffaloes like heavy tropical raindrops on a tin roof. The machine-guns of the Buffaloes started to fire back. German artillery joined in the river battle. But the enemy gunners were rattled by the 8th Corps bombardment and their fire was inaccurate, fortunately for the infantry sweating out those endless minutes in mid-stream. Suddenly everything was noise and chaos – and sudden death.

Back on the Allied bank, the Argylls and the KOSBs were waiting their turn to cross, sheltered in the protection of a large quarry upstream of Artlenburg. Suddenly they came under fire from long-range German guns. The Jocks cowered in their hiding place as the shells dropped all around. A large shell struck the entrance to the quarry. There was a tremendous explosion. A blinding flash of angry flame. When it had cleared, the survivors, shocked and ashen-faced, saw that half the company was sprawled out on the ground, dead and dying. Rallied quickly by their officers and NCOs, the survivors filed down obediently to the waiting craft. As always the 'poor bloody infantry' were paying the butcher's bill.

Behind them came the KOSBs. Their objective was the road leading from the river on the other side up the steep, twisting cobbled rise through Schnakenbek. Already the little inn which lay at that exit was burning brightly and the young Jocks could see their objective quite clearly, almost as if it was day.

The leading craft ground to a halt. The KOSBs surged forward. Hurriedly they searched the burning *Gasthaus*, followed by the owner's weeping wife who was trying – unsuccessfully – to explain in the thick local dialect – *Platt* – that there were no Germans there. She was right. All the Jocks found was her prostrate husband. The shock of the attack had given him a heart attack.

They started to advance up the steep cobbled height. Green-clad German policemen from Hamburg, hurriedly formed into an infantry battalion, tried to stop them. But the middle-aged policemen were no match for these raw-boned, hard young infantrymen. They were swept aside. Relentlessly the KOSBs pushed on, leaving a trail of bodies behind them, fighting their way to the key Route Four – the road from Hamburg to Berlin. The 15th Scottish had done it. They had a foothold on the other side of the Elbe!

The 1st Commando Brigade had also made a successful crossing of the Elbe. At Lauenburg to the Jocks' right. Now, however, they were stopped by a 150-foot cliff. But only temporarily. The green-bereted specialists, who disdained the Army's steel helmet even in the hottest action, were used to scaling cliffs. They'd practised the task often enough on the cliffs of England's south coast. Under the command of Captains Clapton and Cruden they began to climb the cliff, seemingly unaware of the fact that they were carrying sixty pounds or more of equipment on their backs, plus their weapons.

Up above them the German defenders leaned over and began to drop stick grenades on to the heads of the climbing men. They exploded on all sides. Men screamed and fell from the cliff, tumbling to the tiny shingle beach below. But most of them made it. Then it was in among the enemy with the bayonets while someone sounded a hunting horn. As Captain Clapton put it later in his terse report, 'The majority of the enemy in the immediate area were at once eliminated.'

An hour later the Commandos were regrouping at the edge of the sandpit near the shattered railway bridge which the men of the 11th Armoured Division had failed to capture ten days before. As soon as dawn broke, they would launch an all-out attack on the little riverside town which two centuries before had belonged to the English crown. And there would be no doubt of the outcome of the action. Commanded by Colonel Mills-Roberts, who was always at the front of the battle – only the other day he had shot a German sniper, the Colonel firing from the hip with his favourite Garand American rifle – they had fought at the forefront of Montgomery's troops from Holland to this spot, having crossed five great rivers under fire doing so.[1]

At the same time as the Commando Brigade regrouped, the 15th Division had secured the immediate bridgehead and, in the face of light fire from the eight or nine German infantry battalions defending the river, were swinging out to left and right to extend their hold on the riverbank. But the German fire from further inland was intensifying.

The lead brigade of the division, with the Cameronians and the Glasgow Highlanders in the lead, was also beginning to push inland, advancing in a northerly direction and infiltrating between the numerous hamlets and small villages of the area.

The Brigade had been given an 'advance to contact' mission. But so far it had met with little real opposition. The infantry had once bumped into a handful of scared boys aged betwen 13 and 16, clad in overlong overcoats, commanded by an exceedingly tall, gaunt and elderly major. The Jocks had been so angered by this soldier's arrogant attempts to have his young innocents slaughtered when the war was already virtually lost that they had had to be restrained from shooting him on the spot. Instead they allowed the official photographer to take a picture of him looking very glum and out of place next to his line of tousle-haired young 'warriors'.

While the infantry advanced and behind the bridgehead the other divisions which would follow – the 53rd, the 11th Armoured, the 5th and 6th Airborne – piled up waiting for their turn to cross, Colonel Foster's sappers started the task of building the vital bridge. Almost from the start his men laboured under heavy shellfire from further inland. It wasn't very pleasant, but they'd done it before and they were doing it again now.

The big engineer Colonel's worries lay elsewhere. As dawn broke and his men cursed and swore below as they dragged up the girders for the Bailey bridge, Foster started to scan the horizon anxiously. Over and over again. Already the anti-aircraft guns from Corps were in place, and in due course the RAF would provide an aerial umbrella of fighters to guard the bridge which was now beginning to edge its way across the Elbe under fire. But the RAF's 83rd Group of the 2nd Tactical Air Force, flying from bases in Germany to provide this umbrella, had only one squadron of operational jet fighters. They flew the Meteor jet, which was as yet untried. But they would be flying

---

1 At the end of the war, Mill-Roberts slammed Field Marshal Milch's bejewelled field marshal's baton down over the latter's head for 'insolence', then took it away from him. Forty-odd years later the descendants of the two officers were still haggling over the possession of it.

against the combat-experienced German jet pilots, who had been flying battle missions since late 1943. Time and time again the German jets had outflown anything the RAF had been able to send up against them. What if the German jet fighter-bombers now struck his bridge in force? The whole drive to the Baltic coast might well be in jeopardy.

Little did a worried Colonel Foster know it that morning, but his bridge across the Elbe would be the focal point of the biggest air battle between Allied and enemy fighters since Goering's thousand-plane raid on Allied installations on New Year's Day 1945. 'Fat Hermann', as his pilots called their gross commander behind his back, might well be languishing in open arrest (at Hitler's orders) in a castle in southern Germany, but his young, bold pilots were prepared to have one last go before the war was finally lost. This would be the *Luftwaffe's* swan-song.

II

In Hamburg that Sunday dawn, it seemed as if yet another wartime day had commenced for the 600,000 half-starved, cowed civilians still left in the shattered city: a day just as miserable as all those which had preceded it. Around the 'dead zone', the parts of the inner city which had been sealed off after the week-long raid of July 1943 – the same raids which had broken Kaufmann's loyalty to the Führer – the poorly clad housewives started to line up outside the foodshops as soon as it was light. Even outside the *Pferdeschlächter* – the horsemeat butchers, once disdained by even the poorest of housewives – there were long queues. Horsemeat was not rationed and these days there were plenty of dead horses.

Those who were on duty – and most of the menfolk were – went to their stations and posts through streets adorned with patriotic slogans exhorting them to 'Fight Bolshevism to the End' and, in the local dialect, 'Better Dead than Slaves'.[2] The underground and most of the trams still ran, and they were packed with people coming in from the villages and small towns to the north of the great port to work in Hamburg's celebrated 'free harbour'. Besides, two of the area's most popular football clubs – Altona 93 and HSV – would play a friendly game out in the suburb of Rothenbaum and anyone who could wanted to see HSV's star, Seeler, play.[3]

2 As in English, the German word for 'Slav' is very close to the German word meaning 'slave'.
3 Father of Uwe Seeler, the German soccer star of the 1970's.

Rumours flourished, of course, as across the Elbe to the south-east the English guns thundered. Goering had died of heart disease . . . The Army in Italy had surrendered . . . Hitler was fighting at the head of his troops in an embattled Berlin . . . As aged Mathilde Wolff-Moenckeberg wrote in her diary, which she would one day pass on to her daughter Ruth Evans in faraway Wales, 'The end of the ordeal is near and our imagination is working overtime trying to take in all this horror.'

Yet, despite the closeness of the English and the constant dog-fights between British and German fighters further off, Hamburg itself remained peaceful. All the time the air sirens continued shrilling their warnings of impending dread. But nothing happened. All the Hamburgers could make out, as the 65-year-old diarist noted, were 'the reconnaissance planes which circle above with their dark humming noises'.

But Kaufmann thought this the lull before the storm. Already the reports were flooding in from the Lower Elbe about the British crossing and that the 245 German Infantry Division defending the area was preparing a counter-attack. Soon all hell would be let loose and Hamburg would suffer yet again.

Now Kaufmann moved. He signalled Doenitz in Ploen that no purpose would be served by continuing the battle in his area. All that would result would be the destruction of Hamburg and its outlying suburbs and small towns. All further combat with the 'Western enemy' should stop. Instead Doenitz should concern himself with stopping the 'Bolsheviks'.

He turned to Wolz, now his willing ally, and ordered him to remove the two most fanatical formations from his command – the former U-boat men of the 2nd Marine Division and the survivors of the 12th SS Training Battalion. Wolz was also ordered to convince General Erdmann of the 8th Airborne Division, which lay to the north of Hamburg, that he should intervene with his paras if he and Kaufmann had trouble with Hamburg's garrison.

While this was going on, Kaufmann's aides ordered the printers of Hamburg's chief newspaper – the *Hamburger Zeitung* – to prepare a special issue which would be published as soon as the occasion called for it. It began with 'After a heroic battle and tireless endeavour for a German victory . . . our nation has succumbed to superiority in men and material. . . .' It continued with the statement that 'Anyone who has the military ambition to continue the fight, he may do so outside the city . . . I know, however, my duty is to save Hamburg and its women and children . . .' At last Kaufmann had laid his cards plainly on the table. The *Hamburger Zeitung* statement was a declaration of *Gauleiter* Kaufmann's intention to surrender the city to the British. Now it was up to General Wolz.

That afternoon, sponsored by Kaufmann and Wolz, their civilian emissaries made the first contact with the Tommies. They offered to surrender the fuel for the V-1s, the 'doodlebugs' which had plagued London the previous year, which was stored just outside Hamburg. At the same time, three Germans bearing a white flag approached the lines of the British 7th Armoured Division outside Harburg and asked the infantry of the 9th Durham Light Infantry who received them if they could speak to a senior British officer.

The Germans, who had been sent by Kaufmann and Wolz, were the civilian director of the Phoenix Rubber Works, which specialised in tyres and contraceptives, Albert Schaefer; a German Army doctor, Dr Burchard; and their interpreter, Lieutenant Otto von Laun, a member of Wolz's staff. They explained they wanted to arrange immunity from artillery fire for a military hospital located in the cellars of the Phoenix Rubber Works. It was an excuse, but the British didn't know it.

In the event they were blindfolded and driven to the HQ of Brigadier Spurling, whose 131st Infantry Brigade held that section of the front. He heard their request and then told the Germans that 'If hospitals insisted on posititioning themselves within the zone of active operations, the staff and patients must accept the consequences.' They were told to either evacuate the hospital or else surrender Hamburg. For already Spurling had gathered that Schaefer, in particular, was more concerned with the port than his works and the military hospital.

The two others thereupon decided to return to their own lines, but Schaefer hung around. In a conversation with the 7th's divisional intelligence officer, he mentioned that the question of the surrender of Hamburg had already been favourably mentioned by *Gauleiter* Kaufmann in a private discussion with leading Hamburg businessmen. The news was immediately flashed to Corps HQ.

Before Burchard and von Laun left, a German-speaking 'Desert Rat' who was present heard the doctor whisper to von Laun, 'Herr *Leutnant*, this is what we are fighting against – these fine young officers who have such a high level of culture that they might almost be German!' The last part was the joke of officers' mess for the next twenty-four hours. Then they left, only to blow themselves up on a German minefield laid by the 12th SS Training Battalion just before they had been withdrawn from the sector. Fortunately the two of them survived.

Now the discussions moved to a small country inn between the villages of Steinbeck and Trelde. Its name was not very apt in that flat countryside, for it was called *Hoheluft*, mountain air. Schaefer told the British officers that Kaufmann and Wolz were very definitely interested in surrendering Hamburg. That had been the reason for his own presence in the mission.

Schaefer's words encouraged the Intelligence officers present to draft a letter which they hoped the divisional commander, General Lyne, would sign so that Schaefer could take it back with him. It was addressed to his fellow-general Wolz and read:

1. The Reichsführer SS has already made an offer of unconditional surrender to the Western Powers [Himmler was meant].
2. Before attacking Bremen we demanded the surrender of the City. As this offer was refused, we had no alternative but to attack with artillery and air support. Bremen fell in twenty-four hours but not without much unnecessary bloodshed.
3. In the name of humanity, Herr General, we demand the surrender of Hamburg. For you as a soldier there can be no dishonour in following examples of famous generals as Gen. d. Pz Josef Harpe, Genlt Fritz Bayerlein and many others[4] who have surrendered themselves and their commands. From the political point of view there can be surely no reflection on you if you follow the example of the Reichsführer SS.
4. We, therefore, ask you Herr General to send into our lines an officer empowered to negotiate the surrender. Our forward troops have been warned to expect this arrival and not to shoot at him. He will be treated according to Geneva Convention and returned after the parley to his own lines.
5. The population of Hamburg will not easily forget its first large-scale raid by over one thousand heavy bombers. We now dispose of a bomber force five to ten times greater numerically and operating from nearby airfields. After the war the German people must be fed: the more Hamburg's dock installations are damaged the greater are the chances of famine in Germany.
6. If this offer is refused we shall have no alternative but to attack Hamburg with all the forces at our disposal.

It was a long-winded, yet cleverly constructed message, courteous and appealing to Wolz's military honour – after all he had been contemplating suicide rather than dishonour. But the sting in the tail was there all right. If the Germans didn't surrender, they could expect the worst – the very thing Kaufmann feared most – the total destruction of Hamburg!

---

4 Who had just surrendered to the Americans in the Ruhr.

III

As yet Montgomery knew nothing of this first tentative attempt at direct surrender to him, which would change the whole balance of a campaign which he really considered was not much more than a sideshow.

That morning he hurried to the Elbe front where, at a cost of some two hundred young men who would never see the end of the war, the 15th Scottish Division was firmly established on the other side. General Barker, the 8th Corps Commander, thought the Fifteenth were a bit slow. But then, he explained, the division had been in action since Normandy. It, too, had had a complete turnover in personnal in the rifle companies during its ten months in combat. The division, the corps, the British Army were wearing out.

But Montgomery had other things in mind. Hurriedly he conferred with General 'Bimbo' Dempsey, the tall, thin commander of his 2nd Army, and the American General 'Matt' Ridgway, commanding the 18th US Airborne Corps, a craggy-faced officer with a great hook of a nose, who wore a hand grenade pinned to his webbing even when he was miles behind the front.

Ridgway, who didn't particularly like Montgomery (in common with most American generals), was the man who was going to 'build a fire under Monty', according to General Bradley. Now he had no opportunity to stoke the fire. Instead he listened. For as usual Montgomery was doing the talking – and ordering!

Later Montgomery signalled the War Office in London that he had met Ridgway and giving the following orders:

18 US Corps make an assault crossing over the Elbe in the Bleckede area at 0300 hours tomorrow and this will be done with the 82 US Airborne Div. A further crossing to be made in the Darchau area if this is found suitable and possible. 18 US Corps to then operate towards Schwerin and Wismar and it will be joined by 6 British Airborne Div. which will be passed over at Lauenburg and thence eastwards over the bridge at 898250 [map reference] which we have captured intact. II Armd Div. of 8 Corps to be moved forward and to start crossing the Elbe at Artlenburg at 1200 hours tomorrow and this division to be directed straight to Lübeck.

Operations given, Montgomery departed for his HQ once more, leaving his subordinate commanders to sort out the details. A little later, Dempsey and Ridgway set off to find Gavin of the 82nd Airborne, who had just set up his command post further down the Elbe opposite the village of Bleckede.

Gavin liked 'Bimbo' Dempsey. He had, in Gavin's opinion, a quick and scholarly mind and, unlike Montgomery and Ridgway who to Gavin seemed 'a little retarded', an entirely adult personality. Dempsey cared nothing about the newspaper and radio publicity which the new breed of Second World War generals thought so necessary for their careers. Gavin also felt much sympathy for Dempsey, who had been in action with the infantry for most of the war, for Montgomery was always interfering in the 2nd Army Commander's operations; he knew from his own experience during the Battle of the Bulge what it was like to serve under Montgomery and to suffer what Bradley called the former's 'usurpation of authority'. In short he (unlike most of his fellows in the US Army) was prepared to help Dempsey – and naturally through him Montgomery, too – the best he could.

On this warm April Sunday afternoon, with the wind from the north bringing the noises of the battle on the Elbe through the open window of his CP, Dempsey asked Gavin for immediate help to reach the Baltic.

Gavin protested that so far only one battalion of his 82nd had reached the Elbe front: the rest of the division was still strung out between there and Cologne.

Dempsey, using Montgomery's arguments, urged that it was vital to reach the mouth of the Baltic before Rokossovsky's Russians. The latter were already approaching the Baltic port of Rostock, which was only 70 miles away from Lübeck, 2nd Army's objective.

Ridgway stepped in and suggested that he could offer Gavin the infantry from 8th US Infantry Division – 'the Golden Arrow' [5] – which was already on the Elbe and ready for action.

Gavin knew the Eighth. He had fought beside the division in the Battle of the Hurtgen Forest the previous February and wasn't too happy with the suggestion. Although the Eighth had fought through the campaign since August 1944, when the then divisional commander General Stroh had had the traumatic experience of seeing his own son shot down over one of the Division's objectives during a dive-bombing raid, he had not been pleased with its performance. But when Gavin objected, Ridgway said hurriedly he would give him complete charge of the Eighth's men allotted to him.

Gavin agreed and said his 'All-Americans', together with the new men from the 'Golden Arrow', would attack at four o'clock the next morning.

---

5 Nicknamed thus after its golden arrow divisional patch.

Thereafter Dempsey confided to Ridgway, who had seemed a little bored by the whole discussion, that he had hoped the British would have the kudos of making the first contacts with Rokossovksy's Russians in the British sector. However, it now appeared that the Americans would be on his right flank and the ones most likely to make the link-up. Since the Americans had already met the Russians at Torgau on the Elbe a few days before, could not Ridgway let the British 6th Airborne Division – 'the Red Devils' – which came under Ridgway's 18th Airborne Corps have that privilege?

Ridgway frowned and considered the suggestion. He didn't like it much. He explained to the British General, who looked emaciated in comparison to his own powerful physique, that 'this request would throw my attack off stride'. He continued that it would mean throwing the British airborne division diagonally across the path of his own US 7th Armored Division, which 'could cause all sorts of trouble on the road'.

The British Army Commander, whose physical strength was disguised by his gentle speech and sloping shoulders and who affected a goose – 'Gertie of Falaise' – as a pet, nodded his understanding. He said, 'That's quite all right. I understand. You do it your way.' With that he left.

But back at his own command post, Ridgway started to mull over 'Bimbo' Dempsey's request once more. He 'remembered the great fight the British had made throughout the war, the disaster at Dunkirk, the quiet valor of the people of England under the German bombings'. In the end he decided to grant Dempsey's request. The 6th Airborne, the British 'Red Devils', would have the honour (if such it was going to be) of making the first contact with the Red Army.

Ridgway's emotions that day were undoubtedly genuine. But they smacked of the condescension of a representative of a great power, for such had America become over the last four years to that of a second-class one which lived off past traditions, past victories and power. They revealed, too, just how much the American attitude to the British had changed this month. Whatever Montgomery, Dempsey and the British thought to the contrary, it was America, the superpower, which was running the show. They could afford to be magnanimous and allow the British to have their little triumphs. As Bradley phrased it later in his memoirs:

In a courteous gesture, Ridgway positioned the British 6th Airborne in the van of the XVIII Airborne Corps so the British could have the honor and public acclaim of greeting the Russians at Wismar. As it turned out, Gavin's troops actually linked first, but we downplayed the union in order not to upstage the British.

But the battle for the Elbe, which Bradley would later describe as 'almost unopposed' – it had cost Barker two hundred casualties, as we have seen, and on the morrow Gavin would cross without a single fatality – was not over yet. By midday that Sunday, Colonel Foster's bridge was under full attack by the *Luftwaffe*.

At noon, taking advantage of the momentary absence of the 'umbrella', the twin-engined ME 262 jets came streaming in at a tremendous rate, trailing their unearthly shriek behind them. A British officer stalled there in his tank recalled this his first sight of a jet plane:

Six jets in line astern screamed down on the bridge and plastered us with anti-personnel bombs. I felt very small, sitting in the open top turret. With a continuous series of explosions and spouts of water they dropped their load. It was over in a matter of seconds. They missed all of us sitting on the bridge and were gone behind the trees. With an unsteady hand I lit a captured German cigar. I suppose I should have said to myself: 'Well, there opens a new chapter in man's achievement, but I don't think I did.'

Neither did Colonel Foster. By the end of that Sunday fourteen German planes would be shot down. But they were dealing out punishment, too. Each time the squat howling jets disappeared, they left more silent figures slumped on the steel girders of the Bailey bridge across the Elbe.[6]

One group of British fighters that day, under the command of the Battle of Britain ace 'Johnnie' Johnson, ventured a little further than the Elbe though. Against orders probably. The cocky young fighter-pilots, flying from their new base just south of the Elbe at Celle, decided they'd have a look at the advancing Russians on the other side of the river.

They found them soon enough. 'Are they Huns?' Johnson asked his number two, focusing his eyes on the gaggle of planes approaching his squadron.

They decided they were the Russians, their allies seen by them for the first time since Russia had entered the war in 1941. 'All right, chaps,' Johnson ordered. 'Stick together. Don't make a move.' To himself he said, 'I'm for it, if this mix-up gets out of hand.'

---

6   It was reported that in the six days of the air battle over the Elbe, the *Luftwaffe* lost 128 planes at a cost of 29 to the 83rd Group.

The Russian Yak fighters made a slow turn which would bring them behind Johnson's Spitfires. He knew he couldn't allow that. So he swung to starboard and brought his planes above the Yaks, which numbered nearly a hundred. 'Tighten it up,' he ordered. 'Don't break formation!'

For a couple of turns the erstwhile allies circled each other. Both sides were cautious and suspicious. Johnson narrowed the gap between them. When he was opposite the Russian leader, he rocked his wings. The Russian commander did not react.

Suddenly the Russians seemed to lose interest. Without any signal they turned and flew away, rising and falling in the air and reminding Johnson of a 'great wheeling tumbling pack of starlings which one sometimes sees on a winter day in England'. The British and the Russians had met for the first time. But the coldness of their meeting did not augur well for the future. It would be the first and last time that British fighter-planes would venture beyond the Elbe into Russian territory . . .

However sanguine people like Ridgway and Bradley might have been about operations on the Elbe afterwards, that Sunday those who were at the scene of the fighting did not think it was such a walkover. The Germans were making determined attempts to knock out Foster's bridge, not only with aircraft but with floating mines and frogmen from special German 'Ascension Day commandos'.[7] And if that bridge were knocked out, not only would the 11th Armoured Division's and the 6th Airborne's drive be stalled, but probably also that of Ridgway's 7th US Armored Division.

Chester Wilmot, the Australian war correspondent attached to Montgomery's HQ, who over the years had received many of the Field Marshal's confidence, expressed those worries in a dispatch filed for the BBC that day:

Here in the north, there's still an army to be reckoned with: an army whose fighting power Himmler may still regard as bargaining power. We have smashed the German Army as a whole and its Air Force. But we haven't yet broken the power or the spirit of the German Navy . . . In Kiel, Wilhelmshaven and the northern ports there are more than 100,000 German navy personnel – most of them with some training in the use of weapons. And they're being put into the land battle. We're meeting marines, sailors and even submarines crews and they're fighting well.

Moreover when Field Marshal Busch became Commander-in-Chief North-West, he took over an area where the organisation and discipline behind the lines was good because the Navy still had the situation firmly in hand. Busch also found that in

7 One-day missions, i.e. to heaven.

addition to the troops fighting south of the Elbe, he had four other divisions that he could bring from Denmark . . . This combination of circumstances has provided the Second Army with the immediate task of isolating and smashing this force and of seizing the naval bases behind it. We cannot afford at this stage of the war to pause in the task. As long as there are pockets of resistance as well organised as this one, the Nazis may be encouraged to fight on elsewhere. And so here in the north the Second Army is striking at what amounts to Himmler's last hope. . . .

Little did the chubby, broad-faced Australian correspondent realise just how true his words were that day. For, at his villa HQ outside Hamburg, the crusty little Field Marshal Busch was determined not to surrender tamely. His soldier's ethos forbade it. He knew of Kaufmann's plans and rejected them. For he distrusted the whole bunch of 'golden pheasants' who had been running Germany since 1933. He preferred an 'honourable fall' to a 'dishonourable capitulation'.

Perhaps the old soldier knew that he was dying – within two months he would be dead.[8] But before he went, he would fight to the last. That night, as Brigadier Villiers, commanding the leading brigade of the 15th Scottish Division astride the Dalldorf-Lauenburg, reported that the area to his brigade's front seemed empty of enemy troops. Field Marshal Busch was already alerting his men. He intended to strike into the left flank of the Scottish Division which was preparing to march north. As he told his staff crustily, 'A German field marshal does not surrender. He fights to the death . . . '

8 He would die in the 'Generals' POW camp at Aldershot in July 1945.

5

'My Führer, my loyalty to you will be unconditional.'

I

Rain mixed with snow started to fall as Gavin's single battalion of 505th Parachute Infantry Regiment began to move to the boats. Six miles away at Lauenburg they could still hear the boom of the British guns. But here at Bleckede all was quiet. The Germans on the other side seemed to have gone to sleep. Perhaps the rotten night had forced them back into their bunkers and weapon pits. For nothing stirred there, save for occasional flares which hissed into the sky on the other side of the Elbe and made the advancing paratroopers freeze in their tracks, nerves tingling electrically, hearts thumping.

Gavin moved forward with the first wave, mulling over the situation in his head. By now he had gone into combat in North Africa, Sicily, Italy, France, Holland, Belgium and Germany, and he was used to battle. Yet really one never was.

He recalled the time when he had captured his first prisoner, a terrified Italian who had feared castration when Gavin had begun cutting off the soldier's trouser buttons so he couldn't escape. As soon as he had started to slice through the prisoner's flies, the man had grabbed the knife and they had fallen to the ground in a 'kicking, yelling, fighting mass'. In the end the Italian had managed to escape in the darkness, his manhood intact, leaving Gavin 'madder than hell'. It had all been very messy and unsatisfactory.

Now he was going to do it for what was probably the last time. He forced himself to concentrate on the task ahead as the rain dripped off the rim of his helmet. Their crossing spot at Bleckede was narrower than where the British had crossed at Artlenburg, and the Elbe was shallow here, too. There were several handy sandbanks half-way across, spaced out at 6-yard intervals. They'd prove useful. The only problem he could visualise was enemy artillery once he was across.

He knew his paras – 'the devils in baggy pants', as they liked to call themselves. They were used to being surrounded, cut off, living a hand-to-mouth existence without heavy weapons to support them. But what about the four battalions of the 'Golden Arrow' Division, which would follow the first wave across? How would they fare without any real artillery support and without the benefit of the TAC Air Force? The weather forecast wasn't good and on the morrow it was unlikely that the planes would be able to fly.

The tall, handsome Airborne General dismissed the thought and concentrated on the task at hand. Together with his small staff, he entered one of the rubber assault boats and they started to cross. Slowly and carefully they moved into mid-stream. Still no German fire. Gavin blessed the miserably cold rain and sleet. They moved on.

A sudden burst of tracer skimmed startlingly, frighteningly, across the river. His men ducked instinctively. Was this the start? It wasn't. The lone German machine-gunner hadn't spotted them. He was just letting off a routine burst, as he had been ordered to. Now he was probably getting his head down again.

The first boats grated against the sandy opposite bank. Still no firing. Gavin, still on the river, could see his paras as they switched on the flashlights attached to their breast pockets and went hunting for the Krauts. He grinned in spite of the tension. What a way to fight a battle!

The minutes passed as the joyful paras, glad to have survived this far, winkled out more and more German defenders who had been mostly surprised in their shelters. Now the German artillery had commenced firing. Hurriedly Gavin began to dispatch patrols. Soon the Krauts would be concentrating specifically on the bridgehead, and he wanted his positions dug in and established before the really heavy stuff started coming in.

But the German reaction came in a way that Gavin had never dreamed of. In his two years in combat he had never seen anything like it. Behind him, where the engineers were beginning to ferry the first of the paras' vehicles across, there was a sudden, tremendous explosion, followed by a blinding flash that turned night into day. Gavin spun round, completely deafened, just in time to see a jeep sailing 'high into the air, turning over several times'.

As he admitted later, 'We had never seen anything like it and it took me some time to figure out what sort of explosion it had been.' A little afterwards, as the German artillery grew heavier and heavier (later Corps Commander Ridgway would state that the artillery barrage was heavier than that they had faced before the Rhine crossings), the flashlights picked up a huge metal ball, its surface criss-crossed with ugly metal warts, floating towards the ferry site. 'Mine!' someone yelled incredulously, and a mine it was. In the middle of the Reich, the German defenders were floating sea mines down the River Elbe, armed with a massive charge of 1 ton of explosives, enough to sink a warship. The Germans were reacting at last . . .

A dozen miles or so from where Gavin's paras were experiencing their surprise, an all-officer patrol of the Cameron Highlanders, Brigadier Villiers' lead battalion, set off to reconnoitre the road to their immediate front. It was first light and visibility was bad. But they soon spotted the first German infantry slipping across the wet fields and the dripping firs towards the British positions. The officers were battle-experienced enough to know what the Germans were up to: they were trying to infiltrate the Cameronians' lines before an all-out attack. It was standard German operating procedure. Swiftly the three officers slipped away and doubled back to their own positions.

Five minutes later, as they were making their excited report to their CO Colonel Remington-Hobbs, there was a sudden burst of high-pitched firing from the direction of the Cameronians' C Company. Field Marshal Busch's flank attack had commenced!

The Germans of the 245th Infantry Division, a hastily thrown together, understrength formation, attacked with *élan*. The Cameronians countered with a tremendous blast of fire. Hastily the 15th Scottish's divisional artillery on the other side of the river was called upon to give covering fire to the defenders. But neither the infantry fire nor that of the artillery's 25-pounders could stop the Germans. They commenced digging in right under the Jocks' positions and started to slog it out, forcing the Cameronians to pull back here and there. This Monday morning of the last week of the Second World War in Europe, the Germans were seemingly fighting as hard as ever.

By midday Brigadier Villiers knew he was under full-scale attack. Prisoners taken by the hard-pressed Cameronians, revealed that. But Villiers knew he could not simply stay on the defensive. This morning the 11th Armoured Division was scheduled to start crossing over Colonel Foster's bridge, and the way had to be cleared for the vulnerable armour. On this side of the Elbe, the cobbled roads were dead straight, with deep drainage ditches on both sides. Up on the high-crowned roads, tanks were sitting ducks for desperate young men armed with the German *Panzerfausts*.

Villiers decided that the greatest danger was that presented by a large group of Germans dug in in a large wood to his immediate front. Accordingly he ordered another of his battalions to carry out the task of 'winkling them out', as he put it, making it sound easier than it was.

The Seaforth Highlanders, the battalion he had selected for the mission, advanced across the flat open fields in a thin grey drizzle. Now it seemed strangely quiet after the artillery barrage. Stolidly the Jocks plodded forward, rifles held across their skinny bodies at the high port, faces thoughtful as if wrestling with some problem

They came within 100 yards of the dark fir wood in which the Germans were reported to be. Still there was no sign of them. Fifty yards. Abruptly there was one solitary pistol shot. It acted as a signal. In an instant the whole front of the wood erupted into violent, frantic life. Ugly spurts of red flame stabbed the greyness everywhere.

The fire galvanised the Seaforths into action. An officer waved his revolver. NCOs bellowed red-faced orders. The infantry broke into a run bayonets fixed and clasped tight to their hips. This was it!

In the end it took four hours. When it was over, only four Germans remained alive, and the young Scots infantry men were beat, leaning exhausted on their rifles, the barrels of their Bren-guns glowing a dull purple. They looked like men who had just run a long, exhausting race.

But they had won. The way ahead was clear. The 245th's flank attack had failed and Field Marshal Busch had lost. Behind them on the Basedow road they could now hear the first heavy rumble of General Roberts' tanks. The race for the Baltic had commenced!

II

While the Seaforths helped to break up Field Marshal Busch's last desperate attack, far away in Berlin the charred bodies of Adolph Hitler and his long-time mistress and new wife Eva Braun smouldered outside the Berlin bunker which had been his last headquarters. They had committed suicide at three o'clock on this Monday afternoon, ten days after Hitler's last disastrous birthday. Now outside the Russians were everywhere, finishing off the capture of the capital of that empire which Hitler had once boasted would last a thousand years.

The two of them smouldered in their funeral pyre, abandoned by the paladins of old, save for Dr Goebbels, Minister of Propaganda, and Martin Bormann, Hitler's long-time secretary and head of the Party organisation.

Goebbels, the undersized Rhinelander with the quick, bitter tongue and club-foot, had probably decided by now that there was no future for him in a post-war Germany. Of all the Party bosses he was the smartest. He had already probably decided he would stay and die in Berlin with his Führer.

Bormann, the undersized bureaucrat, turning to fat like a boxer running to seed, had other ideas. The skirt-chasing Party Secretary, who seduced most of his female employees and who was known behind his back as the 'General of the Teleprinters' because it was through those machines that he commanded the Party organisation throughout Germany, was determined not to die in Berlin. He thought there was a future for him after the war.

We do not know what went through Bormann's bullet head that Monday afternoon. But as Himmler and Goering had already been branded as traitors, and Goebbels was obviously out of the running, he might have reasoned that there was a place for him with Doenitz in the north. The way was free for him. However he did need an instrument for his personal ambitions, for he was virtually unknown outside the Party.[1] He needed a public figure, such as Grand Admiral Doenitz, whom he could manipulate behind the scenes as he had often done with the Führer. Behind his back, those at Hitler's court who had envied him had called him the 'brown eminence'.[2]

That afternoon, while Rokossovsky's troops advanced steadily through his native Mecklenburg towards the Elbe, Bormann must have considered all the possibilities until in the end he made his decision. The Admiral would be Hitler's successor. Although he had known Doenitz only since 1943, he thought he would be able to manoeuvre the sailor well enough once he arrived at Ploen. Besides he did control the Party and Doenitz would need the Party's organisation in order to rule what was left of Germany.

Without mentioning the fact that the Führer was already dead, Bormann started to dictate a cable to his secretary, 21-year-old Else Krueger who would one day end her days surprisingly enough in Cambridge. It read:

Grand Admiral Doenitz.

In place of the former Reich-Marshal Goering, the Führer has designated you as his successor. Written authorisation on the way. Immediately take all measures required in the present situation.

---

1 When he was sought as a war criminal by the Allies after the war, they had the greatest difficulty in finding a photo of him.
2 On account of the brown Party uniform he wore.

That done, the 'General of the Teleprinters', born survivor that he was, set about finding companions for his hazardous journey out of Russian-held Berlin to Ploen.[3]

Soon, to the surprise of the world, Hitler's death would bring an immediate and abrupt end to National Socialism. It died as if it had never even existed. Overnight virtually all the former fanatical National Socialist leaders were transformed into instant democrats. There would be no fierce last-ditch German resistance to the Allied occupation, as Eisenhower had predicted there would be: a prediction which had helped to change overall strategy for the last campaign of the war in Europe.

The feared 'Alpine Redoubt', which occupied much of America's military might in Europe in the last weeks of the war, turned out to be a chimera. In Germany alone of all the countries occupied in Europe during the Second World War was there no effective resistance to the occupiers (even little Luxembourg, which can be crossed in a fast car in half an hour, had a powerful resistance movement). National Socialism, that most powerful political force in Europe in the 1930s and 1940s, one that at its zenith had ruled over an empire of 300 million Europeans, disappeared overnight. It was all very puzzling for those who were now left to govern Germany's affairs.

It was not, therefore, too surprising that Grand Admiral Doenitz found himself confused and in no way confident when he received Bormann's message that evening at 6.35. As yet Doenitz did not know that Hitler was dead. Yet he suspected it would not be long before the Führer would be gone. That meant one thing only: the end was very close indeed for National Socialist Germany. It would be only a matter of time before the whole structure of what was left of the Third Reich would come tumbling down like a house of cards.

Yet his first action, perhaps an instinctive one, was in keeping with his part and confirmed the worst fears of those close to him who wanted this futile last battle brought to a speedy end. Summoning his loyal aide and confidant, Commander Ludde-Neurath, he drafted a cable to be sent to the already dead Hitler. It read:

My Führer!

My loyalty to you will be unconditional. I shall do everything possible to relieve you in Berlin. Fate nevertheless compels me to rule the Reich as your appointed

---

3 He never made it. After a quarter of a century of 'Bormann spottings' all over the world, it was finally officially decided that Bormann was killed while trying to escape from Berlin. See C. Whiting, The Hunt for Martin Bormann.

successor, I shall continue this war to an end worthy of the unique, heroic struggle of the German people.

Grand Admiral Doenitz

It was a typical piece of hollow Nazi bombast. But it showed that Doenitz was not prepared to surrender, although the power to do so now rested in his hands.

Doenitz's next communication confirmed the fact that he was preparing to fight on. He turned his attention to Kaufmann's request of the day before, demanding a cessation of hostilities in the Hamburg area. Again dictating to Ludde-Neurath, he stated that his main concern now was 'the saving of German territory and people from Bolshevism'. He warned Kaufmann that the line of the Elbe 'must be held' in order to keep open the 'door to the west'. The hundreds of thousands of civilians and soliders streaming westwards before the advancing Russians of Rossokovsky's 2nd Belorussian Front depended entirely on that escape route. Doenitz then rejected Kaufmann's request that Hamburg should be spared the consequences of a battle. 'Any damage to property due to combat is more than justified by the saving of German human beings from the east,' he dictated to his aide. In other words, Kaufmann would have to fight on.

Now he dismissed Ludde-Neurath and rested while he waited for Himmler, who had announced that he wanted to come and visit Doenitz that night. But the former U-boat officer Ludde-Neurath could not rest; he was too worried about the visit of Himmler and his SS thugs. He returned to Doenitz after a while, face creased in a worried frown, and asked, 'What if he causes trouble, sir?' He meant Himmler. 'Don't you think we should have Cremer's men here just in case? You need protection, sir.'

Doenitz hesitated a moment. He hadn't thought of the meeting in that light. Besides Cremer and his ex-U-boat men fighting as infantry were tired. 'All right,' he said in the end, 'Get Cremer's men. But see that he places them round the building in a way that Himmler won't notice them.' Then he rested.

Outside Ludde-Neurath informed Cremer of the 'Big Lion's' decision. He told Cremer that Himmler 'won't like our chief becoming the Führer's successor'.

Cremer, who like all the surviving U-boat officers (they had suffered 75 per cent casualties) was fanatically loyal to Doenitz, nodded his agreement.

Ludde-Neurath said, 'We must be prepared for anything.' So the two of them began hiding the sailors behind trees and in alleyways in order not to arouse the suspicions of 'the loyal Heinrich'.

In the event they underestimated Himmler's nose for trouble. That evening Himmler told Heinz Macher, the tough SS officer who commanded his bodyguard, that he didn't like the situation one bit. 'Take enough men, please.'

Macher, a veteran of the war in the east, picked thirty-six men to accompany him to the meeting – 'the most piratical, bravest and most experienced warriors to be had in the whole of Germany,' he boasted later. They travelled in a convoy of open Volkswagens and armoured personnel carriers, arriving at the meeting place in Ploen by the faint light of the waning moon.

The place was completely blacked out, but by the silver gleam of the moon Macher caught the glint of the medal hanging from the neck of the officer coming to meet him. It was the Knight's Cross, hanging from the neck of 'Ali' Cremer himself. Macher sensed that something was wrong. He half-turned and could just make out the former U-boat skipper's men hiding in the bushes. He thought to himself, 'Oh God, those poor bastards! We'll blow them away with the greatest of ease!'

This last meeting between the 'Big Lion' and Hitler's 'loyal Heinrich' commenced like one between two Mafia 'godfathers', with Doenitz keeping a small pistol hidden beneath the papers on the desk 'just in case'; while outside a nervous, apprehensive Ludde-Neurath plied Macher and his officers with a liberal supply of Cognac.

Doenitz started off by passing over Bormann's cable. 'I would like you to read this,' he said. 'It appoints me as the Führer's successor.'

The SS Chief snatched the cable. He went pale as he read it. Then he let the paper fall from shaking fingers. 'Allow me, *Herr Grossadmiral*, to be the second man in your state?'

Doenitz, reassured by the meek surrender of the most feared man in Europe, shook his head. 'No, Himmler,' he snapped, 'I cannot allow that.'

They talked on. Himmler denied that he had offered to surrender to Count Bernadotte, the details of which Doenitz now knew from Berlin. Doenitz, indeed, had been ordered to arrest Himmler, but he hadn't. He didn't press him on the matter. He knew the pale-faced man opposite him, with his schoolmaster's pince-nez, was finished, but still he needed Himmler's police *apparat* to keep to heel what was left of the Reich under his command.[4]

According to Doenitz, the meeting ended shortly thereafter. According to Macher, Himmler's chief bodyguard, it went on to breakfast time when he and the rest sobered up with coffee. Whatever the length, however, this meeting marked the end of Himmler's bid for power in any new German government.

From now until he decided to flee Allied justice, Himmler would hang around the corridors of power, unnoticed by everyone. Even junior officers on Doenitz's staff brushed him aside impatiently. Occasionally in the first days of May, when the first British officers would spot him on their visits to Doenitz's HQ, they would wonder who this undersized little man in the non-descript uniform could be. They wouldn't realise that this was Heinrich Himmler, the cold-hearted fanatic who had once sent millions to their deaths in the concentration camps.

Now he was a broken reed, a living symbol of the shabby, inglorious end of that vulgar, bombastic, brown-clad dream which had been National Socialism. Hitler's vaunted 'New Order' would end not in a bang, but with a pathetic whimper.

III

In Hamburg that night, another man who had once dreamed of that 'heady New Order' and who, too, would soon be on the run, prepared to carry out his final mission as well. Once he had written, 'As a young man of pure British descent, some of whose forefathers have held high positions in the British Army, I have always been desirous of devoting what little capability and energy I may possess to the country which I love so dearly.' Now, as this Monday night was reaching its end, he staggered into the underground studios of Radio Hamburg quite drunk. Only the week before Speer had recorded his secret message here. Now the little man of 'pure British descent' was going to do the same with his last one.

The little man, with his nose jammed on his face at an odd angle and a deep scar which ran from right ear to mouth, was exhausted as well as drunk. Not that the German technicians on duty cared. The man whose message they would now record was a renegade, a traitor.

---

4 The only account of this fateful meeting is Doenitz's, written after he had been released from Spandau gaol, where he had served a sentence as a war criminal. By then he was naturally attempting to disassociate himself from the taint of having dealings with high-ranking Party members such as Himmler.

Soon the British on the other side of the Elbe would arrest him for having betrayed his country all these years by broadcasting propaganda for the Third Reich. Let him drink; he needed it now!

After Churchill, he was the Englishman whose voice had been the best known to the British listening public, and best hated by them. For six years he had opened his broadcasts with that snarled, upper-class 'This is Jairmany calling', and then poured out his venom and contempt against the land which had nurtured him and which, in his heart, he had loved so much.[5] Now William Joyce, the ex-British fascist known to millions of British listeners as 'Lord Haw-Haw', commenced his last broadcast, perhaps well aware that soon his life would be brought to a sudden and violent end by a length of English hemp.

Most of what he said that night was slurred by fatigue or drink, but when he came to the end of his last broadcast he spoke with a slow, obstinate nasal dignity in that abrasive voice which had sent shivers of fear and rage down the spines of his British listeners for many a year.

Britain's victories are barren. They leave her poor, and they leave her people hungry. They leave her bereft of markets and the wealth she possessed six years ago. But above all they leave her with an immensely greater problem than she had then.

We are nearing the end of one phase of Europe's history, but the next will be no happier. And now I ask you earnestly, can Britain survive? I am profoundly convinced that without Germany's help she cannot.

Then, with a last burst of his old defiant arrogance, William Joyce cried in a drunken mixture of English and German, '*Long live Germany! Heil Hitler and farewell!*'

The mike went dead. The light outside the studio door went from red to white. The engineer waved his hand, having not understood a word probably, and rose to his feet to signify that the recording session was over. Slowly the scar-faced little man, who would prove a better prophet about the future of the British empire in the post-war world at that moment of Allied victory than many a professional British politician, staggered out into the night. The hunt was on for him. 'Lord Haw-Haw' had made his last pronouncement.

Exactly one month before, when the 6th British Airborne Division had been flying into the attack on the Rhine, an officer of the division

---

5 In reality Joyce was not a traitor. He had been born an American citizen and had become a German citizen *before* America had entered the war. Therefore he could have betrayed neither country.

had turned to a sergeant sitting next to him in the glider as they flew over Waterloo and said, 'My great-great-grandfather fought at Waterloo.'

The working-class noncom had not been impressed. He grunted as they stared down at the old battlefield, getting ever closer to the new one, 'So did mine and it was probably your great-great-grandfather that got my great-great-grandfather killed. Try not to do the same to me today!'

That perhaps apocryphal story was a sign of the times. Four years of Army current affairs lectures, brainwashing by earnest left-wingers; the *Daily Mirror* with its Jane strip and 'soldiers' rights'; the *Picture Post* and its vision of the 'New Britain'; the Beveridge Plan and all those other grand schemes for a 'welfare state' – all had had their effect. The 'other ranks' had grown 'bolshy'. Soon they would kick out the old man who had saved their hides back in 1940 and who after years of struggle had taught them – forced them – to fight and win.

Times were changing in Britain, as Joyce observed in that last drunken harangue. Even the ruling class could no longer be relied upon. Soon one of those self-same 7th Armoured Division staff officers who were planning the surrender of Hamburg that night would stand up in Parliament and make his strongly left-wing maiden speech as a newly elected Labour MP. Nye Bevan, radical as he was himself, would call John Freeman 'the most dangerous of us all'. Churchill would stare at this apparition – a major in the uniform of the Coldstream Guards, wearing his medal ribbons, speaking for Labour – and weep.

But now, 'bolshy' as they were, no longer believing implicitly in the old order of things – the class system, the infallibility of their officers, the kind of world they had left behind when they had joined the army – they were still prepared to have one 'last bash', as they put it.

That day those same paras of the 6th Airborne Division, who had seemed so 'bolshy' to the correspondent who had recorded the anecdote in the glider on the way to the Rhine, actually tricked their way over the Elbe in order to go into battle.

No one knew how General Bols's 6th Airborne had managed to get this far after suffering 40 per cent casualties in some battalions on the Rhine and without heavy weapons and transport to speak of. But Bols' men had done exactly that. Leaving the Rhine bridgehead with jeeps as their only transport, they had seized anything with four wheels and an engine to transport them across Germany to the Elbe. They had used post-office trucks, butchers' vans, wood-burning lorries complete with their stove-bearing trailers. Alan Moorehead, the Australian war correspondent, had even noted one para 'dashing' forward at a steady five miles an hour in a 'liberated' steamroller!

Now, turned loose at Ridgway's order, they had no particular priority to cross Colonel Foster's bridge, still under heavy attack. It was reserved for Roberts' 11th Armoured. What were they to do? While General Bols fumed at the delay and his staff officers sought an answer to their problem, the 'Red Devils' acted.

They took the law into their own hands. They placed their camouflaged scarves over the divisional signs of the tanks of the Scots Greys, who had been assigned to help them in their dash for the Baltic at Wismar. Then, turning their red berets inside out so that the black lining showed, making them look like armoured troopers who wore a black beret, they mounted up on the tanks.

Boldly the column approached the bridge. For once the Foster's bridge was not under attack by German planes, and the redcaps on duty eyed the column curiously. They had orders to turn everything back that didn't belong to the high-priority 11th Armoured. Here and there a Red Devil felt a butterfly flutter in his stomach. If they were rumbled now that would be an end to their plan.

The first tank laden with infantry began to clatter up the metal ramp. The MP directing the traffic looked at the men hard. Then he waved his arm. They could move on. They had pulled it off! Now they could be on their way to battle. Triumphantly the first tank commenced rumbling across the long Bailey bridge. Behind it another followed – and another. The 'Red Devils' were beginning their race for Wismar to beat the Russians . . .

All along Montgomery's front his weary soldiers – and everyone from Montgomery downwards agreed that the soldiers were tired after ten months of campaigning – were still fighting. It had been a long road since Dunkirk but they were determined to be in at the end.

Outside Oldenburg on the extreme length of Montgomery's line the 2nd Canadian Infantry Division, which had suffered some five thousand casualties at Dieppe in 1942, was preparing for its final assault. In the last three days one of its brigades alone had suffered 150 casualties and there were no reinforcements coming along. But the Second had not lost its desire to fight.

To the Canadians' right, Montgomery's own old division, the Third, which had fought that disastrous battle in France in 1940, was holding the flank, while the Guards Armoured Division pushed towards the north and Stade. Back in 1940 its commander, tiny, frail-looking General Allan Adair, had abandoned his teaching post at Sandhurst –

'too schoolmasterly a job' – and had driven right up to the front to rejoin the Grenadiers in a cab chauffeured by a French prize-fighter from Boulogne. 'All you guardsmen would have died twice a day for General Adair' Montgomery once told his men. 'Not one of you would have died for me!'

To the Third's right, the Reconnaissance Regiment of the 43rd 'Wessex' Division, which had suffered such grievous losses that first day off the coast of Normandy, was still in the thick of the fighting, leading the 214th Brigade against German infantry and heavy fire from their *Nebelwerfer*: those electrically operated, six-barrelled mortars which the PBI called 'moaning Minnies'.

Nor far away from the 43rd, the 51st Highland Division – 'the Highway Decorators' – was still battling, too, finally coming to the end of that long road – those three long years which it had taken them to redeem the honour of the old 51st after its surrender under commander General Fortune, who had no fortune, to a General Erwin Rommel at St Valery, France, back in 1940.

In their ranks were the young men who one day would determine Britain's future, entertain her, shape her opinions. Captain Edward Heath of the Royal Artillery, Captain Willie Whitelaw of the Scots Guards, Captain Robert Maxwell, Lieutenant Kingsley Amis, Lieutenant-Colonel David Niven . . . Even the Prime Minister's own daughter, Mary Churchill, now a subaltern in a mixed anti-aircraft battery, was on her way to the front with the guns.

Over the years Montgomery had brought together all these disparate young men and women, of different interests, different backgrounds and different classes – the future prime ministers, press magnates, artists, etc. – trained them and made them into a compact fighting team. Now, whatever the future was to bring, and before their paths parted, they wanted to be in on what their C-in-C called 'the kill'.

That evening their chief was on the move himself. Montgomery did not know it but it would be his last move of the Second World War. Since June 1944 his HQ had travelled over 1,000 miles from the Normandy beaches and swollen from twenty-seven officers and 150 men to the size of a battalion, transported by two hundred vehicles. Now this 'TAC HQ', as it was called, moved for the last time until, as one staff officer noted, 'We came to the Luneburg Heath – on a windswept site on the bluff above Deutschevern, with a great view across the barren heath to southward.'

Swiftly the camp, or 'laager' as the staff officers called it, using the old Boer War term, took shape, with Montgomery's own personal vehicles in the centre under a grove of the birch trees typical of the heath. There were his sleeping caravan, complete with 'liberated' chamberpot, office caravan and map lorry, all screened by an enormous camouflage net. And to their front there was a small portable flagpole from which the Union Jack was always flown. One day soon, the photograph of that particular Union flag and 'the Master' standing beneath it would appear in newspapers all around the world.

That night Montgomery did not know that the lonely stretch of heather on which his encampment was now being set up would soon become historic. But he did know that the end was near. One day before, he had written home in a personal letter:

I think we are approaching the moment when the Germans will give up the unequal contest. They are hard pressed; they keep on fighting only because every German soldier has taken a personal oath to Hitler and so long as he is alive they must keep on fighting. Once it is known that he is dead or has cleared out, there will be a big scale collapse.

Now Hitler was dead – though this day, of course, Montgomery did not know that.

Soon the events which would take place in this remote camp on the heath at Lueneburg would change the whole course of Montgomery's last campaign. Abruptly the little Field Marshal would be in the limelight again, his minor role as the flank guard to General Bradley's US armies instantly transformed into the major one. After all the back-biting, the envy, the intrigue, the detested Britisher, 'that little fart, Monty' would gain the kudos of final victory over the Germans . . .

BOOK THREE: THE LONG SURRENDER

TUESDAY 1 MAY – WEDNESDAY 23 MAY 1945

'Es geht alles vorueber. Es geht alles vorbei.
Nach jedem Dezember gibt's wieder ein Mai.'*

German popular song, spring 1945

* It will all pass It will all be over. After every December, there is always a May

1

'It'll be a piece of frigging cake.'

I

The order of march of the 6th Airborne Division that sunny morning of 1 May 1945 was simple but suicidal. The 'Red Devils' advanced on brigade fronts along separate roads, driving for the small town of Gadebusch 15 miles away. Whichever brigade of the Sixth reached Gadebusch first would be the one that would make the final rush to Wismar on the coast to beat the Russians. And now the Russians were reportedly – unofficially – to be some 25 miles away from the Baltic port.

Up front there was a single section of paras, with two other sections to left and right in the fields. Behind them came the bulk of the brigade, riding on the tanks or whatever other vehicles they had been able to 'liberate' from the Germans.

It was a tricky tactic – a thin arrow of underarmed infantry pushing forward deep into enemy territory, packed with German troops, with both their flanks wide open. The Germans had armour, too. They could at will cut off the paras, confined to the dead straight cobbled roads of the area. Besides, even if the *Wehrmacht* was losing heart, there were still the eager young fanatics of the Hitler Youth and the new Werewolf Movement[1] (some as young as 14) who were now completely out of the control of their more realistic, war-weary officers. If they were going to die, well they'd take a few Tommies with them.

But in that heady atmosphere of the last battle and the great race with the Russians, the Red Devils were prepared to take risks. Hadn't they always taken risks in the past, for they were the élite of the British Army, weren't they? After all, of the fourteen battalions of the Parachute

---

1 The secret German resistance movement set up in late 1944, numbering five thousand-odd youths, girls and boys. See C. Whiting, *Hitler's Werewolves*

Regiment which had been formed a mere five years before, six had been totally wiped out.

They came to the small town of Luetzow. As far as the eye could see the narrow cobbled streets of the medieval township were packed with a chaotic mass of German civilians and soldiers. Sergeant Stewart of the Scots Greys, commanding the lead tank, cried out 'Duck!' to the paras piled on the tank's deck. He had a sure-fire way of clearing the main street. They ducked. Sergeant Stewart pressed the firing button of his Besa machine-gun. White glowing tracer hissed crazily over the heads of the milling crowd. They shouted, fled in panic, or simply dropped to the cobbles. Stewart grinned and stopped firing. He had cleared the road ahead. The column of happy, relieved paras roared on.

Now the prisoners started to stream in, hands on their heads, the flaps of their long coats trailing as they ran, bread-bags bouncing at their hips. There seemed no end to the field-greys wanting to give themselves up to the Tommies. They knew what might happen to them if they were captured by the Russians. Hadn't the German 6th Army which had surrendered to the Russians at Stalingrad back in 1943 virtually disappeared? They would be safer with the British.

That morning the gleeful paras of the Parachute Regiment's 12th Battalion took four thousand German soldiers prisoner. Their comrades of the 13th were even luckier, despite that 'thirteen'. They had dispensed with taking common soldiers prisoner. They concentrated on officers. That morning four German generals in full uniform were seen surrendering at the same time to Battalion HQ.

Gadebusch was reached. It was packed full of sullen, heavily armed German soldiers. The Red Devils simply ignored them. In their turn the Germans ignored the British. At each crossroads stood German military policemen directing German traffic. They were known as *Kettenhund* ('chain dogs') from the silver crescent of office suspended round their necks by a metal chain. Now, not knowing what else to do, they waved the paras on!

The lead brigade clattered past fields on both sides full of German infantry dug in in their foxholes, with here and there tanks, their long overhanging cannon directed at the road being used by the British. *Would they fire?*

But apart from sullen looks, nothing happened. The advance to Wismar continued. The small town of Muehlen-Richsen was reached. By now the 6th Airborne had run out of maps. Instead they were forced to use the Germans' own black-and-yellow road signs to guide them towards the Baltic. And they knew they were going in the right direction. For the air was growing cooler and there was the faint salty smell of the sea. Now it was only 20 kilometres to the coast . . .

To the right of the British, Gavin's men of the 8th Infantry and 82nd Airborne Division were also moving fast this beautiful May morning. The day before, the Germans had fired the last of their ammunition and the veteran 505th Parachute Regiment had experienced its heaviest concentration of artillery fire of the whole war. Now the opposition was limited to small-arms fire and mortar rounds. So the 505th and its running mate the 504th Parachute Regiment, which had crossed the Elbe during the night, were able to press on. Again, just as was the case with the Red Devils' advance, prisoners were streaming in. But with them they brought cheering yet disconcerting news.

They told the Airborne Intelligence officers who interrogated them that the retreating formations of the beaten Army of the Vistula, which now existed in name only, were eager to surrender, but that the Russians were on the heels of Manteuffel's and Tippelkirch's armies. The Red Army was advancing west just as quickly as the Anglo-Americans were driving east.

Despite the beautiful day, that news worried Gavin. For he knew, too, the great store being set by the top brass on an Allied formation reaching the Baltic before the Russians did. He urged his veterans to ever greater efforts, and being the kind of general he was, leading from the front, he was up there at the point with his men, checking the situation for himself. He had always done it that way and he would continue to do so, taking his chance of sudden violent death with his soldiers.

But as General Gavin strove to advance quickly and anchor Mont-gomery's flank on the line Eisenhower had laid down for meeting the Russians, he little realised that this was his last day in combat. From now till the day he retired, General Gavin would be a chairborne commander. Soon it would be all over.

To the left of Ridgway's Airborne Corps advance, it did not seem as if 'Bubbles' Barker's advance on Lübeck was going to be that easy. General 'Pip' Roberts had divided his 11th Armoured Division into two mixed brigade groups, a mixture of tanks and infantry so that both arms – the footsoldier and the cavalryman – had plenty of muscle. It was a tactic which the Germans had invented. Now the British were perfecting it.

At 4.30 that morning the Rifle Brigade, supported by tanks, attacked the German village of Sahms on the perimeter of the new bridgehead on the Elbe. The place was defended by two companies of German infantry, supported by a number of anti-tank guns. Behind the Eleventh, the men of the 5th Infantry Division waited until they had cleared the place so that they could begin their own advance towards Lübeck.

Lance Corporal Pinder of the Fifth was an old sweat. He had been with the 'Globetrotters', as the Fifth called itself, ever since it had commenced its travels in 1939. The Yorkshireman had been with it in France, South Africa, India, Egypt, Palestine and through the fighting in Italy. Now he waited in a barn with a section of young soldiers, not one of them over 20. All of them were new to battle and they were apprehensive – and not a little scared, too. Old sweat Pinder reassured them. 'It's too late. The Jerries have stopped making 'em [he meant shells] with your numbers on, lads. It'll be a piece of frigging cake! '

In that very instant a German barrage from a battery located in Schwarzenbek to their left opened up. Suddenly the air was full of shells with their 'numbers on'. The roof of the barn flew off. The place rocked alarmingly. Dust, smoke and straw flew everywhere. Corporal Pinder was flung to the floor, his head ringing, blood streaming from his nostrils.

How long he lay there, he couldn't remember afterwards. But finally, when he started to become aware of his surroundings once more, he saw to his horror that his whole section had 'bought it'. There wasn't one of his teenage warriors who was not dead or critically wounded. As so often in the past, the old sweat Pinder survived (like so many of them did). But his 'lads' were gone before they had really started living. Even now, at this stage of the war, with Germany's leaders almost universally committed to peace, young men were dying and being maimed in a battle that should never really have been fought.

By midday, however, Sahms was cleared and the Eleventh, followed by the 5th Infantry Division, could commence moving towards Lübeck. Thereafter progress was easier. As 'Pip' Roberts recorded after the war, 'The opposition was sporadic, but in places mines had to be cleared and small villages had to be captured, as they were sometimes held by anti-tank guns and say 100 men. It was not difficult but time-consuming.'

Elmenhorst was cleared. An obstinate enemy group at Kankelan, 'dealt with' by an angry barrage of cannon fire, surrendered. Still, even when the regulars of the *Wehrmacht* surrendered, there was still the danger of those knobbly-kneed fanatics of the Hitler Youth in their short black pants taking a pot shot at a passing Sherman with his *Panzerfaust* and then making a run for it.

They came to Trittau, a large village of half-timbered brick houses and large sprawling farmhouses in which animals and men lived under the same straw roof. It was held by a larger and more stubborn party of the enemy and would have to be cleared more systematically. The advance started to slow down.

Still it was clear even to those angry, sweating, frustrated young soliders at the point that the German Army under Field Marshal Busch was in full retreat. Cars, heavily laden with officers and their personal belongings – piled into the suitcases and leather briefcases that made them look like so many clerks in uniform – honked their way through the fleeing civilians and the common soldiers wearily toiling northwards on foot or on carts drawn by skinny-ribbed, drooping nags.

Everywhere armoured vehicles were being abandoned as the petrol gave out. Small blue fires flickered the length of the exit roads as hand grenades were flung in petrol tanks or long rolls of latrine paper leading to the tanks were ignited. As the light started to fade, they flickered everywhere like little beacons, beckoning the pursuing British to come this way.

Everywhere as the British edged forward, they saw that Busch's broken army had littered the countryside to left and right with their abandoned equipment: tanks and trucks, artillery pieces, huge mobile workshops. Occasionally dead men sprawled out in the furrows like bundles of wet, grey rags. Even the most insensitive of the pursuers didn't need a crystal ball to realise that soon the dispirited, weary soldiers retreating before them would be throwing away their personal weapons too. It wouldn't – it *couldn't* – be much longer now.

Up at Moelln, captured by the other one of Roberts' two mixed brigade groups without a shot having been fired, an officer of the 11th Armoured stood in the turret of his stalled Churchill tank and watched the breakdown of National Socialist order and the world's once most powerful army, *die Wehrmacht*. 'A vast quantity of DPs[2] had left their camps nearby and were roaming the streets in search of liquid refreshments,' he noted afterwards with some attempt at British understatement. For these displaced persons were not merely seeking a half-pint of beer; they were out to get blind, stinking drunk!

---

2 Displaced persons.

They had now broken about two thousand bottles and the gutters ran with wine. A POW camp had been opened and RAF personnel were making their way to the rear in joyful mood and in any conveyance they could commandeer – those on carthorses galloping down the road seemed to be enjoying themselves most, but there were several happy parties in smart traps and gigs with slogans chalked on the side.

And in the midst of all this drunken, happy chaos there were the field-greys in enormous numbers, 'bewildered and glum'. They sat or slumped by the roadside passively waiting for orders, or 'walked vaguely' down the road.

A whole division, headed by a general in full uniform, came in to surrender and the advance bogged down altogether. Now the fields outside the pretty little town of Moelln started to fill with surrendered German soldiers, who stood there 'like cattle, silent, tired and beated'. At the crossroads there were feared Panthers, all of them brand-new but now harmless, for their crews had abandoned them in the general flight north. The gunners, true to the tradition of their service that the guns were never abandoned, stayed by their deadly 88mm cannon, but they did so with their hands in their pockets, watching the British tanks with sullen disinterest. As for the SS, so that young tank officer noted, 'They were pretending to be something else and trying to slip away without any idea of where to go . . .'

But while the 11th Armoured's drive to Lübeck started to bog down, the British fighter-bombers, the feared *Jabos*, kept up their attacks hour after hour. In peacetime on May Day, a holiday in Germany, German working men had traditionally celebrated their day of freedom by going from one country inn to the next, their persons decked with 'May green', then come staggering home to their angry wives, sun-burnt, drunk and broke. Now on this terrible 1 May 1945, it was the RAF fighter-pilots who had their 'field day', and the successors of those happy peacetime civilians now decorated themselves and their vehicles with a new kind of 'May green': camouflage nets and branches of trees to protect themselves from the Spitfires and Typhoons, which ranged far and wide, shooting up everything that moved.

Hedge-hopping and machine-guns, cannon and rockets blazing, they came tearing in at 400 m.p.h., chasing the civilians down the streets of their little villages and townships, cracking the windows of the little red-brick houses with their traditional horse-head decora-tions, taking the very tiles of the roofs as they hurtled by at tree-top height. Behind them they left chaos, fire and death. More often than not it was the crumpled body of some unfortunate civilian who had not jumped into the nearest ditch quickly enough.

That day the old men, women and children who were left in the flat plain of Holstein took to their cellars or the trenches they had dug in their gardens. If they were forced to leave them, they ventured out fearfully and swiftly, waving white flags or even wrapped in bedsheets, to indicate that, just like the field-greys, the war was over for them. They were prepared to surrender also.

But during those many sorties that glorious First of May, one pilot spotted a target much worthier of the effort being expended on these lone civilians. Flying to the west of Lübeck, just before his fuel gave out and he had to return to his base at the old *Luftwaffe* field at Celle, he saw before him the glisten of the sea, bathed in sunshine. But it wasn't his first sight of the Baltic which captured the young RAF pilot's attention. It was the vast number of ships congregating in Lübeck Bay!

They were everywhere and of all shapes and sizes. There were destroyers and U-boats, armed fishing cutters and barges; and lying some 3 miles out to sea, anchored and stationary, were two large liners surrounded by smaller vessels. Both of them looked as if they were well over 20,000 tons.

Now, as the flak opened up at Neustadt and the first anti-aircraft shells started to wing their way towards him, exploding in those so-deceptive puffballs, the young pilot told himself that he had seen enough. He pulled the 'kite' round in a tight turn and, dropping virtually to ground level, sped off with his exciting news. *A whole German fleet was assembled in the bay off Lübeck!*

An hour later RAF Intelligence officers were working out the details. The British Army was closing in on Doenitz's HQ at Ploen. So what was he going to do? Why, he and his headquarters were about to flee by sea to Norway and continue the hopeless fight from there. Something had to be done – and done quickly . . .

II

Himmler had given the original order to have Neuengamme evacuated. When he had still enjoyed almost unlimited power in Berlin he had signalled, after the discovery of Belsen by the British, 'Not a single prisoner must fall into the hands of the enemy. Heinrich Himmler, Reichsführer SS'.

But where to put them? The territory still available in which to hide these miserable starved wretches in their striped pyjamas was daily growing smaller. In the end it was *Gauleiter* Kaufmann who came up with an answer. For with the British virtually on his doorstep, he did not want them to discover at Neuengamme a hell camp similar to that of Belsen, which had shocked the world and caused angry demands in Allied countries for instant reprisals.

Kaufmann knew that the 24,000-ton luxury liner *Cap Arcona*, plus the *Deutschland* and two smaller merchant ships, were anchored in Lübeck Bay. They were all empty and serving no useful function at this moment. They would be ideal for housing the dregs of Neuengamme concentration camp. Perhaps in due course they could be quietly sunk, taking with them all evidence of the cruelties carried out against these unfortunates from half a dozen European countries, including a highly vocal German, non-Jewish minority.

At his trial after the war Kaufmann would deny – successfully – that he had given the order to have the prisoners taken aboard what would become the death ships. He passed the buck to the head of Hamburg's Gestapo, who told the court that Himmler had given the original order but that at a 'conference' attended by himself and Kaufmann it had been agreed 'that in the light of the current situation [in April 1945], it would not be advisable to let the prisoners remain where they were in Neuengamme. They had all been concerned with the safety of the inhabitants of Hamburg.' As if the ten thousand half-starved creatures imprisoned at Neuengamme could have harmed Hamburg civilians, protected as they were by at least two infantry divisions plus all the auxiliary troops located in the area of Greater Hamburg!

On 26 April 1945 the first batch of prisoners from Neuengamme had been brought aboard the *Cap Arcona*, which before the war had boasted only first-class passenger accommodation on its South American run and whose owners had maintained was virtually unsinkable. Lashed by the whips of their SS guards and threatened by the guards' Alsatian dogs, which had been trained to go only for the prisoners, the unfortunates shuffled through the dining room where waiters in frockcoats had once served twelve-course menus ranging from chicken fondant to capoletti italienne to elegant upper-class ladies and gentlemen in evening dress. They were forced deeper and deeper into the innards of the former luxury liner until they finally reached what was called the 'banana locker'. Forty years later ex-Polish soldier Tadeusz Kwapinski, one of the few survivors, recalled what it was like:

With blows and cries, they drove us forward. We started to climb down the steep ladders into the great hold. In the haste many fell and broke their limbs, spines etc. Down below we were packed together like sardines. We lay there side by side, hardly able to move in the stinking darkness. It was dark, cold and damp. There was no water and no food.

There was one faint glimmer of hope for the prisoners as more and more of them were packed into the liner. From mouth to mouth the rumour was whispered that they were going to be evacuated to Sweden. But up on the upper deck the SS guards speedily set about securing all life-belts, floats, anything with which a drowning man might save himself in an emergency, and locking them away securely out of the reach of the prisoners. They knew in which direction the *Cap Arcona* was going to sail, if it ever did sail – down to the bottom of the sea!

At three o'clock that same afternoon, when the young RAF pilot first sighted the *Cap Arcona* in Lübeck Bay, the one man who now had the power to avert the tragedy received a second message from Bormann, who was still in Berlin. Speer, who was present as Ludde-Neurath brought the signal from the radio room, noted how the Admiral's face started to flush as he read it:

Grand Admiral Doenitz (Top Secret. Via Officer only.) Führer deceased yesterday at 3.30. Testament of 29 April appoints you Reich President. Minister Goebbels Chancellor. *Reichsleiter* Bormann Party Leader . . . On the Führer's instructions, the testament is sent out of Berlin to you to ensure its preservation for the nation.
    Reichsleiter Bormann will try to get to you today to orientate you on the situation. The manner and timing of announcement to the troops and the public are left to you.
    Confirm receipt.

                                                                                    Gobbels-Bormann

In effect, Grand Admiral Doenitz was now the 'Führer' of what was left of Hitler's Germany.

The day before, Admiral Godt of the German Navy had noted a dramatic change in Doenitz, who had previously been contemplating suicide, when he had learned from Bormann that he was now in full command in the north. Now Doenitz was angry. He snapped, 'This is utterly impossible!'

Speer realised what the angry Admiral meant. The new message made a farce of his new office. Goebbels and Bormann were obviously going to make themselves the power behind the throne and really run things. He was to become a mere figurehead.

Doenitz looked up at Ludde-Neurath. 'Has anyone else seen the message yet?' he queried.

Ludde-Neurath replied in the negative. He and the naval signaller who had received it from Berlin were the only ones who knew of the signal's existence.

Doenitz now ordered that the radioman should be sworn to secrecy immediately and the message locked in the safe. When the adjutant had departed, Doenitz asked Speer what he should do if Goebbels and Bormann turned up at his HQ. Then he added severely, 'I will absolutely not operate with them under any circumstances!'

Speer nodded. He hated Bormann with a passion and stated that Doenitz should have them both arrested if they turned up at Ploen. Doenitz agreed. It was clear that Doenitz felt it would be wiser, if he were going to retain his new office, that he should disassociate himself from the old political leaders of Germany, whom he knew would never be tolerated by the victorious allies, especially the Russians.

A little while later, after Speer had gone, Doenitz was visited by an old comrade, Admiral Godt. The latter described Doenitz as 'developing his views with Speer in a lively manner, full of initiative'. He told Godt, 'There's been enough fighting. We must keep the state together. There must be no more unnecessary sacrifice of blood.'

The visitor thought the words 'fairly bubbled' from the normally laconic, tight-lipped Grand Admiral. 'My impression of that evening', he wrote later, 'was of a complete change in Doenitz now that he had been freed from the immediate influence of Hitler. It was almost as if he had been liberated from a nightmare. A few days before I would still have regarded him capable of ordering total war without any regard for the consequences.'

Speer, watching the events of that day, noted later, 'On this note the Third Reich ended: everyone was betraying everyone!'

Speer was right. Doenitz, by having the radio message locked away, was concealing the key official document, 'the last link in a chain of deception, betrayals, hypocrisies and intrigues during those days and weeks'. Thus Speer characterised the events in which Himmler betrayed his master Hitler, and Bormann had managed to turn the latter against his old comrade Goering of the *Kampfzeit*[3] who, in his

---

3 The Battle Time, i.e. the period before Hitler came to power.

turn, was also attempting to betray Hitler by negotiating with the Allies.

Now Doenitz, the last 'Führer', would continue the chain, betraying and lying to the German people to the very end.

III

While Doenitz worked on a speech he was now going to give to the German people, Himmler appeared unannounced and asked if he could be invited for lunch. These days the man whose very name had once caused strong men to go white with fear was very humble.

Doenitz agreed. Himmler told Doenitz that his spies in the port had brought news that Kaufmann was about to surrender Hamburg without a fight. A leaflet was being printed there to prepare the populace for the entrance of British troops into the city; they were being warned to behave themselves so that there would be no British reprisals.

Doenitz grew angry. If everyone acted on his own, he snorted, his pale face flushed, his new assignment was pointless. Speer, who was also present, then offered to drive to Hamburg and talk to his old acquaintance Kaufmann. Doenitz agreed and then after the other two had left got on with his speech.

That afternoon Speer met Kaufmann. As usual the *Gauleiter* was surrounded by his bodyguard of armed students. Even now he was taking no chances. He was as angry as Doenitz had been. He told Speer about the 7th Armoured Division's ultimatum. Either he surrendered Hamburg to them, or what was left of the city would be bombed to pieces. 'Am I supposed to follow the example of Wegener of Bremen?' he blurted out. 'He issued a proclamation calling on his people to defend themselves to the last and then cleared out while the city was destroyed by a frightful air-raid.'

Speer said nothing.

Then the *Gauleiter* told the Minister that he was very determined to prevent a battle for his city. If necessary, he would mobilise the Hamburg masses to join in *active* resistance against the military defenders of the city. It was the thing that Doenitz feared most – the arming of the workers in these great ports, which even after twelve years of Nazi dictatorship were still known to be 'red'.[4]

4 There had been left-wing activity throughout the NS period in the great ports and cities of the industrial Ruhr. As soon as the system started to break down, small communist groups began to appear everywhere to the horror of the authorities.

Hastily Speer telephoned the new 'Führer' and told him of Kaufmann's threat of open rebellion. Doenitz must have thought it was going to be November 1918 all over again, when the Imperial Navy had mutineed and everywhere in North Germany the 'Reds' had begun forming workers' and soldiers' revolutionary councils. One hour later he *personally* telephoned General Wolz and ordered him to surrender the port of Hamburg without a fight. The ball was beginning to roll. Montgomery's luck was changing dramatically.

At 9.30 that night Hamburg Radio interrupted its programme to state that 'a grave and important announcement' would follow soon. There was a selection of Wagner's operas, followed by the slow movement of Bruckner's Seventh Symphony. Then, as the music died away, a solemn voice declared:

Our Führer, Adolf Hitler, fighting to the last breath against Bolshevism, fell for Germany this afternoon in his operational headquarters in the Reich Chancellery. On 30 April the Führer appointed Grand Admiral Doenitz to take his place. The Grand Admiral and successor to the Führer now speaks to the German people.

Already the lies had commenced. In the original message from Bormann, the latter had cabled that Hitler was *verschieden*, i.e. deceased, and not *gefallen*, the usual German word when someone had died in battle. It was clear to Doenitz that Hitler had actually committed suicide. Now he lied that Hitler had been killed in battle. Again Doenitz, just like the rest of the Party leaders, lacked what the Germans call *Zivilcourage* (roughly, public spirit). He could not bring himself to face up to the truth, even at this desperate moment.

Doenitz said that Hitler had 'fallen'. He had died a 'hero's death':

His life was a unique service for Germany. His mission in the battle against the Bolshevist storm flood is valid for Europe and the entire civilised world ... The Führer has appointed me as his successor. In consciousness of the responsibility, I take over the leadership of the German people at this fateful hour.

Thereafter Doenitz issued an Order of the Day to the *Wehrmacht*:

I take over command of all arms of the services with the intention of continuing the battle against the Bolshevists until the fighting forces and the hundreds of thousands of families of the German east are saved from slavery or destruction.

Against the English and Americans I must continue to fight for as far and as long as they hinder me in the execution of the battle against the Bolshevists ... Who now avoids his duty and thereby brings death or enslavement to German women and children is a coward and a traitor. The oath of loyalty which you gave to the Führer is now due from each one of you to me as the Führer's appointed successor.

Again all was confused and distorted. One thing was clear, however. Doenitz continued to fight and he demanded the same kind of loyalty for himself from the fighting men as they had once given by their 'oath on the flag' to Hitler.[5]

But by now most Germans were beyond caring for such things. They wanted an end to the suffering and wanted to save their own skins. Sitting shivering in her cellar, a mere mile from where that broadcast came, 65-year-old Frau Wolff-Moenckeberg wrote to her daughter, Ruth Evans, by the light of a flickering candle:

When one recalls Hitler's flaming victory speeches, his prophecies and inflated promises that it would all be well in the end, one can only regard our present situation as the quintessence of irony in the whole history of the world. But we will never get over this bloody calvary. We have grown old and weary to death.

Yet even as the old lady wrote, while the wind 'is howling outside, the rain pouring down and from the distance come the sharp reports of enemy artillery', Wolz's letter to the 7th Armoured Division was on its way back across the frontline, carried by a frightened, war-weary messenger. With the kind of understatement that the British traditionally ascribe to themselves, Wolz wrote:

The thoughts for which you have found so lucid an expression in your letter of 29 April 1945 have been considered by myself and by countless other responsible commanders; not unnaturally considering the present military and political situation.

The eventual surrender of Hamburg would have far-reaching military and political consequences for the whole of that part of northern Germany that is not yet occupied, and for Denmark. For this reason the orders given to me to hold Hamburg to the last man can be seen to have a clear justification. But in spite of this I am prepared, together with an authorised representative of *Reichstatthalter* and *Gauleiter* Kaufmann, to discuss with a representative empowered by GOC Second British Army to make decisions on military and political matters the eventual surrender of Hamburg and the far-reaching consequences arising therefrom.

May I ask you to inform the GOC Second Army of these proposals and to request that a time and place for discussion be fixed?

Wolz
Major General

5 In the German Army it is the custom to swear the oath of loyalty across an outstretched flag (*Fahneneid*). In the Second World War all German fighting men swore this oath to Hitler. The legal penalty for breaking it was death.

Now the ball was beginning to roll even faster. Even a cursory glance at the Wolz message told the 7th Armoured's staff officers, including John Freeman, that future Labour MP who would make Churchill weep in Parliament, that there was more than just Hamburg at stake. Wolz was just a mouthpiece for someone more important!

Hurriedly the news was flashed to General Dempsey, commanding the 2nd Army. The commander of the 7th Armoured Division, General Lyne, was empowered to reply that he would see General Wolz the following night if the German would come to offer *unconditional* surrender.

Dempsey, and naturally Montgomery too (for he knew by now what was going on), were still playing the matter strictly according to regulations. Back in 1943 President Roosevelt, heavily disguised as 'Admiral Q', and Churchill, as 'Mr P', had met in North Africa and agreed that the war would be fought until the enemy agreed to 'unconditional surrender'. One year later the formula was supported by the Soviet Union. This time, unlike the First World War, there would be no option of prior conditions, no negotiated armistice and no chance of an honourable end to hostilities.

It went without saying, therefore, that with minor exceptions there would be no piecemeal surrenders. Eisenhower had laid it on the line that any attempt to do so would have to be submitted to him personally. Above all, German troops could not surrender to the Western Allies without also surrendering to their Russian friends. Now here for the first time there was the hint of a partial surrender which might include the continuation of hostilities against the Russians. Doenitz's speech of that evening, with its many references to the 'Bolshevik hordes' and 'storm floods', made that quite clear.

Montgomery was obviously going to bend the rules now, as far as he dare. If, in due course, he could convince Busch to surrender to him all the forces under his command, who would worry about that absurd political ruling made two years before by 'Admiral Q' and 'Mr P'? Weren't the very names indicative of the basic frivolity of the 'frocks', as Montgomery had contemptuously called the politicos back home in World War One who had no knowledge of the bloody realism of the front? Besides, what better ending could there be to the 'Second German War' than a headline which ran 'German Army Surrenders to Monty'?

But still it was early days. Now the officers of the 7th Armoured Division busied themselves with getting the German Colonel who had brought Wolz's letter back to his own lines before dawn broke.

As before Brigadier Spurling accompanied him to the section of the front held by the Durham Light Infantry. As they reached the area, the German asked Spurling if he might speak to him alone.

Spurling said he could.

The German thereupon explained that he feared that he and the rest of Wolz's staff officers would be sent to Siberia by the Russians. 'As soldier to soldier,' he said earnestly to the British Brigadier, 'I ask your advice whether I and the staff ought to commit suicide on our return?'

Spurling considered for a moment, while to their front the usual flares hissed into the night sky and somewhere a machine-gun chattered, its racket muted by the dripping rain. Then he said, without any feeling, 'That's entirely up to you, Herr Oberst.'

With that he turned and left the German. But the German Colonel obviously decided that suicide was not necessary; the Russians would never reach Hamburg. So he lived to collect his pension and the secret peace negotiations continued.

At exactly the same time – 10.30 that evening – that the German Colonel and his interpreter started their return for Hamburg, the BBC's *Your Hit Parade*, consisting of the 'ten most popular tunes of the week', was faded out suddenly. A sensational news flash had just come over the wire. The BBC felt it necessary to interrupt the programme in this unusual manner to relay it.

In the cultured tones typical of the BBC announcer of the time, the upper-class speaker stated:

THE NORTH GERMAN NEWS SERVICE HAS JUST TOLD THE GERMAN PEOPLE THAT HITLER IS DEAD.
THEY SAY HE'S BEEN KILLED IN THE BATTLE OF BERLIN.
ADMIRAL DOENITZ, THE COMMANDER-IN-CHIEF OF THE GERMAN NAVY, HAS BEEN NAMED AS
HITLER'S SUCCESSOR . . .

Doenitz's radio message from Radio Hamburg was having its worldwide effect.

The day before there had still been heavy fighting on the Hamburg front. Captain Maxwell of the 7th Armoured Division dug in above Harburg had written to his French wife:

I am well, but in the same place and especially at night it's rather nerve-wracking . . . they launched a counter-attack with 200 men, one tank and several self-propelled guns. Fighting went on all night and by the morning they had had enough. They lost 47 killed, 56 captured and no doubt quite a few of them were wounded, but the Germans managed to evacuate them – we lost seven killed, 20 wounded and 18 got captured.

Now, however, all was suddenly quiet on the Hamburg front. Back home the General Forces Programme continued with *Music While You Work*. Thus, as far as most Britons back home were concerned, the hated tyrant against whom they had fought for six years passed away in tune to Victor Sylvester and his 'strict time' orchestra.

In the lines of the Royal Welch Fusiliers of the 53rd Division, waiting for Hamburg to fall so that they could move in, the soldiers heard the news of Hitler's death on that same programme. They were billeted in a low-ceilinged farmhouse where one of their officers had been fiddling 'with the knobs' of their command radio. Now they knew it was virtually all over.

One of the Fusiliers decided the event was worthy of record. The soldier, who had been a stonemason in 'civvy street', found a hammer and chisel somewhere and went out into the darkness. In the centre of the village square there was a stone monument, commemorating the fact that the Führer had visited the village in 1935. Now he started to inscribe an unsympathetic postscript, which his surprised comrades would see in the morning. It read, '*Kaput, 1945*' . . .

2

'A proper Fred Karno's, this is!'

I

The first 'Red Devils' of the 6th British Airborne Division reached the outskirts of the Baltic port of Wismar at one o'clock on 2 May. They were eleven light Honey tanks laden with the paras of the division's Canadian Parachute Battalion. For a while they hesitated there. So far opposition had been light. Yet in the distance they could still hear the rattle of machine-gun fire.

Hesitant as they were, they knew the importance of capturing the port before the Russians arrived – and by now they could be only a matter of miles away. But weren't they too small a force for the task – they were in barely company strength? Before them lay two un-damaged bridges leading across a stretch of water into the south-west suburbs of the port. They could use them. But why hadn't they been blown up by the retreating Germans? Were they booby-trapped or mined? There was an air of sullen uneasy tension about their whole front. Were they walking straight into a German trap?

While the paras considered thus, a German officer strolled casually towards them. In a bored manner he raised his hands when challenged by the Canadian paras and then suggested quite calmly that he'd take them across the bridges, if they feared some trick or other.

Again the Canadians, who had seen some very hard fighting on the Rhine, hesitated. Was this German prepared to commit suicide in leading them into some kind of ambush? But in the end the officer's very calmness convinced them. Placing him on the front of the leading Honey tank, the column slowly started to rumble across the bridges. Nothing happened.

Now an hour later the whole of the Sixth's 3rd Brigade was spreading over the north-west area of the port. One group was just approaching a *Luftwaffe* airfield, not marked on any map they possessed, when out of the rain-sodden sky German ME 262s shrieked down on them. Madly the Red Devils ducked. *This was it!*

But the twin-engined fighter-bombers hurtled up into the clouds once more, trailing black oily smoke behind them, without firing a shot. The *Luftwaffe* was no longer killing the British. Their last shells were reserved for the Russians just beyond the horizon. The paras breathed a sigh of relief and continued their cautious progress towards the strangely silent *Luftwaffe* field.

Abruptly a German soldier sprang up from a ditch at the right side of the road. He shouted something and next moment flung a stick grenade at the paras. It missed them and exploded harmlessly in the field behind. The lone German last-ditch defender didn't get a second chance. The officer leading the party whipped out his .38 revolver. It was a notoriously unreliable weapon even at short range, but the para officer didn't miss this time. He fired. The German pitched to the ground, dead.

Now more sporadic firing broke out on both sides and the paras advanced crouched low, loosing off bursts from their little sten-guns. But the mini-battle didn't last long. A bedraggled German officer ran up towards the suddenly startled British with his hands in the air. 'Sorry . . . I'm sorry we fired at you,' he panted, chest heaving. But we didn't realise you were British . . . Give us five minutes and we'll surrender.'

The Red Devils gave him his five minutes. They told each other it was obvious the Russians had not reached Wismar. For it had been against the latter that the Germans had expected to defend this strange mysterious *Luftwaffe* field.

While they waited, further down the field a light German plane attempted to take off. Immediately one of the tank drivers gunned his engine and lurched forward. It burst through a hedge and on to the runway. Cheered on by the delighted paras, the tank gunner pumped shell after shell at the speeding plane. But luck was on the pilot's side. As the tank braked to a skidding stop at the edge of a deep ditch which marked the edge of the runway, the pilot of the light plane jerked his stick back and the aircraft zoomed up into the lowering sky and safety, leaving the tank commander standing upright in his turret, shaking his fist impotently.

Moments later the bedraggled officer emerged from the bunker into which he had gone. Behind him filed two hundred unwashed, shabby German soldiers, their hands raised above their heads in surrender. One of the watching paras, shaken by the confused events of these last hours, shook his head in astonishment and breathed, 'This is a proper Fred Karno's, this is!

But the capture of Wismar, just before the Russians arrived there, was not all a confused, impossible knockabout farce – a proper Fred Karno's. Major Watts, a medical officer with the Sixth, also witnessed tragedy that day. Just as his jeep approached the outskirts of the port, the doctor spotted a pitiful column of *Wehrmacht* wounded, hobbling and hopping down the road.

The wounded were in a terrible condition, the blood seeping through their paper bandages (cloth ones were no longer available in the *Wehrmacht*). Here and there lightly wounded men supported those who could hardly walk. Exhausted Red Cross nurses tried to assist the amputees the best they could, here and there carrying those who had lost both legs. For two miserable, blood-littered miles, this column of misery stretched back along the road.

Watts, who had seen much of misery during his war service, felt his heart go out to the Germans. He got out his jeep and asked the first young nurse what had happened. Tearfully she explained that the hospital train in which they had been fleeing west had run out of fuel. While they had been stalled, wondering what to do next, a band of marauding Cossacks had descended upon them. They had set about looting and sacking the train, stealing even from the dying, and shooting anyone who tried to resist. Before they had galloped away with their booty, they riddled the length of the train, containing those of the wounded who couldn't be moved, with machine-gun fire.

Watts acted. He ordered his medical staff to select the worst cases and load them on to the medical jeeps. He then told the nurses and their charges to stay where they were until he could bring help. There was a large *Luftwaffe* hospital in Wismar. He'd try to find out if they could be accommodated there.

But when he returned later, having dumped the more serious cases, he found the Germans gone. Their fear of the advancing Russians was so great that nothing was going to be allowed to arrest their slow progress to the west and safety.

To the rear of these frightened wretches, the German 102nd Infantry Division, which had been conducting a fighting retreat against the Russians for weeks now, had already made contact with elements of the 6th Airborne in Wismar. The day before, the divisional commander had sent out a small column under Captain Spindler to find out what the British thought of his surrendering to them. Spindler had first bumped into the Canadian paras, who had swiftly relieved him of his wristwatch. But finally they had taken him to a senior officer, who commanded a squadron of tanks.

The unknown Tommy had given Spindler a strange order. Instead of surrendering, the 102nd Infantry Division should continue holding the line at Bad Doberan to the east of Wismar. As soon as Wismar was completely in British hands, the division could then withdraw and head for Lübeck, and the British would take it over.

It was all very strange. As one of the division's staff officers, Major Erich Mende, one day to be a senior German politician in the *Bundestag* recalled afterwards, 'Now we were British prisoners and under the protection of Field Marshal Montgomery. But at the same time we were soldiers of the German *Wehrmacht* who, as grotesque as it may seem, were holding a 20-kilometre stretch of the front against the Russians – on the orders of a British-Canadian Officer!'

But not for much longer. Already the 3rd Parachute Brigade was beginning to pass through the port heading for the harbour and the Baltic, their final objective in the Second World War. A sinister stillness hung over the shattered, silent streets. In the lead Captain 'Titch' Wade, who had already won the Military Cross for bravery in action, was worried. Was he leading his men of the 3rd Para Engineer Squadron into some sort of a trap?

Ready for anything and followed by Sapper Jones, armed to the teeth, he burst into the Post Office brandishing a captured German Schmeisser machine-pistol. Everywhere the Germans shot up their hands. Wade might be small but he looked exceedingly fierce, every inch a killer.

Wade ordered the sailors and soldiers among the group of Germans to drop their weapons, and he began searching the surrounding area. Everywhere the Germans, civilians and military alike, surrendered peacefully. They were all obviously glad it was all over. They were pleased, too, that the British and not the Russians had won the race for Wismar.

One small, blond-haired Hitler Youth in short pants was defiant, however. 'Heil Hitler!' he shouted at the para engineers. In poor English he added, 'We will win the war yet!'

Half-amused, half-angered, the sappers told the boy to shut up.

He was defiant. He persisted in crying, 'Heil Hitler!'.

In the end Sapper Jones and the rest had had enough. They grabbed him by his skinny legs, up-ended him and stuck his blond head in the nearest lavatory pan. Someone pulled the chain. Thereafter the defiant little Hitler Youth stopped shouting.

The 'Fred Karno's' continued . . .

To the 6th Airborne's left, was the 11th Armoured Division, followed up by the 5th Infantry Division, was pushing hard for Lübeck, fighting mines and the odd last-ditch resister all the way. At the same time that the paras were infiltrating into the port at Wismar, the 15/19th Hussars in the van of the 11th Armoured, bearing the infantry of the Shropshire Light Infantry on their tanks, had cleared the county town of Bad Oldesloe and were now ordered to head for Lübeck itself. The port was to be captured by that same evening. It was an order welcomed by the troops. As the divisional history recorded; 'Theirs had been a long journey and it should have a fitting end. The capture of Lübeck would set the seal on their achievements.'

So the tanks of the Fife and Forfar Yeomanry and the infantry of the Cheshire Regiment now took the point. They got off to a fine start, cheered on their way by 1,600 liberated RAF officers who had been shot down over Germany during these last terrible years, some of whom were terribly disfigured and would soon be heading for 'Max Factors'[1] for treatment before they could be sent home.

By quarter past three the famous twin spires of the city's medieval city gate, *das Holstentor*, were in sight. Now the men of this mixed force of infantry and armour could see the damage wrought by 'Bomber' Harris's first major raid of 1942, which had escalated the air war so dramatically. But if the inner city was destroyed, the bridges were all intact. So the tanks were able to move into the city itself within fifteen minutes, opposed only by a little sporadic machine-gun fire from some last-ditch fanatic.

Minutes later it was all over. The victorious British soldiers were overwhelmed, not only by the thousands of German soldiers and sailors prepared to surrender but also by thousands of freed prisoners of war from half a dozen Allied nations. They flooded the streets of the old Hanse city, cheering, looting, drinking, careering around in German vehicles they had just 'liberated'.

As photographer Margaret Bourke-White described it, 'The streets were full of merry Englishmen driving fantastically luxurious motor-cars which the *Wehrmacht* officers had abandoned – red-upholstered

---

1 The name the patients and staff gave to No.5 Maxillo-Facial unit, which was located close behind the front during most of the campaign.

Mercedes-Benzes, Hispanos, Renaults and other top-drawer limousines ... The British supplied Lugers and dress swords by the bushelful for anyone who wanted German souvenirs.'

A. J. Evans, who was up front with the leading troops looking for liberated POWs (for the one-time ex-Kriegie[2] himself was in the business of finding out what had happened to the 130,000 British prisoners in German hands), kept his gaze firmly on the beaten enemy:

Lübeck district was an extraordinary sight that day. On every road, in every street and in many of the fields were columns, convoys and masses of German soldiers. There seemed to be far more German soldiers in Lübeck than British ... Many times I saw a column of Germans marching three abreast up the road in perfect order with their packs and full equipment on their backs and an officer at their head. For the most part they looked neither starved nor desperately tired. But they had been given an order to surrender and they were obeying this with the same patient discipline as they had obeyed an order to die heroically at their posts.

The ex-POW concluded, at this moment of personal triumph, 'The Germans are an extraordinary race. I feel sure that no other army would surrender *en masse* in such good order with such superb discipline and with so few signs of despondency.'

But not all German soldiers were prepared to surrender that day 'in such good order' and 'with such superb discipline'.

That day of victory the 3rd Royal Tanks and 4 KSLI of the 11th Armoured Division were confronted in Forst Segeberg, a large forest of the area, by a strong body of SS men. They were not prepared to surrender. 'Pip' Roberts of the 11th Armoured was faced with a dilemma. He did not want to lose any more British lives in this moment of triumph. He thought hard and then came up with the ideal, and ironic, solution to his problem. General Erdmann's 8th Parachute Division was prepared to surrender. The surrender was accepted and then the undersized tank General ordered the German paras to operate against the SS. They obeyed instantly and, as the General put it years later, 'in due course, the SS yielded'.

Now not only were the Germans fighting the Russians at British command, they were also fighting their fellow Germans. Truly this was a real 'Fred Karno's' ...

---

2 From the German *Kriegsgefangene* for POW

II

At the same moment as the Yeomanry's tanks were rumbling through Lübeck, surrounded by the cheering throng of DPs, an officer of the German Navy at the port was speaking on the phone with Doenitz's adjutant Luedde-Neurath in Ploen. Suddenly he spotted the Yeomanry's Churchills and cried 'British tanks are passing by'.

Abruptly the line went dead.

Impatiently the Lieutenant-Commander rattled the receiver. But the phone stayed obstinately dead and Ludde-Neurath guessed what must have happened. The British had cut the link-up. He dropped the phone and burst into Admiral Doenitz's office. He told the new 'Führer' the unpleasant news. The British had reached the Baltic, and the 'door to the west', as Doenitz liked to call the escape route between the Elbe and the Baltic, was finally closed.

Doenitz considered for a few moments. Obviously there was no future in continuing the policies of 1 May. Those left east of the Elbe-Baltic line would have to be abandoned to their fate. Meanwhile he was not going to be captured himself here in Ploen. He would have to find a new and safer headquarters. He selected the little coastal town of Flensburg, which possessed a large naval barracks that he could use as his HQ. Flensburg was on the border with Denmark and he probably reasoned that the RAF would hardly be likely to bomb the place and chance killing their allies, the Danes, at this stage of the war. Flensburg would be safe from the British *Terrorflieger* of 'Bomber' Harris's terrible merciless air fleets.

On that same afternoon, while his staff officers hurriedly threw their bags and secret documents into the waiting staff cars, their drivers already gunning the engines impatiently, he called his old comrade and new head of what was left of the German Navy, Admiral von Friedeburg. In the three weeks that he still had to live, the sallow-faced, sad-eyed Admiral would emerge from the obscurity of his past and make the headlines – before it all became too much for him and he took his own life. Now Doenitz told von Friedeburg to meet his convoy as it travelled north to Flensburg, at a bridge over the Kaiser Wilhelm canal near Kiel.

That meeting would seal von Friedeburg's fate. But the flight to Flensburg also sealed the fate of many thousands of other men and women that day, of whom the world would never hear. For now, as all German authority broke down in Holstein and those who might have prevented tragedy fled north, the survivors of Neuengamme concentration camp were left to the SS.

By now the seven thousand-odd prisoners on board the *Cap Arcona* and the other two ships knew Hitler was dead. The German prisoners among them knew this from their own secret grapevine, and in a mixture of languages they had passed on the tremendous news to the Russians, Czechs, Poles and all the rest who didn't understand German.

They could also hear the sound of firing from the land and knew it would not be long before they were freed. Their SS guards were obviously scared, and seemed to be making preparations to flee once the Tommies reached the shore some 3 or 4 miles away.

On the afternoon of 2 May, the prisoners' suppositions seemed to be supported when two barges packed to overflowing with prisoners from another concentration camp outside Danzig appeared off the *Cap Arcona*. The two barges trailed behind them a wake of dead men, women and children in striped pyjama uniforms who had been tossed overboard when they had suffocated in the mêlée. Captain Bertram, the skipper of the *Cap Arcona*, refused to take any more prisoners on board. Then, to the joy of the concentration camp inmates already on the *Cap Arcona*, and to the terror of those on the barges, their SS guards abandoned them. That could mean one thing only – the SS men, who had once been so arrogant and brutal, were now scared. They were going to save their own miserable hides before the English appeared. The mood of the prisoners on board the *Cap Arcona*, many of whom were now being allowed on the upper deck so that they could see what was going on, rose mightily. Soon their long suffering would be at an end.

So, as the two barges drifted away, carried towards the shore by the prevailing wind until they disappeared from sight, all eyes on the *Cap Arcona*'s top deck were directed towards Lübeck. Who would see their rescuers first? Who?

On the front of the US 18th Airborne Corps that Wednesday afternoon everyone was on the lookout too. Their commander, General Ridgway, had ordered his men to be on the alert for the approach of the Russians. He knew that General Eisenhower had laid down some sort of guideline on what to do when the two armies linked up. His main concern, however, was that there should be no outbreak of fighting between the Allies.

As for the emotional scenes which had taken place at Torgau on the Elbe the previous week, Ridgway wanted none of those. He preferred to abide by the 'canny' British directive which set the pattern for the conduct of British troops when they met the Russians. 'Our Russian allies should be treated with civility.' the directive stated, 'but there must be no excessive overture of friendship. Such efforts on the part of the British, it was pointed out, would be taken by the Russians as a tribute to their superiority as soldiers.' Ridgway agreed. 'Neither the British nor the American soldier at that time had any reason to look up to any other fighting man that walked the earth.'

The tall, craggy-faced General was worried that he was losing control of his three American divisions – the 7th Armored, the 8th Infantry and the 82nd Airborne – which were pushing deep into Mecklenburg against token German resistance. What if they bumped into the Russians and a fire fight started by accident?

Indeed Gavin's paras were so spread out that even their own troops more than once nearly fired upon them. That day Colonel Rubel of the 740th Tank Battalion of the US 7th Armored Division called one of his platoon commanders to check whether the troops on the horizon were enemy or friendly forces. The commander assured him they were paras – and American. A minute later another tank commander came on the radio and reported, 'Believe it or not, Captain, four paratroopers on bicycles just passed my tank and are now spearheading. More power to them!' A few minutes after that the same officer radioed once more. 'Good lord', he cried, 'Here comes a horse and buggy loaded with about eight paratroopers – they are passing me! . . . Colonel, this is the damnedest thing I ever saw. Look over there to the left. There's about twenty men riding horses! They are paratroopers and they are rounding up Jerries!'

It was under these circumstances that Ridgway decided something had to be done to make sure that the Russians knew exactly where the Americans were. He ordered the 7th Armored Division to select an officer to find the Russians and brief them.

General Hasbrouck, Commander of the 7th Armored Division, was no friend of Ridgway. Once, during the Battle of the Bulge in December 1944,[3] Ridgway had briefly sacked him after his week-long defence of St Vith, which had decimated his division. Now he didn't like the idea of sending off his men on this journey into the unknown. After all the Seventh was opposed by some five German divisions, even if they were no longer fighting very hard.

But orders were orders and Hasbrouck selected for the task a young

3 See C. Whiting Death of a Division.

lieutenant who had just come to the division from West Point as a replacement. First Lieutenant William Knowlton of the 87th Cavalry Reconnaissance Squadron was given a handful of bottles of Hennessy three-star Cognac, which he was to give to any senior Russian he met 'somewhere to the east – between fifty and a hundred miles'. The drink was to be used as a bribe to persuade the Russian to come back to the US lines and be briefed on the American positions.

Thus the young officer, new to the front, set off into the confused unknown, leading a little team of ninety men in twenty jeeps and eleven Staghound armoured cars, fast, six-wheeled vehicles armed with a light cannon and machine-guns. They would provide the muscle if Knowlton needed it.

Meanwhile other elements sought to re-establish contact with the British 6th Airborne Division, which lay somewhere on the 7th Armored Division's left flank. Riding at point in a jeep, Colonel George Rubel of the 740th Tank Battalion battered his way through a German strongpoint and suddenly found himself in the middle of a German SS flak battery that was 'at that moment firing like the very devil at some of our airplanes'.

The Colonel and his little team were 'too startled and too scared' to stop. Seeing 'visions' of his wife collecting 'her insurance money',[4] the hatchet-faced Colonel braved it out and managed to convince the SS to surrender. Thereupon he ordered the sullen gunners to destroy their weapons there and then – he thought it safer – before setting off with a German officer parked on the front of his jeep in the direction of a nearby German Corps HQ.

In due course Rubel and a fellow officer, Colonel Kunzig, found the German HQ and were introduced to the Corps Commander, whose corps was made up of five divisions. They told him that they were there to accept his surrender.

The German General bristled at this. He snapped that he had no intention of surrendering – now or at any time! They showed him the dispositions of the American troops on their maps. The German did the same, showing them the Russians' positions. Now the German was convinced that any further resistance would mean the useless spilling of blood. He told them, through his interpreter that he would still not surrender, but he was going to order his corps of some forty thousand men to 'withdraw' westwards, whether the Americans liked it or not.

---

4 All GIs overseas were insured to the extent of ten thousand dollars, which their next-of-kin could claim if they were killed 'in the line of duty'. Needless to say, there was no similar scheme in the British Army.

The two American colonels agreed, informing him that the 'withdrawal' would have to start immediately. Soon the highly indignant troopers of the 740th Tank Battalion would find themselves being told by a German commander to move their *'panzers'* off the road at once so that his soldiers could withdraw. The 'Fred Karno's' had spread to the American zone of operations!

By now Knowlton and his little force were rolling through the little town of Parchim, 20 miles behind the crumbling German line. Here to their surprise the Germans welcomed them more like liberators than conquerors. German MPs directed them down the main street, lined with cheering soldiers and civilians who (as the puzzled Americans found out later) obviously believed Goebbels' propaganda line that the Americans were moving east to fight the Russians!

They rolled on. Six miles up on the road further east, heading for the small town of Lubz, the young American officer met up with a German major. They chatted more like friends than foes before setting off once more to Lubz, where Knowlton would set up his command post for the night in the local *Gasthaus*.

Whatever he had said to the German is in doubt now, but the latter radioed his divisional commander, General Ernst von Jungenfeld, that he had spoken to an American captain in charge of twenty tanks.

Both of us tank leaders with forty tanks request you personally order an attack against the east to start the morning of 4 May. We believe that with Hitler dead, it is the moment to finally defeat and crush the Russians and thereby communism. Therefore, we request you and expect from you a clear attack order against the east and we are convinced that we will defeat and drive out the Russians and we are also sure that everywhere comrades will immediately follow our example.

Perhaps the Major was drunk and his message was never acted upon. But it was reported to General von Tippelskirch, Commander of the German 21st Army with its HQ at Parchim, that the Americans were now deep to their rear. He made a decision. He ordered his Chief of staff, Colonel von Varnbuhler, to see if he could sound out the Americans on the subject of surrenders. So yet again someone set off into the unknown. The American he would meet was General Gavin of the 82nd Airborne.

Gavin had just experienced his last fire fight of the Second World War. He had been riding down a country road in his jeep when he had spotted a German dispatch rider in helmet and ankle-length leather coat. The German had seen the American General, turned, and drove away at top speed, with Gavin firing at him with his carbine from the wildly bouncing jeep. As Gavin commented afterwards, 'He was the last German in the war we were to see running away.'

Now he was standing in a village street, surrounded by thousands of cheering Germans, watching his paras moving on to attack another objective. He described how he 'was standing near the curb of the main street intersection wearing a parachute jump suit, faded from three years of war, carrying an M-1 rifle over my shoulder and looking like any other GI in the 82nd except for the two stars on my collar and my helmet' when a GI approached. He said there was 'a German general' looking for the 'American general in charge'.

'Send him over'!, Gavin ordered.

Colonel von Varnbuhler, 'the German general', eyed Gavin somewhat haughtily. When Gavin said he was the American commander, von Varnbuhler said he couldn't be; he looked too young and didn't look like a general to him. As Gavin later recalled maliciously, 'it took only a minute to change his mind' for him.

Convinced, von Varnbuhler told Gavin that his commander wanted to send civilians and their own wounded through the American front to safety. Politely Gavin refused. He said that would mean support for a German army fighting against the Russian ally. Americans couldn't do that. Then von Varnbuhler tried another tack. Could they talk terms about the surrender of the whole 21st Army?

Again Gavin turned him down. He said von Tippelskirch would have to surrender to the Russians against whom he was currently fighting. This was bad news for the German staff officer. He told Gavin that no German soldier who had ever fought against the Russians would voluntary go into Soviet captivity; it was virtually a death warrant.

Here the discussions broke off for a while. Gavin disappeared for half an hour. When he returned he said that a *modus vivendi* might be found so that the Germans could surrender to the British or Americans. Later von Varnbuhler reasoned that Gavin had talked with Montgomery, who was visiting Ridgway's Corps HQ that day.

Earlier that day Gavin had told the commander of his 325th Glider Infantry, Colonel Charles Billingslea (who was soon to break his leg demonstrating to drunken Russian officers how airborne troops left their planes by jumping out of a window), to set up his command post in the eighteenth-century palace at Ludwigslust. Gavin had not seen the HQ yet, which he thought would be a fitting setting for the last day of combat.

Now he suggested to the German Colonel that he would 'be happy to see General von Tippelskirch at the palace that evening'. The two men agreed that the historic meeting would take place at eight o'clock that night. With that, von Varnbuhler returned to the 21st Army, still occupied in fighting and retreating before the advancing Russians.

Thus, while the Germans were still fighting the Russian ally, a second divisional general under Montgomery's command was beginning to break the agreed formula of no partial surrender to individual allies.

III

While Gavin journeyed that evening to the command post where the fateful meeting would soon be held, Doenitz waited impatiently at the bridge over the Kaiser Wilhelm canal near Kiel.

It had been a nightmarish journey. Burning trucks and cars shot up by the dreaded British *Jabos* littered the roadsides all the way. Twice the Grand Admiral had been forced to abandon his armoured Mercedes and cower in a ditch as British Typhoons came hurtling in, rockets flashing from their wings. But he had persisted, urging his driver to force a way through the mass of fleeing soldiers and civilians.

Now, by the time he had reached the agreed meeting place, it was dark and there was no sign of von Friedeburg. Anxiously Doenitz waited, flashing glances in the direction from which his old comrade would come. Had the other admiral been killed by marauding RAF planes? If he had, where would he find a substitute for him? He didn't trust the Army.

Then, just when he was about to give up and order his driver to drive on, von Friedeburg's car appeared out of the glowing darkness; for nearby Kiel was under attack again. He explained that he, too, had been attacked all the way by the damned *Jabos* and had been forced to take cover from them several times.

Doenitz waved aside his apologies. Time was running out – fast! Taking the smaller man by the arm, he led him a little way from the others and explained in a low voice what he wanted von Friedeburg to do. He was not prepared to surrender to the British yet. He needed more time to allow von Tippelskirch's army and the civilians to withdraw into the American lines. He also wanted the bombing of Schleswig-Holstein stopped and medical supplies sent in for the thousands of wounded now arriving daily in the peninsula. Therefore he was going to send him, von Friedeburg, personally to see Montgomery. It would be his task to obtain a truce, a partial surrender, anything that would allow him to achieve his new aims. 'You must play for time,' he said urgently, almost passionately for such a cold-blooded man, '*time!*'

Thus they parted, these two admirals. One would be dead within the month and the other would spend ten years of disgrace in prison. Now each went on his separate mission, important, honoured, experienced men who still believed that they were making the real decisions . . .

Later in Flensburg, Doenitz went to the local radio station with another man who believed like Doenitz that he was still in control. It was his new 'Foreign Minister', Count Schwerin von Krosigk, a former Rhodes scholar at Oriel College, who had been Hitler's Minister of Finance. Devout Catholic and admirer of England, he read the first speech of his new office. It reflected exactly the Grand Admiral's hopes and illusions, for Doenitz still cherished the mistaken notion that the Anglo-Americans and the Russians, now linking on the Elbe, would begin to fight each other and that the Anglo-Americans would need Germany as a new ally.

'German men and women,' the new 'Foreign Minister' warned, 'the iron curtain in the east moves closer and closer. Behind it, hidden from the eyes of the world, all those people caught in the mighty hands of the Bolsheviks are being destroyed.' The conference currently being held at San Francisco to draw up the constitution of the United Nations attempt to end all war would, he maintained, fail if the Bolsheviks weren't stopped in Europe. For, he predicted, a Bolshevik Europe would be the first step to the world revolution which had been planned by Moscow for these last twenty-five years.

Therefore, we do not see in San Francisco what anxious mankind is longing for. And we also believe that a world constitution must be established, not only to prevent further wars, but to remove the tinder boxes which start war. But such a constitution cannot be established if the Red incendiary helps establish it . . .

The world must now make a decision of the greatest consequence to the history of mankind. Upon this decision depends chaos or order, war or peace, death or life . . .

Dramatic, perhaps even prophetic words. But now the Germans were no longer making the decisions. The decisions were being made for them!

Outside the palace where Gavin met von Tippelskirch, one of his troopers played 'Lilli Marlene' on a 'liberated' concertina as hundreds of German soldiers marched by, heading for the cages. Tears started to roll down the cheeks of the passing Germans. But as the trooper played, his victorious comrades bent over with the laughter at the sight, holding their sides. The German Army was well and truly beaten. Now the Krauts were bawling.

General Gavin, too, was inclined to be less than kind to the man who would soon become his prisoner. Von Tippelskirch told Gavin that he hoped the American would take good care of the palace in which they found themselves because it had once been his home. Gavin replied acidly, did the General know how the Germans had taken care of Coventry back in 1940? The 82nd Airborne had trained near the British city and knew of the devastation wrought by the *Luftwaffe* there.

Von Tippelskirch said, 'Not especially, but I know what the Allies did to Cologne.'

Gavin said they did, too. They had just come from the shattered city. 'We had walked over the high piles of rubble out of which weeds were growing in what once had been the lovely downtown part of the city.'

Thereafter, the subject was dropped and the two of them got down to the subject of surrender. Von Tippelskirch offered to surrender his 21st Army to the Americans if Gavin would tell the Russians to stop their attacks on him. Gavin said he had no control over the Red Army. Von Tippelskirch would surrender unconditionally or Gavin would continue his own attacks until he linked up with the Russians.

Von Tippelskirch gave in. He ordered the document of surrender to be drawn up. While it was being done Gavin, who was keeping his distance from von Tippelskirch – 'by the time we reached Germany there was much ill feeling on the part of the troopers toward the German military establishment[5] – heard the latter ask an American if he could stay the night in the palace. Gavin butted in and snapped that if von Tippelskirch stayed the night there it would be as an American prisoner of war! Hastily von Tippelskirch changed his mind and went to his car. He had just signed over a whole army group to the youthful Airborne Commander. For the next three days a steady stream of 150,000 Germans, their equipment and accompanying civilians – in-

5 Later Gavin became friendly with his former enemy and many year later the American returned the sword he had taken off von Tippelskirch that day at the palace.

cluding quite a few mistresses of their higher ranking officers – passed into the American cages.

The first limited surrender, *without the approval of the Russians*, had taken place and Eisenhower knew nothing of it. Nor did the Russians. But soon they would find out, for now they were on the very heels of the retreating Germans. That night, at precisely 9.30, the van of Rokossovsky's 2nd Belorussian Front reached the Baltic at Bunz, some 10 kilometres east of Wismar. Here the British paras were waiting for them.

Two motor-cycle combinations were in the lead, followed by two lease-lend scout cars from the USA. Each contained seven ragged Red Army men, all with dirty faces and shaven skulls, and one female soldier armed with a Tommy-gun.

Cautiously the little column approached the para's positions, bringing with them their own distinctive and unmistakable smell. As one eyewitness remembers it, 'a mixture of stale male sweat, sweet black bread and the coarse *mahorka* tobacco they smoked, rolled in chutes of old newspaper'.

Finally they recognised the British uniforms and relaxed the pressure on the triggers of their weapons. They broke out the vodka, which all of them carried with them it seemed. There was the usual dumbshow of hand-shaking and signs, slapping each other on the back in hearty good will – for neither side understood the other's language. As was customary in the last spring of the Great Alliance, exaggerated toasts were drunk and gestures of eternal friendship made. On the morrow it would be repeated for the last time when, as the history of the Red Devils notes, 'a brigadier noted for his courage, his abstemiousness and his gentle smile, was in due course found asleep in his car in a convenient but fortunately shallow ditch!'

Then the impromptu party started to peter out. The Russians were obviously tired and the paras had covered an amazing 60 miles in the course of the single day. It was time to sleep so they went to their separate camps.

As the paratroopers, very tired and a little drunk by now, started to sprawl out in the luxury of their requisitioned beds or on the bedrolls under the stars, the Russians began to build an enormous roadblock, cutting off their lines from the British. No one knew it then and the paras, who all believed that the future lay with 'Uncle Joe's boys' and themselves, would have laughed with derision if anyone had suggested that they might have to fight these same Russians one day, but that night the Iron Curtain had begun descending on Central Europe.

Back at his headquarters just outside Luneburg, Montgomery knew something of what might soon come. That night he signalled London's War Office:

There is no doubt that the very rapid movement from the Elbe bridgeheads north to the Baltic was a very fine performance on the part of the troops concerned. There is no doubt also that we only just beat the Russians by about 12 hours. All's well that ends well and the whole of the Schleswig peninsula and Denmark is now effectively sealed off and we shall keep it so.

He added that 'the flood of German troops and civilians fleeing from the approaching Russians is a spectacle that can seldom have been seen before and it will be interesting to see how it sorts itself out tomorrow'. The little Field Marshal concluded with prophetic words, 'We have had a remarkable day today and tomorrow may be even more so . . .' Then he went to bed in his sleeping caravan, with his glass of hot milk and the 'liberated' chamber-pot.

3

"We're celebrating! We're going to have bread and margarine tonight!"

I

Dawn, Thursday 3 May 1945

It was then that they started slaughtering the prisoners. All night the panic-stricken former inmates of the Danzig concentration camp, packed in the two barges, had been trying to make their way to the shore. They had fashioned a crude rudder from boards and the light south wind had helped. Just before it had grown light the two barges had grounded just outside the little Baltic seaport of Neustadt. Exhausted, half-starved, the surviving hundreds of men, women and children had spread out to search for food and shelter.

Almost immediately the alarm was sounded in Neustadt. Police, SS, the trainees of the nearby U-boat school, even the Hitler Youth, were alerted. Their orders were simple – shoot to kill!

Now, on this hazy morning, with victory in the air everywhere, the young fanatics commenced the slaughter. Margot Weidemann, aged 15, was on her way into the town to fetch some bread for her mother when she came across the line of dead men, women and children in their striped pyjamas on the beach. Standing in front of them was an SS man.

'It doesn't look good,' he told the ashen-faced girl. 'There are dead everywhere.' Suddenly he held up his hands proudly, fingers outstretched to indicate that he, personally, had shot ten of them.

'I've got to go home,' Margot said hurriedly.

He nodded his approval and, clutching her loaf to her skinny chest, she fled, trying – and failing – not to see the corpses which littered the beach all the way to her house. 'I can never forget them,' she recalled forty years later. 'Everywhere one looked, the bodies were piled up.'

220

Frau Magdalene Lange who lived in Neustadt itself watched in horror as an SS man plus some sailors shot a group of men, women and children huddled in blankets on the quay. They went from prisoner to prisoner, standing there like dumb animals waiting to be slaughtered, and blew off the backs of their heads so that they fell straight into the water.

Next to Magdalene her three small children watched in fascinated terror this brutal mass execution carried out in front of their house. Later her little son Eckehard, when the British finally arrived, asked, 'Will the English hang us now?'

They wouldn't. No one would pay the price for the slaughter that went on all day at Neustadt, though the first British officer to arrive on the scene threatened to burn the place to the ground in his anger at what he saw along that dread beach – hundreds upon hundreds of dead bodies, lying packed there like bundles of abandoned wet rags.

On the *Cap Arcona* and the other two smaller ships, packed with thousands of their fellow sufferers, the sound of the firing on land roused once again the hopes of the prisoners. By now there were 4,500 prisoners on the *Cap Arcona*, a further 2,800 on the smaller *Thielbek* and 1,998 on the *Athen*. Guarding and attending them there were seven hundred SS men, plus twenty-four SS *Maiden*, female soldiers.

The latter were becoming increasingly nervous. They had already hidden all life-saving equipment, as we have seen. Now they proceeded to slit the fire-fighting hoses on the three ships, while the commander of the *Cap Arcona*, Captain Bertram, watched passively. Although he had violently protested to the SS commander about placing all these thousands of unfortunates on his ship, he would be one of the first over the side when the tragedy struck, abandoning them to their fate.

But, as the sound of firing off-shore grew ever louder, the former concentration camp inmates seemed not to notice these preparations for their destruction. They were carried away by the thought of their immediate liberation and the fact that they had been able to plunder some of the ships' supplies. As Polish Dr Borucki recalled long afterwards, 'We moved about crying to one another, "Have you heard? There's peace. We're celebrating! We're going to have bread and margarine tonight!" '

For most of the thousands packed on the three ships there would be no 'bread and margarine' this night, or any other night for that matter. This day of victory they were fated to die.

In Hamburg, some 100 miles away, Kaufmann, who had indirectly sentenced them to die this day, knew he had saved Hamburg and its citizens. At that same dawn, the cavalry of 1945 outside the besieged city heard the end announced, not by a trumpet call as in the past but through the earphones of their tank headsets: 'In Hamburg all resistance has ceased!'

The veterans of six years' fighting in two continents prepared to move into Germany's second greatest city. NCOs rapped out orders. Officers pointed with their swagger canes. Vehicles were loaded, given a last check. As always on such occasions in the British Army, 'bull reigned supreme'! Then, as the first light of dawn flushed the sky, the order to mount up was given. Tank engines coughed into life.

In front of the great procession of armoured vehicles came the Infantry Brigade in their trucks and Bren-gun carriers. One of them, Captain Maxwell, already showing a keen eye for publicity, would write the following day to his wife, 'Look out for the newsreel about Hamburg, you will see me in it issuing orders and carrying my faithful stick.' But at that particular moment the infantry were wary, more concerned with keeping a lookout in the ruins for some last-ditch fanatic armed with a *Panzerfaust*. They were led by the only two tanks of the 7th Armoured Division which had survived the campaign since it had first landed in Europe in June 1944. They were named 'Sharpshooter' and 'Jerboa', the latter being the desert rat which had given the division its name.

Now, as they started to rumble into the outskirts of the port, they saw for the first time the real extent of the damage wrought by 'Bomber' Harris's boys. Whole sections were brick wastes, with here and there a ruined wall still standing, or a chimney stack. Everywhere there were mountainous heaps of twisted metal, girders and rubble. The 'Desert Rats' had seen destruction and devastation enough before – in London, Foggia, Naples, Caen – but never anything like this. To some of them it seemed the city would have to be abandoned after the war; nothing could be rebuilt here, they told themselves. Suddenly the men fell silent, awed by the grim spectacle.[1]

Now there was no sound except the rumble of their tracks and wheels. The brick waste was deserted save for the elderly policeman in their leather helmets who were there to direct the victors. The cheering throngs of newly liberated cities in France, Belgium and

---

1 The ruins were so bad in some places that one column got lost and had to ask directions from a German policeman! The CO was not amused.

Holland were absent naturally, but there weren't even the sullen crowds they had encountered in other German towns they had captured.

Kaufmann had ordered that everyone was to be off the streets when the Tommies arrived. All offices, shops and public buildings were closed and public transport was at a standstill. The Hamburgers stayed at home in their ruins, wondering what the future would bring. 'No more bombs, no bunkers, no hiding in the cellars, no sleepless nights, no panicky packing of suitcases,' old Frau Wolff-Moenckeberg wrote to her daughter in Wales, with a mixture of relief and sadness. For 'our Germany will no longer belong to us; and our once proud and free Hamburg will have to submit to English rule'.

But for the time being the British were not behaving at all like conquerors. Indeed some of them appeared decidedly casual and offhand. Way up front of the division, as was customary, its divisional reconnaissance regiment, the 11th Hussars – nicknamed 'the Cherry-pickers'[2] – was, in its usual carefree fashion assessing the opposition, if any. Colonel Bill Wainman, its CO, sailed into Hamburg's great *Rathausplatz* in his armoured car to find a host of bemedalled dignitaries waiting for him there. Apparently they wanted to surrender the keys of the city to him.

As the Colonel in his GI combat jacket and baggy civilian trousers sprang down from his vehicle, the Germans jumped to attention in front of the town hall with its pseudo-Gothic spires. One of them advanced on the decidedly shabby British officer and asked in English if he would accept their surrender then, if he did not want the city's keys. Airily Wainman waved him away, saying that he'd leave that job 'to the Brigadier'. Then he bent and started feeding the pigeons with crumbled Army biscuits.

But Colonel Wainman knew something that few other British officers present that day of triumph did. The surrender of Hamburg had now become insignificant. For that morning the 'Cherrypickers' had escorted not only General Wolz, the Battle Commandant of Hamburg, through the British lines, but also Admiral von Friedeburg. And the sallow-faced Admiral with the sad spaniel's eyes had not been taken to see the Seventh's divisional commander but had been whisked straight off to meet no less a person that General Dempsey, commander of the whole British 2nd Army. Something big was in the wind!

2 After its cherry-red beret.

It was. At his headquarters in a smart middle-class house at Haeck-lingen, General Dempsey had already sounded out the German delegation under Admiral von Friedeburg, using his Intelligence officer, Colonel Murphy, for the task. At this stage of whatever was going on, he did not want to have any direct contact with the Germans. From Murphy he had gathered that they were attempting to drag out the negotiations. They would surrender, however, if they received certain terms.

As Colonel-General Jodl, Hitler's cunning, pale-faced Chief of Staff, was noting that day in Flensburg, in any discussions with the former enemy it must be made clear that 'Germany, in the midst of its total defeat, is once again a factor in Europe . . . The day will come when we can play off the Russians against the Anglo-Americans . . . Important, the basic principle is not to annoy the English!'

Dempsey ordered Murphy to call Montgomery's military assistant, Colonel Dawnay, and relay to him his thoughts on the matter, knowing that only Monty himself could deal with the hitch. Immed-iately Montgomery heard, he snapped into action. He ordered a four-man German delegation, headed by von Friedeburg to be sent to his own TAC HQ as quickly as possible. That done he pressed his button and ordered his Canadian personal assistant, Colonel Warren, to arrange the 'drill'.

The Union Jack had to be hoisted at once. When the four Boche arrived they would be lined up directly beneath the British flag, facing his office caravan. In the meantime everyone else in the camp was to get out of sight, save for Warren and Dawnay who would wear their side-arms. Colonel Ewart, the Intelligence officer, would act as his interpreter.

Hastily the camp started to prepare for the Germans' arrival, while Montgomery 'dressed' for the occasion. As usual he was 'sloppy', as King George VI had once characterised him. He was wearing a battle dress and khaki trousers which didn't quite match and a black beret which he was not entitled to wear, adorned with two badges – those of a general and the Royal Tank Corps – again quite contrary to King's Regulations.

What went through his head at that moment we do not know. He did not confide his thoughts to anyone. But Montgomery surely must have been aware that he was on the verge of something big. Already two of his generals – the commanders of the British 7th Armoured and the 82nd US Airborne – had accepted piecemeal surrenders. Now this unknown 'General-Admiral' von Friedeburg was coming to offer, perhaps, an even larger surrender. But yet again he guessed one of the German's conditions would be surrender *solely to the Anglo-Americans*. Another piecemeal surrender, which would not gain the Americans' favour.

Now this Thursday morning the right course of action for Montgomery would have been to hand over the whole affair to Eisenhower and his political advisers, all of whom were fearful of any course which might offend the Russians. They, then, would have been able to stand by the official policy of total, unconditional surrender to all three major Allies, Britain, the USA *and* Soviet Russia. But vain and opinionated as he was, Montgomery was not prepared to allow this triumph – this large-scale German surrender – to be gained by other and, in his opinion, lesser men. They had thwarted him on Berlin. They had relegated the British Army, which had been fighting since 1939 – one year of that time all on its own against the might of Nazi Germany – to a supporting role without any great political or strategic importance. They had starved him of men and then made fun of his slowness in attacking. Now he was *not* going to be cheated of his final victory. Come what may, he, Bernard Law Montgomery, would accept the surrender of what was left of Hitler's Germany . . .

While the von Friedeburg party, led by a British armoured car, drove to his HQ on the heath, the first of the fighter-bombers which had taken off that morning from the RAF base at the nearby town of Celle came out of the clouds over the Baltic. Squadron Leader Martin Rumbold leading the flight saw the ships first.

Forty years on he would state, 'The *Cap Arcona* looked very small. I thought she wouldn't displace more than 5,000 tons.' Below the prisoners started to wave frantically as they spotted the eight British fighter-bombers. But they waved in vain. Rumbold didn't spot them. He was far too high. Besides, the German flak was already beginning to pepper the sky all around with those familiar lethal puffballs.

He rapped out a single command: 'Peel off!' His pilots needed no urging. They were all running out of fuel. Their attack would have to be quick and decisive. Then it would have to be back to Celle 'toot sweet' to fuel up again.

One after another the pilots broke off and zoomed down in a steep dive, fingers poised above the firing buttons which would activate their rockets. None of them had had great experience with firing rockets. But Rumbold did his best. Then there it was – the target. The

Cap Arcona lay in his sights. 'Group – fire a salvo!' he commanded over the R/T. The other pilots pressed their firing buttons at once.

Flying above the squadron, Pilot Don Saunders could see the rockets surge downwards towards the stationary ship. 'There were 64 of them,' he reported long afterwards. 'One single rocket fell in the water. The other 63 ripped into the ship. It was as if a gigantic fire ball had suddenly burst!'

Down below the cheers changed to screams of fear and rage, as that monstrous salvo ripped the *Cap Arcona* apart. Prisoner Heinrich Mehringer, one of the few survivors, recalled afterwards:

'The ship started to burn in several places straightaway. The whole ship trembled, as if an earthquake . . . Panic . . . panic! The prisoners rushed for the gangways and exits. Everyone was shouting and pushing. But the three exits were too small. Some of the prisoners tried to fight the fires with the hoses. They pulled them from the drums. But only a few metres appeared. The remainder had been cut off!'

The SS had done their work well. Mehringer, a German political prisoner, managed to fight his way on to the deck. 'There were prisoners everywhere on the deck, their clothing already blazing. A Frenchman came up. His clothes were afire, too. All he could stammer was *"Alles Wasser . . . Alles Wasser . . . Feuer . . . Alles kaputt!"*[3] Then he dropped down dead.'

Directly behind Rumbold's planes, which had now broken off the action, a new flight of fighter-bombers appeared. Flight Lieutenant J Hargreaves, who commanded the flight, recorded afterwards, 'As soon as we reached Lübeck Bay, I saw two very big stationary ships. One was burning fiercely and the other a passenger ship with two funnels had a small fire.' Just like Rumbold, Hargreaves did not hesitate. He thought like his predecessor that these were German ships about to run for Norway, perhaps carrying Doenitz's staff with them. 'I ordered my own section – Green – to attack.'

They went in, this time to drop bombs. The attack was not a great success, for most of Green Section's bombs missed their target completely. But after his next attack Hargreaves could see that they had hit the ship with their bombs. Now it was suddenly beginning to slip into the water.

Now a third squadron joined in. Led by Squadron Leader Johnny Baldwin, the nine Typhoons from 198 Squadron spread out, attacking

3 All water . . . All water! . . . Fire . . . Everything kaput!

all four ships below. The *Cap Arcona*, the *Deutschland* and the *Thielbek* were all hit, and already Baldwin could see the first boats being lowered. The Jerry sailors were abandoning their ships. They had done their job well. It was time to go home to the traditional meal of bacon and eggs, and – if they were lucky – a good stiff glass of whisky.

Now it was every man for himself. The German concentration camp inmate Erwin Geschonneck watched as Captain Bertram of the *Cap Arcona* carved his way through the panic-stricken mob of prisoners with a large machete, cutting down anyone who attempted to stop his flight. Then, together with his crew and officers, he abandoned the big liner and its 'passengers' to their fate.

Meanwhile those of the SS who had not already flung themselves over the side were firing at the mob to keep them at bay while they escaped. Geschonneck watched as one SS man, armed with a revolver in each hand, fired to left and right until his ammunition was all gone, then he was overrun by his former prisoners and trampled to death.

But most of the prisoners had no time for thoughts of revenge. They were primarily concerned with saving themselves as the *Cap Arcona* started to list frighteningly – and already from below the flames were reaching up for fresh victims, the deck beneath their feet nearly red-hot.

Heinrich Mehringer, who had already survived two shipwrecks, thought that the *Cap Arcona* would soon settle on the bottom of the shallow bay with her superstructure clear of the water. But he now found the danger was not the sea – but the fire. 'Suddenly we were all ablaze,' he recalled afterwards:

I was burning at my back and my head. The roar of the flames now drowned the piteous screams of the dying and burning. In the very last moment I saw an iron stanchion above me. With my one good arm I could just reach it and somehow with a superhuman effort, I managed to draw myself up on it.

Now Mehringer was above the heads of the packed, screaming, burning crowd of panic-stricken prisoners below. He spotted his friend Max, whose both arms were badly burnt, with the charred flesh hanging down in black streamers. He pulled him up to the stanchion and then, as the flames consumed those below, he and Max stepped from head to head to safety, leaving behind them 'a terrible picture. More than 200 human beings, charred and burned, were melted together in one revolting lump.'

By the time Mehringer rescued himself and his friend Max, more than three thousand people had been burned to death on the *Cap Arcona*, many of them trapped below in the 'banana locker', others overcome by the flames and smoke in the ship's great lounges, which before the war had been described to the prospective first-class passenger as 'completely fireproof'.[4] Some of the prisoners had been so emaciated after months in Neuengamme that they had been able to squeeze their way into the portholes. But they hadn't quite made it through in time. Now they sprawled there grotesquely, the upper halves of their bodies apparently untouched but the bottom halves totally burned to a cinder.

Russian prisoner Vassili Bukreyev was one of those who managed to escape through the porthole nearest him and drop into the sea, where he met his fellow prisoner Geschonneck. But the two of them soon changed their minds about swimming for the shore, which was clearly visible. For already they could hear the single dry cracks of rifles and the hiss of machine-pistols and guessed what was happening. The many small boats hurrying towards the sinking, burning ships were coming not to rescue the inmates fortunate enough to have escaped from the disaster, *but to shoot them* as they paddled and swam frantically for safety.

Watching from the shore a 15-year-old boy, Gerhard Schnoor, could see the sinking, burning ships quite clearly, and the hundreds of heads – 'a sea of heads', he called them later – of those attempting frantically to save themselves. He saw too the fleet of little boats heading out into the bay, but they weren't there to help the prisoners. For, as he could hear plainly, 'Only German soldiers are coming on board!' an officer called to the shipwrecked men through a loud-speaker. Then 'the Germans struck at those who were clinging to the sides of the boats, striking their hands and throwing them back into the water mercilessly'. But it didn't end there. As more and more of the swimmers tried to save themselves by clinging to the boats, 'the Germans started to fire. They shot at the people in the water, too. Silently those hit sank beneath the waves.'

Bogdan Suchowiak, a Pole, clad only in a German Army shirt, was one of those threatened with death as he approached a German naval cutter. Standing at the bows stood a young German officer, crying through a megaphone, 'Don't take any prisoners aboard! Only SS and

4 If Captain Bertram had operated the fire-control system which was possible from the bridge of the *Cap Arcona* – forty years later the stricken British ferry *The Herald of Free Enterprise* still did not possess the pre-war German system of bridge control – he might have been able to stop the fire. But Captain Bertram was already safely on dry land.

sailors!' Suchowiak was already exhausted by his long swim from the sinking Thielbek. He knew he could swim no more. This was the sentence of death for him. But he could speak fair German and he was clad in a German shirt. He decided he would pretend to be German.

Somehow he got aboard and discovered there were other Poles and Russians in the group of shivering, exhausted survivors. Obviously the crew had paid little heed to the young officer's orders. Still Suchowiak was taking no chances. He pulled off the shirt, huddled himself in blankets, and feigned sleep in one of the crowded cabins.

But his stay on board didn't last long. One of his former concentration camp 'comrades' at Neuengamme, a German criminal, cried out to a passing sailor, 'Hey, there are foreigners aboard!'

Swiftly Suchowiak and a Czech fellow prisoner named Koubek were forced on deck at bayonet point. The sailor behind the Pole gave him a hefty kick in the rear and roared, 'Over the side quick!'

Through the thin, cold rain which had now commenced falling, the Pole could see the coast was quite close. He stood a chance of making it. It was better to try than be stabbed to death. He went over into the water once more. A few minutes later he felt sand underneath his feet. He had reached a sandbank, some 100 metres from the shore. He slumped down exhausted in the water.

'I have triumphed!' he told himself joyously. 'I have saved my life. Now the war is behind me, the September campaign [he had fought in the Polish Army in September 1939], my time as a prisoner of war and the 37 months I spent in a concentration camp!'

Exhausted but happy he struggled the last 100 metres to the shore, only to be met by the harsh command in a boyish voice, 'Bandit, get down or I'll shoot!' He looked up, frightened out of his wits, and was faced by 'boy soldiers': 16-year-old recruits dressed in the uniform of the German Navy, armed to the teeth.

The Pole and another fifteen survivors who had followed him to the beach were forced to lie full-length on the wet sand, until after half an hour the 'boy soldiers' ordered them to rise, put their hands in the air and start marching. 'They were very nervous, kept shouting orders all the time and striking us with the butts of their rifles.' The fifteen nearly naked men wondered if they were going to be shot; the boys seemed capable of anything.

But instead of shooting them, the 'boy soldiers' led them into a hut filled with canvas. The Pole wrapped himself up in a piece to keep warm, tying it around him so that it looked like a toga, while all around him his comrades in misery moaned with the pain of their wounds and burns.

After a long time they were ordered out and into a waiting naval truck. Again Suchowiak though he was going to be taken away to be executed; the boys looked very grim and determined. But as the truck ran into scattered small-arms fire, with in the distance a machine-gun rattling, it stopped and they were ordered to get out. To his surprise, standing in the middle of a group of German officers, with a German major saluting him, was an English captain! He was saved.

The Pole gathered the last of his strength to make the first speech in English he had ever made in his life. He went up to the English officer, clad in his 'Roman toga', and said hesitantly, 'You have brought us freedom. We thank you.'

The English officer looked down at the bedraggled, comic Pole and barked, 'Shut up!'

The 'Shipping Strike' attack – the result of a genuine mistake of identification – was the greatest marine disaster in history, greater even than the loss of the *Titanic*. Of the ten thousand prisoners on board the prison hulks, some 7,500 were killed by the RAF pilots, who didn't know till forty years later that they had slaughtered their own allies. On the same day twenty-two other German ships, submarines, destroyers, tankers, etc., were also destroyed in the Baltic, with no records of how many were lost. It was a great unwanted tragedy on this day of Allied victory.

II

The German delegation came in a grey Mercedes. As they stepped out of the vehicle they seemed to present a perfect caricature of the Nazi officer, complete with gleaming jackboots, long belted coats that came to their ankles, and a general air of pent-up, hard-faced defiance.

At 11.30 precisely they strode across the damp heather to where Montgomery's two staff officers were waiting for them. The doomed men – for only one of them would survive the next few weeks – strode through the tents, past a half-concealed self-propelled gun, to Montgomery's office caravan.

There they stood to attention under the flag and waited while the Canadian Lieutenant-Colonel Warren surveyed them, thinking that General Kinsel, soon to kill himself and his mistress, was 'a magnificent-looking officer ... complete with monocle – a real professional Prussian'. Montgomery let them wait. To Warren it seemed like an age, though in reality it could only have been five minutes.

Finally he appeared at the door of the caravan, hands behind his back. Very slowly he came down the five steps to the ground, while the Germans saluted woodenly. He savoured every minute of it. Casually, almost sloppily, Montgomery saluted back and the Germans could drop their arms at last.

His piercing blue eyes looked at von Friedeburg, who was on the verge of tears as he would be all the time he was at Montgomery's HQ, and bellowed in a sharp voice, 'Who are you?'

The 'General-Admiral' snapped back, '*Generaladmiral* von Friedeburg, Commander-in-Chief, the German Navy, sir!'

Montgomery was as cruel as he had been as a young cadet at Sandhurst when he had been nearly dismissed for toasting another cadet's bare bottom over an open fire. 'As quick as a flash and in a loud voice,' as Colonel Warren recalled many years afterwards, 'he shouted back, "I have never heard of you."'

He turned to the next German, Major Friedl, whom Warren thought had 'the cruellest face of any man I have seen', and asked the same question.

Friedl replied in the stiff German fashion with a slight bow from the waist, 'Major Friedl.'

Montgomery pretended rage. 'Major! How dare you bring a major into my Headquarters?'

Montgomery was having his revenge for Dunkirk. Standing next to Dawnay, the Canadian Warren whispered that the 'Chief' was putting up a pretty good act. Dawnay whispered back, 'Shut up, you son of a bitch, he has been rehearsing this all his life!'

So he had. Now he was trying to impose his will upon the Germans. He knew he didn't have the troops to continue the campaign into Denmark and Norway. He wanted the surrender and he wanted it quickly, whether the Americans liked it or not.

'What do you want?' he snapped now.

Von Friedeburg, eyes watery again, offered the surrender to the British of all the German troops fighting the Russians in Mecklenburg on the other side of the Elbe. He meant the Army of the Vistula. 'Certainly not!' Montgomery answered. 'The armies concerned are fighting the Russians. If they surrender to anybody it must be to the Russians. Nothing to do with me.'

While his interpreter, Colonel Ewart, translated, Montgomery's mind raced. He knew he must not be too hard on the Germans. They had to be offered the carrot as well as the stick. So he added that he would 'naturally take prisoner all German soldiers who came in to my area with their hands up'. Now he jumped in with both feet and told the crestfallen Germans what *he* wanted.

It was a lot.

He wanted the surrender '*to me* [of] all German forces on my western and northern flanks. These are to include the following. All forces in West Holland. All forces in Friesland, including the Frisian Islands and Heligoland. All forces in Holstein. All forces in Denmark.' In essence, Montgomery wanted the surrender of all Doenitz's command, though he wasn't including the Vistula Army forces in this total surrender.

The delegation refused 'in anger'. They pleaded that they needed to concern themselves with the civilian population to the east. They would suffer under the Russians.

The plight of German civilians cut no ice with Montgomery. He said, 'Do you remember a little town in England called Coventry, which six years ago was blown off the face of the earth by your bombers? The people who took the brunt of it were women, children and old men. Your women and children get no sympathy from me.' Strangely enough it was the same argument that 'Slim Jim' Gavin had used to General von Tippelskirch the day before. Then Montgomery proceeded to tongue-lash the white-faced Germans about the concentration camps, especially Belsen which he had visited.

By now Montgomery knew his brutal, even cruel tactics were succeeding. Von Friedeburg's bottom lip was trembling again and, as he explained to his joyful staff later, 'By this time I reckoned that I would have not much difficulty in getting them to accept my demands ... But I thought that an interval for lunch might be desirable so that they could reflect on what I had said.'

Again Montgomery was calculating. Taking Dawnay and Warren to one side, he told them to give the Boche the best lunch they could find, adding that they should be given all the drink they wanted. Teetotaller Montgomery knew well the effect of drink on emotionally upset human beings. The Germans were being set up even more.

Very swiftly a first-class meal was produced from whatever Compo rations were at hand, accompanied by a bottle of red wine and, more importantly, a bottle of Cognac. One of Montgomery's officers who could speak German was quickly disguised as a mess sergeant – he was fitted into the over-large white jacket of the real mess sergeant by means of carefully concealed safety-pins – and was sent into the Germans to apologise for the poor food. He explained that the day's rations had not yet been brought up; the Germans had been fed on leavings.

One of the delegation responded by saying, in surprise, 'We have not eaten food like this for months.'

The 'mess sergeant' shot back swiftly, 'Our private soldiers won't touch this muck!'

While the great set-up continued even at lunch, Montgomery prepared to conduct his own part in the 'squeeze'. He ordered two maps to be prepared, giving details of the front this day. While the two colonels and Ewart the interpreter should be armed, though concealing their weapons, he would personally 'brief' the Germans on the military situation. Then, after the Germans had had 'a really good whack' at the coffee and Cognac after lunch, they were led to the slaughter.

Briskly he put to them three points:

You must surrender to me *unconditionally* all the German forces in Holland, in Friesland, including the Frisian Islands, in Schleswig-Holstein and in Denmark. *Two:* Once you have done that, I shall be prepared to discuss with you the implications of that surrender – that is how we shall dispose our forces, our occupation and so on. Accept Point One and discuss Two. *Three:* If you don't agree to Number One, I shall go on with the war and will be delighted to do so and all your soldiers and civilians will be killed!

The last part smacked of child's talk the way Montgomery said it with such obvious relish, but it had the effect he sought. The Germans blanched. Now Montgomery piled on the agony. 'I wonder if any of you know the battle situation on the Western Front?'

Numbly they shook their heads. Montgomery briefed them, telling the Germans that he had tremendous strength and sufficient aircraft to fly ten thousand bombers day or night – and all of the Germans who had lived with constant air-raids for two years now knew what that meant. Montgomery could and *would* bomb their remaining cities of the north into ruins if they didn't agree to his harsh terms.

Von Friedeburg, who had already broken down and sobbed at lunch, said in a low voice, 'We came here entirely for the purpose of asking you to accept the surrender of our armies on your eastern flank. And we have been given powers to agree to that only. We have not the power to agree to your demands. Two of us will go back and two will remain until we return.'

Montgomery nodded his agreement curtly and returned to his caravan to let the Germans get on with their arrangements. He was not interested in them basically. They were merely minor actors in a great drama and they had now played their part. His performance had, he was confident, completely overawed them. He could see that from their pale, shaken faces. They had lost the war and they knew it. Now there was no hope for Germany. They would return to Flensburg, he was quite sure, and recommend surrender on *his* terms.

As he sat down in his caravan, still decorated with the picture of his old, now long-dead opponent, the 'Desert Fox', Field Marshal Rommel, Montgomery must have realised the die was cast. He had gone ahead without prompting from his staff. He had made the decisions without advice from the War Office in London or from the redoubtable Churchill himself. Nor had he consulted Eisenhower, though now his staff was telephoning Eisenhower's Chief of Intelligence, Scottish Brigadier Ken Strong, to let him know what was going on.

Of course, Montgomery must have realised he was taking a great risk by talking surrender terms on a major scale without reference to the Russians. If his negotiations and decisions didn't meet Eisenhower's approval because the latter thought they might offend the Russian ally, he might well be, in his own often-used phrase, 'for it'. Only the week before in Italy there had been a tremendous fuss and outcry because 'Alex' (Field Marshal Alexander) had approved a similar partial surrender of the German forces there without consulting the Russians first. Eisenhower was now so powerful that he could ruin the rest of Montgomery's career if he wanted to. Montgomery was under no illusion on that score.

Yet if he pulled off this unexpected surrender on his front he would achieve a great triumph for British arms, and overshadow the fact that his army had been relegated to a side-show through Bradley's machinations. It was a risk worth taking.

Down at his new HQ in Wiesbaden, Bradley was still obsessed with his silly, mythical 'Southern Redoubt'. 'We may be fighting *one month* from now and we may be fighting *a year* from now,' Bradley's ADC had quoted him saying on 24 April 1945. Meanwhile Montgomery was actually bringing about the surrender of all German troops in the North commanded by the new 'Führer', Doenitz. Surely the rest of Germany's armies in the south would follow suit immediately and then total victory would be *his*.

As the two Germans were escorted back to Lueneburg, and from thence to their own lines, Montgomery personally started to draft a surrender document. It would be brief and allow of no misunderstandings. When it was finished Montgomery would hand it to his ADC for typing.

Thereafter he would take a bath – he had a marble one in his sleeping caravan – and turn in. Outside his guards would see the light go out promptly at 9.30. It was the time he always put out his lights on the eve of his most decisive battles . . .

III

Eisenhower, the Supreme Commander, liked to regard himself as the 'common man'. He was fond of making comparisons between his present elevated status and his humble beginnings in Abilene in rural Kansas. Now for years he had been mixing with the great and near-great. Since 1942 when he had emerged into the limelight from the obscurity of a two-star general, he had learned to deal with all kinds of prima donnas, military and civilian alike – Patton, Montgomery, Brooke, de Gaulle, Churchill, etc.

Despite his fiery temper, he had exercised great personal restraint, based on what he believed was his ability to see the 'other guy's' point of view. He did not dismiss de Gaulle out of hand as a would-be dictator. Nor did he see Churchill as an old-fashioned imperialist whose main aim was to save the British Empire.

It was the same with the Russians. He did not share the almost paranoid attitude to them of not only Churchill but also members of his command – such as 'Georgie' Patton, the commander of his 3rd Army, who was already advocating 'a shooting war' with them. 'I believe that Germany should not be destroyed, 'Ole Blood an' Guts' was already declaring, 'but rather should be rebuilt as a buffer against the real danger, *which is Russia and its Bolshevism!*'

To Eisenhower, the Russians were a people who bore 'a marked similarity to what we call an average American'. In addition these people who, so Eisenhower believed, had never been tainted by the stigma of colonialism like the other European powers,[5] would obviously emerge as the other post-war superpower. It was right and just, therefore, that America should learn to co-operate with the Soviet Union. There had to be no deception and no double-dealing. The Russians had to know *exactly* what was going on in North Germany!

As soon as Strong told him what Montgomery was about, Eisenhower immediately informed the Russian liaison officer to SHAEF, General Susloparoff (some of Eisenhower's anti-Russian staff thought of him as a spy). He also laid down instructions that, if a general surrender did

---

5 Eisenhower, whose staple literature was westerns, had obviously not read about Russia's nineteenth century policy of imperial expansion – at the expense of her southern and eastern neighbours.

result from the Montgomery negotiations, he would arrange 'for a more formal and ceremonial surrender with the Russian representatives present'.

Eisenhower was leaning over backwards to accommodate the Russians, and Montgomery was treading on dangerous ground if he exceeded the Supreme Commander's guidelines for the talks. They were that Montgomery had to refuse the surrender of German armies facing the Russians, though 'individual soldiers of these Armies surrendering would be accepted as prisoners of war'.

On the surface, however, there appeared to be no tension between the Anglo-Americans and their ally, Russia. Eisenhower's fears of angering them seemed groundless. Even as Montgomery slept in his caravan, his Signals Corps personnel were tapping out his nightly report to the War Office in London. It would read, when deciphered 'We are now in contact with the Russians [from Domitz to Wismar on the eastern flank] and everything is very friendly and it has been agreed that we remain in the positions we now hold.'

The reality was different as, for the first time in four years of war, the Americans met 'Uncle Joe's boys' in the shape of the advanced guard of Rokossovsky's 2nd Belorussian Front. From the highest to the lowest ranks they would be surprised, shocked, angered – and invariably disillusioned – with these representatives of the new super-power which, together with America, would shape the future of the post-war world.

That day young First Lieutenant Knowlton, who had been sent out by Ridgway to look for the Russians, found them. He bumped into a 'military procession' which was beyond the West Point recent graduate's wildest dreams. It was not an army convoy; it was a *horde* on the march!

There were farm wagons, cabs, rusty old field pieces, German vans, bikes, even wheelbarrows. And with the advancing Russians in their earth-coloured blouses and baggy breeches, there were women and children and herds of cattle and goats. To Knowlton, the correct regular Army officer, this collection of yelling, waving Russian soldiers was more like a great nomadic caravan.

The drinking started immediately. The 'Russkies', as Knowlton's astonished tankers called them, swarmed drunkenly all over their vehicles. One stumbled over an American machine-gun and slugs ripped the earth all about the Russian colonel in charge of the ragged, shaven-headed soldiers. His men laughed uproariously and slapped each other on the back.

The Colonel pointed an imperious finger at a large house nearby. Immediately half a dozen Cossacks, with their black fur hats tilted rakishly to one side, swung on to their horses, galloped off and broke into the place. There were screams, a splintering of wood, glass shattered. Two elderly Germans shot through the front door. A boy was carried out by a Cossack, who was holding the screaming child by the seat of his pants. With a shrug he tossed the little German over a hedge, then they rode off yelling and hooting like a bunch of Mexican *banditos*.

Knowlton gave up. He decided it was safer to leave his men and have a drink with the Colonel. As he did so, he flung a glance at the amazing scene over his shoulder. A Russian major was poking his head through the assistant gunner's seat in one of his armoured cars. He was laughing drunkenly. Over one arm he had a towel just like a barber back home. With his free hand, which shook badly, he was attempting to shave one of Knowlton's badly frightened men with an open straight razor. Knowlton looked away hastily ...

General Gavin was not impressed either when he made his first visit to the Red Army. All the way to the Russian commander's command post he met drunken soldiers. It struck him that as they didn't recognise his uniform he might have a problem on his hands.

But he arrived at the Russian HQ without problems until he was faced by two guards with Tommy-guns slung across their chests, who looked at him menacingly. They let him through, however, and he met the Russian divisional commander. Over their maps they discussed the boundaries between their two divisions and Gavin was reminded that 'this must have been like what it was in 1939 when the Russians met the German army in Poland. I suppose I thought along these lines because the Russians acted distrustful as if we were combat enemies.'

His boss Ridgway felt the same. He made his first contacts with the Russians that afternoon too, and found them 'suspicious, stubborn, ill-mannered'. It was his duty to entertain them, and he selected as his first guest General Smirnov, who commanded one of the three Russian corps opposite his own. Smirnov, a short, stocky fellow, was all right. But with him he brought:

[a] great hulking giant of an officer, a mountain of a man about six feet four inches high and broad in proportion, whose only social function, so far as I could tell, was to try to intimidate me. He never smiled, never shook hands, but stood by the side of his

commander, glowering at me – one of the most formidable-looking creatures physically I have ever seen. I could not help but think what an excellent target he would make, seen over the sights of my Springfield [Ridgway, in addition to his grenade, always carried a First World War vintage Springfield rifle with him], though, of course, I was careful not to let the feeling be reflected in my manner.

Privately, however, Ridgway thought that he would like to hang on to what he called the 'Wismar cushion', and the area around the port captured by the British 6th Airborne and the American 7th Armored Division. 'We took it by force of arms' and 'a soldier always hates to give up land he has conquered, even to an ally'.

Ridgway knew that in due course his 'Wismar cushion' would have to be given to the Russians because it belonged to the Soviet Zone of Occupation. But on 3 May 1945 the area still belonged to the Allies, and some of them, namely the Red Devils of Ridgway's 6th Airborne, were determined to hang on to what they had fought for, if necessary by force.

That evening, with total victory just round the corner, the paras celebrated. Wismar, which the day before had seemed dead, was now full of drunken displaced persons and hundreds of ragged *Wehrmacht* soldiers, wondering how and to whom they were going to surrender. In the main square were hanging the bodies of half a dozen German civilians. They had belonged to the Werewolf Movement and had fired on British troops. Now, where once jolly brass bands had played, they swayed in the wind, a grim reminder that all further resistance was senseless.

Not that the happy paras were inclined to any further violence. They had seen enough of war – Normandy, the Ardennes, the Rhine and now this last battle for northern Germany. The paras were more interested in the 'frauwleins'. '*We'd rather fuck than fight!*', they chortled as they staggered off, drinking looted schnapps, in search of 'the other'.

They were not alone in their desire for the pleasures of the flesh. Russian soldiers, who had left their own lines, were looking for them, too. Some time that night, a score of drunken Russian soldiers staggered to the entrance of the port's main hospital, which was occupied by the paras. Pushing by the sentry at the gate, they cried in broken German '*Frau komm 'raus!*'[6]

The sentry realised that the Russians must have found out that the

6 'Women come out!'

hospital sheltered a large number of German Red Cross sisters and female German Army auxiliaries, the 'officers' field mattresses', as the ordinary German soldier called them crudely. 'There are no women here!' the sentry said.

The leading Russian thrust his face closer to that of the sentry. The para pulled back a pace. 'Here – women!' he growled in barely intelligible German. 'We want, *da?*'

Now other men of the 7th Parachute Battalion, who had been enjoying themselves with some of the more willing German nurses, poked their heads from the upper windows of the hospital buildings. The Russians spotted them and made threatening gestures with their round-barrelled Tommy-guns, swaying wildly as they did so – later the officers of the Seventh would find out that the Russians had been drinking a potent mixture of vodka and V-1 fuel! Again they made their drunken demand, '*Frau komm 'raus!*'

A half-naked para on the second floor shouted down, 'They're our girls – bugger off!'

The Russians didn't understand the words, but they did understand the para's threatening gesture. Suddenly a shot rang out. It was followed almost immediately by the rattle of a British sten-gun. The Russians scattered wildly. Shooting broke out on all sides. Scarlet flashes stabbed the darkness. Someone fell heavily. There was a yell of pain. In minutes it was all over and the Russians retired to their own lines. Behind them they left six of their number stretched out silent and motionless on the cobbles of the courtyard below . . .

One shooting war was about to end and another to commence. That first drunken, purposeless skirmish over German women had been the first shots fired in the new global conflict between the two great superpowers that would spread to all continents and embrace all races and colours. It would involve West and East in long, protracted all-out wars in Korea and Vietnam, and in obscure little battles in remote countries whose very names meant little to the great mass of people in the West – Angola, Cambodia and the like. It was a war that goes on right into our own time . . .

4

'Now togedder, we fight the Russians!'

I

The Canadian, Lieutenant-Colonel Warren was worried.

The night before he had escorted Admiral von Friedeburg and the cruel-looking Major Friedl back to the German lines just beyond the small town of Quickborn, some 9 miles north of Hamburg. There they had been met by two German tanks commanded by a tough-looking officer with one arm. Warren hadn't liked the look of the tanks or the officer one bit. He had commanded in a loud voice to his escort, 'Get in your jeeps, turn around and let's get the hell out of here as quickly as we can!' But before they had fled, they had arranged with von Friedeburg to meet at the same spot at 1400 hours the next day. Warren had stated specifically that he would wait for two hours only. If the Germans hadn't come back by then, he would assume they had turned down his chief's proposals and the war could go on.

Now Warren and his escort from the 11th Hussars, plus the inter-preter Colonel Ewart, waited anxiously for the appearance of the Germans. But the *Kielerstrasse* to their front, running into the woods which were the German front line, remained stubbornly empty. It seemed as if the war had gone to sleep and the world was empty.

Two o'clock came on this overcast, blustery Friday and still no sign of them. The Canadian Colonel started to frown. Were they coming or weren't they? Warren decided to wait a little longer. For he knew 'the Chief' was certain the Germans would return with an offer of surrender. As the latter had explained to Brooke at the War Office:

the forces to surrender will total over one million men . . . there are four hundred thousand Russian prisoners of war in Schleswig-Holstein . . . and there has been an influx of two million civilians . . . the food situation in the area is such that there will be nothing for them to eat in about ten days time . . . It is almost certain that Keitel will

240

surrender tomorrow because it is not possible to get the German soldiers to fight any more and they cannot cope with the frightful civil problem.

Another hour passed in tense, nervous anticipation. And another . . . Warren was really desperate now. Suddenly the afternoon stillness was broken by the sound of motor-car engines at low gear. Captain Horsford of the 11th Hussars's No. 4 Troop looked at the Canadian. Warren nodded.

The young 'Cherrypicker' moved forward as the big squat Mercedes with the canvas hood topped the rise to their front and began coming towards them slowly on the cobbled country road. It was the Germans all right, over two hours late admittedly, but it was the surrender party. Hurriedly someone called Montgomery's HQ on the other side of the Elbe, where he had just called a news conference for his favourite correspondents. He had barely finished telling them that he had shown the Germans his battle map. 'It was a great shock for them. They were amazed and upset. The General-Admiral broke down and cried. He burst into tears and he wept all through his lunch.'

He beamed at them, Canadian, British, Australian, and said perkily, 'The *General-Admiral*' – he dearly loved that strange title – 'will be back about five. Ha! He is back. He was to come back with the doings. Now we shall see what the form is!'

As Montgomery had confidently expected all along, they *had* brought the 'doings' with them, and 'the form' was – *surrender!*

'No doubt that if the piece of paper is signed,' he told the correspondents before leaving, 'forces to be surrendered total over a million chaps. *Good egg!* And with that schoolboy's expression of another age, he was gone . . .

It was six o'clock and getting dark. It was raining and cold. Overhead fighter-planes wheeled and droned – just in case. For now the Germans knew the location of Montgomery's HQ. But the enemy had had enough. There would be no last-minute, fanatical attempt to kill the soldier who had brought them to their knees.

Montgomery emerged from his caravan. He was dressed as informally as ever – duffle coat and black beret. One hand was thrust deep in his pocket and in the other he held the 'piece of paper' on which the fate of so many millions depended. He vanished into the brown army tent with its simple wooden trestle table covered with a grey army blanket upon which the surrender would be signed.

Then the Germans came, making their way a little awkwardly on the springy, pot-holed heather to the slight incline on which the tent

241

stood. Admiral von Friedeburg, escorted by two British officers, led the procession. He had already told Montgomery privately a few moments before that he had come to sign the surrender document. Behind him came General Kinzel, Admiral Wagner, Major Friedl and a new German delegate, Colonel Pollek. The only splash of colour in the whole sombre scene was the bright scarlet of Kinzel's broad general staff officer's lapels. They halted on the white line – even now, this being the British Army, the usual 'bull' could not be dispensed with[1] – and waited.

The minutes ticked by. Then they were all ushered into the tent and, after saluting Montgomery, they seated themselves. One of them took out a cigarette and lit it to calm his nerves. Montgomery shot him a sharp glance. He put it out swiftly.

Now Montgomery read out the 'Instrument of Surrender' which he had prepared. It was very simple: 'The German Command agrees to the surrender of all German armed forces in Holland, in Northwest Germany including the Frisian Islands and Heligoland and all other islands, in Schleswig-Holstein and in Denmark to the C-in-C 21 Army Group.'

The surrender was to be a personal triumph for the little man, now wearing simple tortoiseshell reading spectacles on his sharp, foxy nose. For he was ordering the Germans to *surrender to him, Montgomery, personally*! Not to Eisenhower's SHAEF or to the newly formed United Nations. He had beaten the Americans after all. He would enjoy the personal kudos of final victory over the Germans in what he liked to call 'the Second German War'.[2]

Finally Montgomery stopped reading. He looked up and commanded, 'The German delegation will now sign. They will sign in order of seniority.' For British war correspondent R. Thompson who was present his words were 'like hammer-blows on an anvil, each one dropping into the minds of us all indelibly and into the minds of the Germans like pins of fire in raw wounds'.

'General-Admiral von Friedeburg first,' Montgomery ordered.

The Admiral rose and took the army-issue wooden pen, which Montgomery commented could 'have been bought in any post office for twopence'. He signed rapidly, as if he wanted to get the whole miserable business over with once and for all. He would be dead by his own hand before the month was out.

---

1 In the British Army in the Second World War the ordinary soldier quipped, 'If it moves, salute it. If it doesn't, paint it white!'
2 Montgomery made it such a personal triumph that he refused to hand over the surrender document as Eisenhower ordered him to do. Instead he kept it for himself and Churchill had to defend his right to do so in the House of Commons. In 1968, after his home was burgled, Montgomery gave it to the Imperial War Museum.

Kinzel followed and did the same. He, too, would commit suicide this summer of defeat, shooting himself and his mistress.

'Major Freide,' Montgomery called, mispronouncing the young officer's name, 'will sign last.' The man with the cruel face did so. He would be dead in a motor accident within the month. In truth, they were all doomed men.

Montgomery paused, then, raising his voice above the whirr of the newsreel cameras, he said firmly, 'Now I will sign on behalf of the Supreme Allied Commander, General Eisenhower.'

Bending down, his lips set and hard, he signed and added the date. It was 4 May, but he wrote the 5th. Seeing his mistake, he crossed out the original, initialled the erasure 'BLM' and wrote '4 May 1945, 1830 Hrs'. He sighed faintly and sat back in his chair, saying, 'That concludes the formal surrender.' The erasure was the only hitch in the procee-dings which had sealed the fate of a beaten Germany.

They filed out and Montgomery called for the Army photographer who had snapped the German group as they approached the tent a few minutes before.

'Did you get that picture – under the Union Jack?' he demanded, pointing to the flag flapping above his head.[3]

The photographer said he had.

'Good, good,' Montgomery said happily. 'An historic picture.'

A little while later Montgomery saw a crestfallen von Friedenburg for the last time in his caravan. The latter asked what the status of the German High Command at Flensburg would be now. After all they were still conducting operations against the Americans and Russians.

Montgomery was in a good mood. He cracked one of his rare jokes. He informed von Friedeburg that, with effect from 0800 hours the next day, the German High Command would be his prisoners. 'And I cannot allow you to conduct operations against the Russians and Americans after that time.'

Von Friedeburg was in no mood for jokes. He remained glum and, as Montgomery related with a chuckle afterwards, 'I do not think the German delegation saw the humour of the situation.'

For most of Montgomery's commanders the news of the ceasefire came in the dry, unemotional officialese of the signal from General Belchem, Montgomery's Chief of Administration:

3 The flag now rests in a church in Bath.

From: Exfor Main.
To: For Action: First Cdn Army: Second Brit Army L of C: GHQ AATPS 79 Armd Div:
Exfor Rear.
For Infm: Second TAF; Exfor TAC: 22 Liaison HQ

GO 411 Secret: all offensive ops will cease from receipt of this signal. Orders will be
given all tps to cease fire 0800 hrs tomorrow saturday 5 may full terms of local German
surrender arranged today for 21 Army Gp front follow, emphasize these provision
apply solely 21 Army Gp and are for the moment excl. of Dunkirk. [4]
In cipher if liable to interception.

ACK
DOP
Emergency
R.M. Belchem

Here and there, while this message was being sent, there was still
sporadic fighting on the British Army's front. Major Tonkin of the
SAS's D Squadron was preceeding cautiously in the direction of Kiel.
He knew that virtually all resistance had ceased, but he had only one
hundred men under his command in his column of jeeps, each
armed with twin machine-guns at the front like a First World War
vintage fighter-plane, and there were armed Germans everywhere.

Up front his sergeant-major, named Bennett, was driving along a
canal bank when he spotted a large barge pulling away from the quay.
A fluent German speaker, Sergeant Ridler, was whistled up. He asked
a passer-by what was in the barge. The answer he received had the SAS
troopers dashing for their jeeps. Angrily they fired a burst from the
twin Vickers right across the barge's bows.

A few minutes later the ship returned and started unloading several
hundred concentration camp inmates of various nationalities. With
tears streaming down their emaciated faces, they told the tough SAS
men that they were the fourth bunch of prisoners destined for a
watery grave that day. The Germans had planned to sink them in the
middle of the canal – as they had done the other unfortunates.

Tonkin, although his men were stretched to the limit in the middle
of the hostile city, sent off hasty patrols to liberate other prisoners in
small concentration camps at Ochtumsand and Neumunster. The SAS
troopers were in an ugly mood and it was recorded in the unit history
that 'there were incidents' and 'some SS guards got hurt' . . .

Behind the British line at Celle there were still casualties being

---

4 Dunkirk, from which the British had fled five years before, was still in German hands and surrounded by a Czech brigade.

brought to the 'Max Factors' to have their terrible facial injuries temporarily repaired before they were evacuated to 'Blighty' for further treatment. For the last eleven months the young nurses of the hospital had seen some terrible sights. How often in those months had they stood tensely by while Lieutenant-Colonel Harding, their boss, had done a running commentary: 'Stomach here . . . Quarter of morphia, Sister. Straight away! . . . Two pints of blood . . . Gunshot, mortar blast mines, incendiaries. Limbs, eyes, abdomen . . .' And so the litany of dread went on, while the waiting doctors chewed their pencils and wondered who of these desperately wounded men would be given priority.

The nurses had learned to reach into the throats of men shot in the face to pull out the fragments of broken bone and teeth, and then sew the end of the man's tongue to his tunic so that he couldn't swallow it. They'd learned to recognise the ominous sucking noise of a man wounded in the chest and to prop him in the upright position straight away. They had learned, too, to sniff dirty field dressings for the telltale sweet stink of gangrene. They had learned that, if a foot was cold in a man, shot through the popliteal vein, there was no time to be lost – 'cut it off!'

But now, on this last day of action at No. 5 Maxillo-Facial Unit – 'the Max Factors' – the catering officer decided that the grievously hurt needed a treat. He sent up a case of captured German champagne. So they celebrated – these men who might spend years in the future having their faces repaired – drinking champagne even if it meant slobbering it through a straw wedged in a splinted jaw.

One patient, however, was put out. He was the one with a nasal tube. He found no elation in the draft the happy nurses poured down his funnel – only a bad case of wind!

Right to the very end, soldiers continued to be killed in action.

As the Guards Armoured Division consolidated their hold on the Upper Elbe, taking forty prisoners that day, they were just about to move into the small village of Hechthausen when a forward observer, Captain R. Wheaton of the West Somerset Yeomanry, went over a hidden mine in his vehicle. He and his whole crew were killed instantly.

Not far away the Jocks of the 51st Highland Division had, at the time Captain Wheaton and his men were killed, just fought a stiff fight for the village of Kuhstedt against their old opponents of the 15th Panzer

245

Division. Now, as war correspondent R. Thompson recorded on a self-imposed mission to find the last British unit still in contact with the enemy, they were still manning their weapons in their foxholes, waiting 'dourly'.

Just at that moment a crowd of shabby German soldiers started to move towards their lines. But they didn't want to fight; they wanted to surrender and no one knew quite what to do about it 'Oh, Lord!' the company commander exclaimed, 'You can't really be prisoners now!'

But for the most part the soldiers just held their positions. Here and there units celebrated. In Bremen the men of the 52nd Lowland Division got drunk and fired off huge quantities of live ammunition, much to the fear of the local populace and fellow soldiers on the receiving end of British mortar bombs. It was later rumoured in the division that thirteen soldiers disappeared that night never to be found again. The Guards, too, fired a final *feu de joie* – 'Fire Plan Grand Finale' – a ten-minute bombardment with every available gun at an area of supposedly desolate marshland. It wasn't desolate, however, and the Guards did not stay long enough in the area to find out 'whether the effect was thought pretty at the receiving end'!

On the whole, though, the strain and fatigue of eleven months of campaigning and fighting was such that when the news finally reached the front it was greeted by a subdued reaction. There was almost a sense of anti-climax noted by most observers that day.

The war correspondents who went up front found that at this moment, the turning point of their lives for most of the men who had done the fighting, there were no cheers and few signs of emotion. For although only 45 per cent of Montgomery's army had actually heard a shot fired in anger in the campaign, they – the engineers, artillerymen, tankers and infantry – had suffered enormously.

That evening Colonel Martin Lindsay of the 'Gay Gordons' of the 51st Highland Division took stock. His battalion had taken part in thirty-two actions during the eleven-month campaign. The 'butcher's bill' had been 986 casualties, plus seventy-five officers, of whom rather more than a quarter had been killed in action or died of wounds. In essence, there had been a complete turnround of the battalion due to casualties. As the Colonel noted:

I don't believe that anybody can go through a campaign with such men as these and watch them killed one after another and know that their joyous personalities are now but blackened broken corpses tied up in a few feet of Army blanket under the damp earth – and remain quite the same. For my part, I felt that this had made a mark upon me that will never be effaced. It is as if some spring deep down inside me has run down.

It was the same everywhere as the survivors counted the cost of this last battle. As one soldier of the US 8th Infantry Division – 'the Golden Arrow' – on the other side of the Elbe told a correspondent from the *New York Times*, 'We've left too many of our guys behind to feel like raising hell.' Not far away at Plauen, combat medic Private Atwell heard the news casually from a comrade as he was munching ham sandwiches. 'Really *over*?' he queried, putting down his bread.

'Yeah, there'll be no more fighting,' his comrade repeated.

The two men relapsed into a moody silence. Atwell later recalled, 'I searched for some feeling, waited for it to develop. There was hardly any sensation at all. A moment later I was aware of an inward caving in, followed by a sore-throat feeling for all those who had been forced to give up their lives for this moment.'

Writing about these young British soldiers that year, the Australian war correspondent Alan Moorehead, who had followed the fortunes of the British soldier over five years and ten countries, felt that the youthful survivors knew that:

[the] thing they were doing was a clear and definite good, the best they could do. And at these moments there was a surpassing satisfaction, a sense of exactly and entirely fulfilling one's life, a sense of purity, the confused adolescent dream of greatness come true . . . Not all the cynicism, not all the ugliness and fatigue in the world will take that moment away from the people who experienced it. Five years of watching war have made me personally hate and loathe war, especially the childish wastage of it. But this thing – the brief ennoblement inside himself of the otherwise dreary and materialistic man – kept recurring again and again to the very end, and it refreshed and lighted the whole heroic and sordid story . . .

Corps Commander Brian Horrocks, whose 30th Corps had fought and suffered so much in the campaign, had often wondered how the war would end. 'When it came,' he recalled later, 'it could hardly have been more of an anti-climax. I happened to be sitting in the military equivalent of the smallest room when I heard a voice on the wireless saying, "All hostilities will cease at 0800 hours tomorrow morning 5th May."' It seemed a strange end to a war that had seen his meteoric rise from infantry battalion commander, commanding eight hundred men, to that of the command of a corps which, at times, consisted of one hundred thousand soldiers.

Further north at the former POW camp at Westertimke, one of Horrocks' divisional commanders, General Thomas – or 'von Thoma', as Horrocks preferred to call him – was planning his 43rd Division's attack on Bremerhaven the following morning with Brigadier Essame, whose brigade would execute the attack. There was a thunderous knocking on the door of his caravan. It was opened and there stood the tall, excited figure of the Brigade Major, W.J. Chalmers.

Essame and Thomas stared at him. As Brigadier Essame recalled afterwards, 'only an event of world-shaking moment could justify an interruption when the General was giving out his orders'.

'Sir!' the Brigade Major said, crouching in the low doorway of the caravan, 'The BBC have just announced the unconditional surrender of the German Forces opposing Field Marshal Montgomery in North West Europe.'

Thomas looked at the Major coldly. 'I take my orders from the Corps Commander and not the BBC', he snapped.

Chalmers disappeared swiftly and the briefing continued without comment.

Half an hour passed while the two generals examined their map of the front in detail with the aid of magnifying glasses, marking in positions through the marshes the troops would take and other details of tomorrow's attack. Outside the thunder of the permanent barrage had died away. Now the only sound was the low hum of the signals' section charging batteries for the Brigade HQ. Somehow Brigadier Essame, a veteran infantryman yet a man sensitive to mood and place, couldn't believe that the battle of the morrow would take place. Thomas, however, worked on the maps with the same energy as ever. His superior seemed confident that his division would fight tomorrow morning.

Again there was a knock on the caravan door. 'Come!' Thomas bellowed angrily.

It was Chalmers once more, this time armed with a signal message. 'A personal message to you, sir,' he announced, 'from the Corps Commander, timed 2115 hours, sir.'

Horrocks had hurriedly left that 'smallest room' and composed the signal himself. He wanted no further bloodshed on his corps' front.

'Read it!' Thomas snapped.

' "Germans surrender unconditionally at 1820 hours. Hostilities on all Second Army front will cease 0800 hours tomorrow 5th May. No, repeat, no advance beyond present front line without further orders from me." '

Without a word the horsey-looking General with the trim First World War moustache packed his papers and maps. Together with Brigadier Essame he walked in silence to his armoured car. To their front, where the Germans waited, all was darkness, save for an occasional flare sailing into the night sky. There would be no wild rejoicing in the lines of the 43rd Division this night. The infantry had fought too long and suffered too much. In the last eleven months the division had lost 12,483 men, killed and wounded: the population of one of those small Wessex towns from which most had come, vanished in one short year.

Just as Thomas was about to climb into his armoured car, he turned to Essame, standing there in the glowing darkness, and said, 'The troops have done us damn well!'

Brigadier Essame stiffened to attention. Thomas saluted and, standing upright, shoulders braced as if on parade, he was borne away, his eyes set on some distant object known only to him . . .

II

The night after that triumphant surrender ceremony, a cocky, cheerful Montgomery had told the assembled correspondents, 'It looks as if the British Empire's part in the German War in Western Europe is over . . . I was persuaded to drink some champagne at dinner tonight.' And then the teetotal Commander-in-Chief had gone off to his caravan, laughing.

Now Montgomery woke on this Saturday morning, 5 May, to find that, while Britain was indeed no longer fighting Germany in Europe, *America and Russia were!* Russian soldiers were still dying east of the Elbe. In Bavaria and Austria on their way to Czechoslovakia, Patton's 3rd Army was engaged in what the official historian called, 'a comic opera war carried on by men who wanted to surrender but seemingly had to fire a shot or two in the process'. For another thirty-six hours, while Montgomery's British and Canadians enjoyed their first days of peace, American divisions, such as the 1st Infantry – 'the Big Red One', as it was nicknamed – would continue fighting – and dying.

Lacking the kind of ruthlessness that Montgomery possessed, and his ability to impose his will on others, Eisenhower dithered. He allowed the surrender negotiations to continue a further three days. He personally, he announced, would not meet the Germans until they had signed the surrender document. He allowed the talks between the German delegation and the Allies to be carried out by two of his staff officers, his Chief of Staff Bedell Smith, an American, and his Scottish Chief of Intelligence, Ken Strong. Both were 'office soldiers', who had never heard a shot fired in anger throughout their military careers, and the Germans seemed to sense it. Doenitz, Keitel and Jodl continued to string them along, while at the front fighting men still continued to die and Eisenhower virtually hid in his office, smoking sixty cigarettes a day and reading paperback westerns.

Montgomery, being Montgomery, naturally enjoyed the spectacle of Eisenhower and the detested staff at SHAEF being made fools of by the Germans, while the world cried out for an end to the fighting and dying. He had bullied von Friedeburg into surrendering by threatening to start once again bombing of Germany's remaining cities and offensive ground operations; and the 'General-Admiral' had been able to see by the look on the little Englishman's sharp, boney face that he meant it. But Eisenhower would not even *see* the Germans.

Naturally Montgomery could have speeded up the process if he had wished. He had the power to order all German troops in northern Germany to be disarmed immediately. He knew too from his own liaison officers that Doenitz had given Colonel-General Jodl full authority to 'surrender everything to everybody'. All he would have needed to do was take over Doenitz's HQ at Flensburg – for he was sure the Germans wouldn't put up a fight; even Doenitz's beloved U-boat crews were now hopelessly demoralised – and the whole remaining governmental structure in Germany would collapse. Field Marshal Kesselring's last remaining resistance in Austria would end immediately.[5]

But Montgomery did not take that course. He wanted to see Eisenhower squirm, make a mess of things, as (in Montgomery's opinion) he had done so often in the past. So he contented himself with sending General Roberts and a brigade of his 11th Armoured Division to Doenitz's HQ in Flensburg. The little Divisional General's mission was to make clear to the Germans that 'in all local matters they were under orders from us pending the arrival of a special mission from SHAEF'.

That Saturday General Roberts' young interpreter, Lt Peter Heath, faced up to 'a portly, rather fishy-eyed old gentlemen', who was Keitel, and introduced his chief. The German staff gasped when they saw the youth of Heath's boss; they thought he was 'not tall enough, nor old enough, nor pompous enough' to be a general. However they soon accepted the fact and they were passed on to Colonel-General Jodl, who was told that the British needed a nearby Luftwaffe barracks to house the division's 131 Brigade under the command of Brigadier Churcher.

---

5 Kesselring was now in command of the southern half of Germany, but acted under Doenitz's orders.

Jodl, who had once directed the activities of millions of German troops on three continents, now got down to the business of shifting a couple of hundred German soldiers out of some huts so that the British could take them over. Later Heath was amused to find 'this trivial business was conducted with a tremendous display of maps, movement charts and timetables and all the panoply of a major military operation which perhaps he knew was to be his last'.

While this was going on Heath wandered through the corridors of Doenitz's HQ looking at the doors, each with a typewritten label pasted on it – *von Ribbentrop . . . Speer . . . von Krosigk . . .* and all the rest of the Nazi bosses who had once ruled an empire as big as that of the Romans. How had all these fetched up here? *And where was Himmler?*

That was the question which occupied the mind of perhaps the strangest Intelligence officer on Eisenhower's staff that week. He was Arthur Calder-Marshall, who had fought at Dunkirk in 1940 but was best known as a female impersonator. As 'Nurse Dugdale', he had starred in his own radio series before the war. Now, as a lieutenant-colonel on Eisenhower's staff, it was his task to find and arrest Himmler forthwith.

To the British of that time, there seemed nothing particularly incongruous about a well-known female impersonator, doubling as an Intelligence officer, being sent to an enemy headquarters to arrest the most wanted war criminal in the world. Later, though, Calder-Marshall did admit that he felt a strange twinge when he bumped into both Field Marshal Keitel and Colonel-General Jodl, both to be hanged at Nuremberg the following year, and as Regulations demanded saluted them. Keitel frowned and then, in response to 'Nurse Dugdale's' salute, the fishy-eyed Field Marshal raised the marshal's baton which had been given to him personally by the Führer!

On board the SS *Patria*, Doenitz's floating mess, Calder-Marshall felt a similar twinge when he was accompanied there by another Intelligence officer – 'a giggly don who looked as incongruous in uniform as I did'. When the immaculate, very professional *Wehrmacht* clicked their heels, bowed and saluted, he sensed 'a look of wonder and amazement . . . in their eyes, as if they were thinking: How on earth could we *possibly* have failed to win the war?'

Calder-Marshall, as we shall see, was not fated to capture the 'most wanted man on earth'. Himmler had already gone underground, to the relief of Admiral Doenitz, who was attempting to drag out the surrender negotiations, perhaps half hoping, as many at his HQ were, that the trouble predicted by Goebbels so confidently before his death would break out between this disparate coalition of West and East.

That day, as von Friedeburg protested to SHAEF that he was not empowered to surrender to Britain, the USA and Russia, Doenitz sent Jodl to Montgomery at Luneburg. The clever Chief of Staff told Montgomery that he was empowered to surrender everything to everybody. This caused an embarrassing situation, even for Montgomery, who revelled in Eisenhower's discomforture. Here was the new 'Führer' – Doenitz – empowering Jodl to surrender everything to Montgomery rather than to his superior. As Montgomery reported to London that Saturday, Jodl tried to 'make his point about surrender to the Russians'. Montgomery wouldn't have it, though it must have pleased and appealed to his somewhat malicious nature. Instead he sent off Jodl and his aide Major Oxenius to see Eisenhower and to plead their case there.[6]

Jodl left, bearing in his pocket an authorisation from Doenitz and written instructions which read:

Try once again to explain the reasons why we wish to make this separate surrender to the Americans. If you have no more success with Eisenhower than Friedeburg had, offer a simultaneous surrender on *all fronts* to be implemented in two phases. During the first phase all hostilities will have ceased but the German troops will still be allowed liberty of movement. During the second phase this liberty will be withheld. Try and make the interval before the introduction of Phase Two as long as possible and if you can get Eisenhower to agree that individual German soldiers will in any case be allowed to surrender to the Americans. The greater your success in these directions, the greater will be the number of German soldiers and civilians who will find salvation in the west.

Back in 1940, when Jodl had been present at the French surrender at Compiégne, he had told his opposite number, French General Huntzinger, when the latter had protested against the harshness of the German terms, that all he could do was 'give explanations and clear up obscure points'. The French would have to accept the surrender document as it was – or else! Now he was no longer in a position to limit himself to giving explanations and clearing up obscure points.

At Rheims Jodl told Bedell Smith, Eisenhower's Chief of Staff, that

---

6 Interestingly enough, after the war Major Oxenius served in the Federal German Embassy in London. There he sent his son to St. Paul's School, Montgomery's old school, whose headmaster by then was none other than the former Major Howarth, one of Monty's 'eyes and ears' in May 1945!

America would soon find itself fighting Russia. Give him time and he would evacuate a large number of German soldiers west of the Elbe who would be useful for the Western Allies in the new battle to come.

Bedell Smith believed, like Eisenhower, that the future would be shaped by America and Russia (he would soon change his mind once he had become America's post-war Ambassador to the Soviet Union). He told the Scot, Strong, just before they parted on the break-up of SHAEF, 'Britain is old-fashioned and out of date' and offered Strong the chance of becoming an American citizen. Now he rejected Jodl's ploy to sow the seeds of discord immediately.

He said, 'You have played for high stakes. When we crossed the Rhine you had lost the war. Yet you continued to hope for discord among the Allies. I am in no position to help you out of the difficulties that have grown out of this policy of yours. I have to maintain the existing agreements among the Allies.' He went on to say, 'I don't understand why you don't want to surrender to our Russian allies. It would be the best thing to do for all concerned.'

Jodl must have thought Smith had fought the war out on another planet. Did he not understand the degree of bitterness that existed between Russian and German? Had he no inkling of the savagery of the kind of battle which had been fought in the east, where both routinely did *not* take prisoners?

But Smith had spent his war in headquarters, had eaten his three squares daily and spent every night between clean sheets. There had been flirtations with female soldiers – 'GI's with built-in foxholes', as he and his cronies called them crudely – and American Army nurses. He had not the least idea of what the front, any front, including his own, was like.

Jodl shrugged and said, 'Even if you are right, I should not be able to convince a single German that you are.'

But the man who had planned all Hitler's campaigns was no mere toady like Keitel. He was a smart, quick-witted staff officer and knew when it was no use pursuing a lost cause. General Strong, acting for Eisenhower, told him 'You can tell them [the Germans] that forty-eight hours from midnight tonight, I will close my lines on the Western Front so no more Germans can get through. Whether they sign or not – no matter how much time they take.'

Jodl knew he was beaten. He told Strong, 'I shall send a message to Marshal Keitel by radio. It is to read – We sign or general chaos.'

Afterwards the apologists for Eisenhower's part in the protracted surrender negotiations maintained that Keitel was enraged by the Supreme Commander's ultimatum and characterised it as 'sheer extortion'. In fact Keitel was delighted, for Jodl had been granted yet another forty-eight hours, making a total of three priceless days since they had surrendered to Montgomery.[7]

But to Montgomery's amusement, Eisenhower's troubles with the German surrender were not over yet. It was planned to come into force on 9 May 1945, two days after the actual surrender document had been signed by Jodl. Now Eisenhower slapped on a forty-eight hour top-secret ban on the news being released to the general public. He hadn't a hope. The news of the great surrender was the biggest scoop of the year. Almost immediately the news was 'leaked' back to New York. Not only that, but Doenitz himself released the information that Germany had surrendered at three o'clock on the afternoon of 7 May.

To cap it all, when Stalin heard from Eisenhower that the Germans had surrendered to him, *he refused to recognise the surrender!* It must have been a bitter blow for Eisenhower. All this spring he had been attempting, against the opposition of Churchill and Montgomery and even some of his own generals, particularly Patton, to accommodate the Russians. He had surrendered Berlin to them and had followed that by virtually allowing them to take Prague when Patton was only a jeep-ride away from the Czech capital – some of Patton's patrols had even penetrated Prague before the Russians. Now 'Uncle Joe' was not accepting a surrender which had taken him so long to achieve!

In the end, Eisenhower had to repeat the surrender ceremony in Berlin on 8 May, with Keitel signing for Germany this time, while Churchill, who had already recorded his victory broadcast to the British nation, was waiting furiously to have it delivered.

So it was all over. It had started as a dramatic personal triumph for Montgomery and had ended four days later in a kind of tragicomedy, with Allied soldiers still being killed purposelessly days after the Germans in the north had put down their arms. As Montgomery wrote in a special note to be inserted at the end of his war diary:

And so the campaign in northwest Europe is finished. I am glad; it has been a tough business . . . The Supreme Commander had no firm ideas as to how to conduct the

---

7 It is interesting to note that General MacArthur on the other side of the world gave the beaten Japanese two full weeks between the surrender and the Allied occupation of their islands. This gave the Japanese authorities ample time to burn all incriminating documents relating to their numerous atrocities (e.g. that 27 per cent of Allied POWs died in their hands compared with 3.7 per cent in German captivity). There would be no holocaust stigma to be borne by post-war Japan as a result.

war and was 'blown about by the wind' all over the place . . . The staff at SHAEF were completely out of their depth all the time. The point to understand is that if we had run the show properly the war could have been finished by Christmas 1944. The blame for this must rest with the Americans.

But whatever else he may have been, the little Field Marshal was a realist when it came to great matters. He concluded that note with a rider: 'To balance this it is merely necessary to say one thing, i.e. if the Americans had not come along and lent a hand, we would never have won the war at all!'

The men, Canadian, British and American, who had fought Monty's Last Battle for him knew nothing of these great matters. Even if they had, they would not have cared. What did the rivalries of the top brass concern them?

Now it was all over officially. The 'Grand Old Man', Churchill, whom they would soon vote out of office, had told them so, and their poor stuttering king had, too. Some celebrated. Some mused. Perhaps they realised that this would be the last time they were together in the way they had been in the line – moving up again as the guns rumbled uneasily in the distance, the horizon flickering the silent, ugly pink, laden down like pack animals with equipment, their faces red and weatherbeaten, their clothes an odd assortment of British, American and German pickings which defied the description of uniform, going up once more, moving into those first high-pitched, hysterical bursts of the German machine-guns . . . Or perhaps they simply got drunk.

Paramedic James Byrom, who had been in the fighting right since D-Day, was on duty that 'Victory-in-Europe Day' as Churchill had declared it. While his comrades of the 6th Airborne at Wismar, according to a 'long-cherished plan' got drunk, he remained as 'sober as a judge'. Long afterwards he recalled:

as the glow of their cigarettes [those of the wounded Germans in the hospital ward below him] confirmed it was dark, the victory celebrations began. Up from the British lines came brilliant flares, singly and in clusters, but without pattern or prodigality, as if one soldier in each platoon had been given an official coloured hat and told to fling it into the air. But further away in the Russian lines, the glow of bonfires steadily lit up the sky. Distance subdued the flickering making static cones that were slightly blurred by smoke or mist; and I could fancy that they were ghost fires, the fires of other historic triumphs, so strongly did I feel them as a symbol of the unreality of victory in relation to the recurring failure to keep peace.

Fifty miles away at Plauen, another combat-medic, the American Lester Atwell, who had been in the thick of the fighting since the previous November, was approached that day of victory celebrations by a 'small, humourous-looking German' who grinned at the American and stretched out his hand. 'Ofer', he announced, 'war ofer. Gut friends.'

Atwell looked around to check if there were any MPs watching. He didn't want to risk the sixty-dollar fine that General Eisenhower had ordered for anyone found 'fraternising'. There weren't any. Cautiously he took the 'old codger's' hand and his own was shaken heartily.

'Now,' the German grinned at him, '*togedder, we fight the Russians* . . .'

5

'A tin of corned beef means true love!'

I

The Germans called it *die Stunde Null*.[1]

It was a time without precedent; a chaos without parallel. One of the world's most prosperous, civilised countries had broken down almost completely. In most places there was no gas and no electricity, and precious little water and food. There was no public transport and no mail. The telephones didn't work and in the border areas only, conquered by the victorious Allies months before, were there Allied-controlled newspapers limited to a single sheet. Most Germans without a radio might have been living on the moon and not in Central Europe, for news of what was happening outside Germany was a precious rarity.

Over three and a half million Germans had been killed fighting with the *Wehrmacht*. Half a million civilians or more had been killed in the air-raids which had destroyed fifty-three major cities up to 70 per cent. There were another two million cripples in the country. And currently one and a half million Germans were fleeing westwards from the Russians. In addition there were ten million displaced persons from a dozen European countries to east and west, now released from their camps. They wandered the shattered former Third Reich, some trying to reach their country of origin, others simply living off their wits, looting, stealing, raping, marauding in armed bands from camps in the forests, trying to make up their minds what to do next before the Occupation forces caught up with them.

David Niven, the movie star, now Lieutenant Colonel Niven, making his way through 'liberated workers' wandering 'dazedly all over the place', came across another little group with farm sacks thrown across

1 Literally 'the hour zero', i.e. nadir.

their backs against the bitter rain. They were led by an elderly man. 'I had never seen such utter weariness, such blank despair on a human face before.' The German, for it turned out he was a German trying to escape with the rest, told Niven that he was a general. Niven nodded and then, noting that despite the ragged civilian clothing the General was still wearing his army boots, said, 'Go ahead, sir,' adding sharply, 'please cover up those bloody boots!'

That little encounter was typical of that May – millions of Europeans crowding Germany's roads, still littered with the tanks and self-propelled guns of the recent fighting, each one surrounded by little crosses, hung with helmets, which marked the graves of their crews. For the great majority of Germans, however, especially those who lived in the bomb-shattered cities, life was a matter of squalor and hunger. Some had fashioned themselves caves in the ruins, where they eked out a miserable existence as if they were back in the Stone Age. Others lived high up in bombed-out apartments, reaching their crude perches by rope ladders or planks balanced precariously from one wrecked floor to another. In that ruined Germany of May 1945, ten people now lived where six had lived before.

The black market thrived, of course, as the supply system broke down and the mark became valueless. On the whole Germany had had a good war as far as food was concerned. There had been none of the British 'one egg per week – per-haps'. No stringent food rationing, where even the fish-and-chip shops which had brought the British poor through the Depression had been without fish. Now, in this month of defeat, the Germans were starting to realise what hunger was. Their fat ration was two ounces, meat three and a half, fish limited to three ounces. Bread, the great staple of the German diet, was cut to two pounds per person per week. By the end of the year, the Germans would be existing on half the calories given to the poor wretches in Belsen concentration camp.

Thus the Germans turned to the black market for survival – and the black market was the Allied soldier, with his plentiful supply of ration cans and cigarettes. Family heirlooms went – and family honour, too.

'Don't get chummy with Jerry,' the US Army newspaper *Stars & Stripes* exhorted its GI readers. 'In heart, body and spirit, every German is Hitler.' Despite that warning, and the monetary penalties of being caught 'fratting', very few of the troops took any notice. They wanted women – and they were going to get them. To the victor belongs the spoils.

'Fratting' had its consequences of course. In the six months from

May to December 1945, twenty to thirty thousand illegitimate children would be born in the American Zone of Occupation alone. In Germany as a whole, the rate of illegitimate births rose by 10 per cent during the period. Today there are thousands upon thousands of middle-aged Germans whose real fathers were British, American, Canadian, French, Russian, and so on.

Venereal disease spread like some medieval plague. Whole divisions were struck down by the several types of the scourge. In Frankfurt, the new site of Eisenhower's HQ, for example, the syphilis rate rose by a whopping 200 per cent on the 1939 figure. It was no different at Hamburg.

The military authorities, desperate that they were losing whole battalions weekly to the scourge,[2] would organise surprise raids, pulling in any women between the age of 60 and 16. Prostitutes, grandmas, housewives, schoolgirls, virgins – they were hauled away in army trucks to be examined for VD at the nearest clinic. But if and when the disease was discovered, there was little the harassed German doctors could do to cure it; there was no pencillin for them. They had to resort to the kind of treatment current before Paul Ehrlich discovered his 'magic bullet' – steam baths, painful scrapings, anti-malaria fever cures and the like.

'In this economic set-up,' one survey stated, 'sex relations, which function like any other commodity, assumes a very low value . . . the average young man in the occupation army is afforded an unparalleled opportunity for sexual exposure.' As the cynical young victors quipped, 'A tin of corned beef means true love!

On 8 May, while the world celebrated the end of the Second World War, Montgomery took over the military governorship of the British Zone of Occupation. He now had under his personal leadership the most populous and industrialised area of the beaten Third Reich. Twenty-three million German civilians, plus another two to three million soldiers in an area ranging from Cologne on the Rhine to Flensburg on the border with Denmark in the north, came under his control, with all their problems and deficiencies. Now the man who had beaten Germany into the ground was expected to raise that part of the country he controlled to its feet once more.

There'd be opposition, of course. The long, bitter war, the personal

---

2 In summer 1945 a secret Royal Army Medical Corps report estimated that one in every eight British soldiers would be suffering from VD by the end of the year.

sufferings of his own troops and the new animosity engendered by
the discoveries of the many concentration camps had created a mood
of great personal hatred against the 'Hun'. Forty-four years later, one
of his soldiers, the future movie star Dirk Bogarde, recalled seeing
Belsen concentration camp and:

entering a hell which I should never forget and about which for many years I was
unable to speak. Sometimes, perhaps if I'd had a drop too much, I might try to explain
and usually ended in unmanly tears . . . I was then 24, now I am 67. My actions [vis-à-vis
Germans] are more controlled. I just leave the elevator if a German enters. It's the voice
which disturbs me so dreadfully; a rather futile gesture.[3]

But, as his Last Battle came to an end, Montgomery was faced with
this monumental task, in the face of opposition from his own men
and from the people back home. Montgomery, who had himself
suffered grievously at the hands of the Germans, being left for dead on
the battlefield in the First World War and losing every single possession
due to German action in the Second, never shirked what he considered
his duty, in war and in peace. He told his staff, 'Our task is to
rehabilitate this great nation [Germany]. The people back home must
be told the truth. Who is going to do it? I shall have to. The politicians
will say that I am interfering in politics. But never mind, I'm used to
that. The truth must be told!'

One of his first problems was that of the Festungen. On 8 May 1945,
when peace reigned everywhere, there were a dozen ports and
harbours, ranging from the French port of Lorient in the south to the
Dutch island of Texel in the north, which had been declared by Hitler
to be Festungen, or fortresses. Although Admiral Doenitz, the new
'Führer', had already surrendered to Montgomery four days before,
the 'fortress commanders', as they were called, had not. Many refused
to obey or recognise Doenitz. Now that the fighting had ceased in the
Reich proper, would these 'fortress commanders' surrender too, or
would they fight on?

All of the fortresses had been occupied by the victorious Germans
back in 1940. In the intervening years the local commanders had had
ample time to dig themselves in. They had underground hospitals,
their own brothels even, hundreds of locals working for them and
serving them, making them – cut off as they were on the North Sea
and Channel coast from the Reich – virtually self-sufficient.

3 *Daily Telegraph*, 26 November 1988.

Back in 1944 General Bradley had tried to capture one of them –
Brest – and it had cost him ten thousand casualties. Thereafter it was
decided in both the British and American armies to contain the
'fortresses' and let them 'wither on the vine'.

But they had stubbornly refused to do this. In the Channel Islands,
Fortress Commander Admiral Huffmeier – 'the madman of the
Channel Islands', as he was called by his own mutinous soldiers and
the local civilians – had actually engaged in offensive operations. On
the same day that the Americans made their first crossing of the Rhine,
9 March 1945, Huffmeier had launched an audacious commando raid
from the only part of Britain occupied during the Second World War.
That night his commandos had captured the French port of Granville,
sunk several ships, released a couple of dozen German POWs and
taken captive some fifty Americans working there. A few days later
Admiral Huffmeier had held a parade for the victorious commandos,
awarding several of them the Iron Cross, followed by something
more precious for them than the piece of enamel – a packet of
cigarettes and a jar of looted American jam for each man!

It had been no different at Dunkirk, still in German hands five years
after they had run the British out of Europe there. Under the command
of another fanatical admiral – Friedrich Frisius – the port's defences
stretched 45 miles and were manned by twelve thousand men with
four hundred guns, supported by torpedo boats of the German Navy.
On the afternoon of 2 May, as British tanks rolled into Lübeck 600
miles away, Frisius attacked and captured eighty-nine men of the
Czech brigade which infested Dunkirk. On the very day of total
surrender, two British officers were killed by German gunfire from
the defences, and as a result the Czechs ignored Montgomery's
ceasefire order. They continued to fire at anything that moved in
Dunkirk.

In Texel, the Dutch island further north, a strange shooting battle
was still continuing too. There a battalion of renegade Russians, who
had surrendered to the *Wehrmacht* in Russia and then had volunteered
for that same army, the 822nd Georgian Infantry Battalion, had mutinied
against their German masters back in April. Now, while everywhere
else peace reigned, a cruel, small-scale war was being conducted on
the island. When the Germans captured a Russian, they stripped him
of his uniform and shot him on the spot. The Russians, for their part,
were even simpler in their method of 'liquidation'. They tied their
prisoners together, attached a single grenade to them, pulled the pin
and ran like hell. It was their way of saving ammunition . . .

In his headquarters at Flensburg it was understandable that Doenitz was not enjoying his first day of peace. He had problems with his reluctant fortress commanders. Both General Boehme in Norway and General Lindemann commanding in Denmark had shown themselves unwilling to co-operate with the British and with how Jodl was attempting to play off the Anglo-Americans against the Russians.

That was not all. Now the thing he had dreaded most was happening: There were rumblings of mutiny in his beloved *Kriegsmarine*, the German Navy. Was it going to be November 1918 all over again?

At the beginning of May, the captain of the minesweeper M612 had told his crew, 'In spite of everything we are going to carry on fighting. Now we're the Free Corps Doenitz!' The crew had not been very enthusiastic. Now Lieutenant Kropp, the young skipper, ordered them to sail for the Hela Peninsula in the Eastern Baltic, where many Germans were trapped by the Russians. The crew refused. Indeed under the command of a teenager, Heinrich Glasmacher, they mutineed – though it was a very polite mutiny, with the former telling the skipper, '*Herr Leutnant*, in the name of the crew we want to go home. It's no use anymore.'

Lieutenant Kropp, the skipper, pretended to agree. He took the minesweeper 'home' to the mother-ship, *Hermann von Wissmann*, which immediately turned its heavy guns on the thirty-odd mutineers. They surrendered tamely, were imprisoned in chains and put on 'trial' – all sixty minutes of it. Naturally all of them were sentenced to death, even though Germany had ceased fighting. For as Captain Pahl, who confirmed the sentence, later stated, 'All of us, from the highest to the lowest rank, were then of the opinion that we were going to fight together with the Western powers against the East. That was our only chance against the Communists. That was Doenitz's great aim too. It was our last chance to stop communism.'

That night, at the stroke of midnight, the reluctant heroes were shot on the deck of their own ship. The last man to die was 19-year-old Glasmacher. The guards pushed him forward and he slipped on the deck, wet with the blood of his comrades, some of whom had been slaughtered like animals. Then he drew himself to his full height in front of the firing squad and cried out at the top of his voice, '*Long live Germany!*'

Two hundred miles away at Amsterdam, now under Canadian control, two deserters from the German Navy, Bruno Dorfer and Rainer Beck, the latter the son of a Jewish mother, were shot that day – *with the approval of the Canadians!* As naval staff judge Wilhelm Koehn explained after the war, 'the whole business was occasioned by the Canadian commander' of the internment camp in which they all were imprisoned. 'The Canadians organised everything and even told us where the site of the execution would be.'

Bruno Dorfer and Rainer Beck, the one 20, the other 28, were led out to the range at Schellingwoode just outside Amsterdam, where a firing squad of captive German sailors, armed with Canadian rifles, was waiting for them. Both men were hit the first time, but only Bruno Dorfer died at once. Beck continued to live, bleeding from the corner of his mouth. He was propped up against the wall again. Five minutes later a volley rang out. The Canadian officer who was there as an 'official observer' saluted his German 'comrade'. Then the rifles were taken from the POW firing squad and they marched tamely back to the Canadian cage. *Crazy!*

II

General der Artillerie Fahrmbacher, the 'fortress commandant' of Lorient, was the first to weaken. The elderly artilleryman commanded Germany's largest submarine base in Occupied France. Doenitz's 'wolf packs' had once sailed from the great underground submarine pens, which the RAF had never been able to knock out,[4] to create havoc in the North Atlantic. In those great days of 1942–3, Doenitz himself had stayed at the base for weeks, welcoming back his victorious skippers with Knights' Crosses, brass bands, champagne and whole battalions of French whores to relax his 'Lords', who had lived off their nerves for weeks, perhaps months on end. But by the time the port had been overtaken by a mixed force of French and American soldiers those days had been over and the submarine pens had been empty. For nearly nine months the 15,000-man garrison of Lorient under Fahrmbacher had fought for their naked existence. Time and time again the desperate General had organised company-strength attacks into the surrounding countryside in order to bring in badly needed food.

Now on this day Fahrmbacher called his chief quartermaster to his office and asked with all seriousness, 'How many railway sleepers have you got left?'

The Quartermaster, whose former comfortable paunch had long

4 They are still there.

vanished, replied, 'One, *Herr General*.'

That did it. For weeks now Fahrmbacher had been having the sawdust from the sawn-up French railway sleepers mixed up in the dough to make the bread which was his troops' staple diet. Now he knew he couldn't feed fifteen thousand men on one sleeper. It was time to surrender. He sent off one last signal to Doenitz, which stated, 'Wish to sign off with my steadfast and unbeaten men. We remember our sorely tried homeland. Long live Germany!' Then he buckled on his pistol-belt and prepared to meet the Franco-Americans.[5]

Across the water in the Channel Islands, the 'madman of the Channel Islands' Admiral Huffmeier decided he had had enough, too. As the two British destroyers *Beagle* and *Bulldog* made landfall off St Peter Port, Guernsey, an ancient trawler flying the battle flag of the German Navy chugged out to meet the two senior British officers, Admiral Stuart and Brigadier Snow.

A few minutes later a Lieutenant-Commander Zimmermann, the man who had planned the commando raid on Granville two months earlier, came on board. His drenched, chinless appearance, plus his extreme youth, made an unfavourable impression on the middle-aged senior British officers who met him. They regarded the 'whole performance' as a calculated insult to them. Zimmermann's first words raised their tempers even more. He demanded to hear the terms of the 'armistice', and he would 'communicate them to his superiors for their consideration'.

Brigadier Snow, a stout, well-fed officer, flushed a choleric purple. He told the arrogant young German that he had come to arrange the islands' surrender, not to discuss terms.

Zimmermann, who had been living off nettle and turnip-top soup for the last few weeks, looked at the Englishman's bulk with scarely veiled contempt. He nodded pointedly in the direction of the German heavy guns across the bay and snapped. 'Admiral Huffmeier will regard your presence as a breach of faith and a provocative act.' If the two British craft didn't move away after he had left, Huffmeier's coastal batteries would open fire on them.

Snow's colour deepened even more. 'Tell Admiral Huffmeier that if he opens fire,' he growled menacingly, 'he'll hang tomorrow!'

The threat worked. On the morning of 9 May 1945, the *Beagle* sailed into St Peter Port to meet the Germans for the last time. Now the Germans were subdued and polite. One of them, General Heine,

---

4 The General would spend five years in French gaols for having 'defaced French property'. He had overprinted French stamps with the word 'Lorient'. Today stamps of that kind are worth thousands.

produced a letter from Admiral Huffmeier, the latter was in virtual hiding because there had been an attempt on his life, not by the British but by his own demoralised troops – 'the Canadian Division', as they called themselves cynically.[6] Huffmeier's letter read in part: 'I allowed the English population to fly flags and hold religious services and had therefore to foresee that a certain agitation might be created among my soldiers. This has happened. I was and am therefore not in a position to meet you personally.' He was too scared to venture out and remained in his heavily guarded hiding place.

So the surrender of the only part of the British Empire to be occupied by Nazi Germany was signed on the *Beagle's* rum cask.[7] Two hours later men of the Hampshire Regiment landed in brilliant sunshine, while surly Gestapo men in their ankle-length leather overcoats lurked on the edges of the cheering crowds . . .

Frisius followed suit, however reluctantly. He didn't think he should surrender Dunkirk to a mixed group of British, American, French and Czech allies. He thought 'the French especially have been most annoying trying to elicit information and take part in the negotiations. It has been pointed out to them that the surrender was being accepted on behalf of the Supreme Allied Commander and that the surrender is to the three major powers.' France, in his prejudiced opinion, did not belong to those 'three major powers'.

Next day, when the surrender document was at last signed, five French officers and a number of other ranks turned up for the ceremony to represent their country; after all Dunkirk *was* French. But the British, with absolutely no sympathy for injured French pride, told them there was no place for them at the ceremony. So the French left to return the next day and ceremoniously hoist the *tricoleur* by themselves over the newly liberated French city.

Only in the 'fortress' of Texel was there no surrender. The Canadians had accepted the surrender of the German troops in Occupied Holland on 5 May 1945 at Wageningen, with German-born Prince Bernhard of the Netherlands hovering in the background. When General Blaskowitz, the German commander in Holland, realised this, he asked General Foulkes, in charge of the Canadian delegation, to point the Prince out. Foulkes obligingly did and the whole German command sprang to attention and looked at their former countryman, who had flown bombing raids over his own country. Bernhard ignored them and casually lit a cigarette.

---

6 Because they felt they were bound for POW cages in that country.
7 Now displayed in the German Occupation Museum in Castle Gornet, Guernsey.

But after the surrender, there was so much to do in a starving Holland, packed with German troops, that the Canadians were unable to reach the far north coast off which Texel, an important naval base, lay. So it was that the Germans continued this strange, bitter little war within a war for two long weeks after the real shooting war had officially ceased.

When the Canadians finally did cross the stretch of water that separated the island from the mainland, they found exactly two hundred Russians left of the eight hundred who had mutineed. This mini-war, of which the world never heard, had commenced as a massacre when the Russians slaughtered many of their officers and NCOs in their beds, and now it had ended as one.[8]

Here and there armed pockets of German troops did still hold out, refusing to acknowledge Doenitz as 'Führer' and to obey his orders. In due course the Soviets would complain that there were armed German soldiers still active, presumably with Allied connivance, right into September 1945. It was certainly true that there were German wireless teams, composed of civilians and soldiers, still at liberty in the frozen wastes of the Arctic until that month. Throughout the war, a secret battle had been fought in that remote area between Russians, Danes, British, Canadians and Americans, who were trying to find the various undercover German weather teams who were broadcasting the vital weather statistics back to the Reich.

To the south, too, the German garrison in Crete did as it wished. The *Daily Express* correspondent, New Zealander Geoffrey Cox, returning to the island after four years (he had fought there back in 1941 during the great German para-invasion) reported 'THE JACKBOOT MEN STILL STRUT IN CRETE' and felt 'It was as if we had stumbled on a Hollywood set where masses of extras were dressed up to play the parts of Rommel's army in a desert war film'.[9]

But, with these exceptions, Doenitz had by the end of the second week of that May of Allied victory, managed to quell all indiscipline within the immediate control of his 'Flensburg Enclave' (as it was now being called), and at the same time he had managed to convince his reluctant 'fortress commanders' that there was no future in further

8 Even when it was all over and the surviving Russians were repatriated, most of them, it was assumed later in Holland, were executed as traitors to the Soviet Union. .
9 *Daily Express*, 28 May 1945.

resistance. By naked force at the lowest level and veiled threats at a higher one, he had put his own house in order.

For Doenitz was still confident, after his early depressions, that he had some role to play in Germany's post-war future. In his broadcast to the 'German people' on 8 May announcing the surrender, he had stated that everyone must face the 'difficult times ahead' with 'dignity, courage and discipline'.

He had already distanced himself and his 'administration' from the crimes of the Nazis and from those Nazis, such as Himmler, who were lurking somewhere or were on the run in the north. Now he felt he could deal with the Allies on the basis of international law. As Jodl expressed it for him on 15 May:

The attitude towards the enemy powers must be. They had conducted the war for the sake of the law. Therefore we wish to be handled according to the law . . . We want the Allied Control Commission to come to the conclusion that we are proceeding correctly; thereby we will gradually gain their trust. Then, once the ground of our loyalty is prepared, the *Grossadmiral* will go to Eisenhower in order to discuss questions about the future with him.

Jodl, Doenitz and the rest of the 'Administration' were living in cloud-cuckoo land. During the course of Germany's war of aggression they had thrown every moral scruple overboard to win that war. Now they thought they could still act on the basis of their old cynical, amoral attitude. After the most devastating defeat in the history of Europe, they had learned nothing!

Von Krosigk, the new 'Foreign Minister' and the only one among them who knew anything about the real mentality of the Anglo-Americans, warned Doenitz that his patently anti-Russian attitude would cut no ice with Eisenhower. He was leaning backwards to accommodate the Russian allies. Their only hope for the continuation of the 'Doenitz Administration' was Churchill and his agent, Montgomery. Churchill had once announced, back in 1941 when Britain had been alone, that he would make a 'pact with the Devil' if it saved the British Empire – which he had promptly done with Stalin. Would he now be prepared to make a similar pact with what was left of Nazi Germany?

The former Rhodes scholar von Krosigk didn't know. How powerful would the British Prime Minister be against Eisenhower's determined opposition? That was the question.

III

Back in 1940, after that young ADC Charles Sweeney, who had been with him on the beaches at Dunkirk, had been posted back to his unit, the Royal Ulster Rifles, Montgomery had noted:

I have lost my Charles. I really do miss him terribly and life seems quite different without him. We have been through a good deal together and I have a very great and real affection for him. I had to let him go though. He is a dear lad and I hope and pray no harm will come to him in this war.

Well, no harm had come to Sweeney during the war. He had returned to 'the Master' and had been one of his longest-serving 'eyes and ears'.

Now, on 12 May, seven days after the shooting war had ceased, Charles Sweeney was dying, the victim of a motoring accident while escorting a German admiral back to Doenitz's HQ at Flensburg. On this Saturday, while great things were afoot in the world outside, Montgomery was primarily concerned with the problem of how to deal with Sweeney's young wife. They had just married. Now that her husband was dying in Germany she wished to fly out and be at his bedside. Montgomery was torn between letting her come and knowing that Army regulations forbad such things. In the end he refused her request, though Major Warren, the Canadian, noted long afterwards, 'it was one of the hardest decisions he had made throughout the war, but if he let her come where would he stop?'

On the morrow after Sweeney's funeral, Montgomery would write in a special personal obituary for The Times: 'He [Sweeney] had a very strong character and was utterly incapable of any mean or underhand action; his sense of duty was highly developed and his personal bravery very great . . . I loved this gallant Irish boy and his memory will remain with me for all time.'

Thus in the last month of the campaign Montgomery had lost three 'eyes and ears' out of the eight serving him in that highly dangerous job, and suddenly he felt deflated again and miserable, as he had been at the death of John Poston. So it was that he accepted the chance of going on leave to England to get away from it all, while the events which would bring about the end of the 'Doenitz Administration' took their course.

On the same Saturday that Sweeney died, Churchill sent a long, carefully worded cable to Truman, President of the United States. It read:

I am profoundly concerned about the European situation . . . The newspapers are full of the great movements of the American armies out of Europe. Our armies are also, under previous arrangements, likely to undergo a marked reduction. The French are weak and difficult to deal with. Anyone can see that in a short space of time our armed forces on the Continent will have vanished except for moderate forces to hold down the Germans . . . Meanwhile what is to happen about Russia? . . . What will be the position in a year or two, when the British and American Armies have melted and the French has not yet been formed on any major scale, when we have a handful of divisions, mostly French, and when Russia may choose to keep two or three hundred on active service?

An iron curtain is drawn down upon their front. We do not know what is going on behind . . .

The famous 'iron curtain'[10] telegram revealed just how desperate Churchill was to stop the Russians making any further inroads into West Germany and thence into Western Europe. As he said privately himself while London still celebrated the victory over the Germans though 'these views are very unfashionable', he was determined that a vacuum should not arise in West Germany, which could be utilised by the Russians. Already he was concerned about the destruction of German weapons. Three days before he had signalled Eisenhower: 'I have heard with concern that the Germans are to destroy all their aircraft in situ. I hope that this policy will not be adopted in regard to weapons and other forms of equipment. We may have great need of these some day.'[11]

If, as Churchill thought, the Americans were abandoning Europe, leaving its defence to a weak France and a Britain with vast overseas commitments and a war with Japan still to be fought, there had to be a need for some kind of state in West Germany. Was Churchill, that second week of May, possibly considering that the 'Doenitz Administration' might form the nucleus of that future German state? The 'Doenitz Administration' was definitely anti-communism. It included two million German soldiers who, although disarmed, were only interned, looking after their own affairs. It was based on territory controlled by Montgomery.

But even as Churchill ordered Brooke, the Chief of the Imperial General Staff, to look into the possibilities 'of taking on Russia should trouble arise in our future discussions with her' (Brooke's conclusions were negative), his hopes were being dashed. Briefed by General Strong, who would not survive for very long in the British Army now

---

10 Churchill did not invent the term as many people think. That doubtful honour went to Goebbels
11 As late as 23 July 1945 Churchill was writing to General Ismay: 'What is being done with German rifles? It is a great mistake to destroy rifles.' One wonders whom he needed those rifles for.

he had made an enemy of Montgomery) that 'every independent act of the Doenitz government' was intended to 'embroil the Allies with the Russians', Eisenhower sent his civilian adviser Robert Murphy to look at the situation in Flensburg.

Murphy flew to Flensburg on 17 May. Doenitz received the American cordially and immediately put his foot in it. He had absolutely no concept of the prevailing American mood. Instead he declared 'solemnly that all Westerners, including the Germans, must work together now to prevent the Bolshevization of Europe. He related how he had organized a radio campaign which had induced an estimated million Germans to flee westwards to escape the Russians. He boasted that he had arranged to bring out the ablest German scientists.'[12] As Murphy concluded, 'this attitude of Doenitz was precisely what Eisenhower had asked us to watch for. It never occurred to the Admiral that Germany was to be deprived of a national government, headed by himself under a Nazi mandate.' Such a government, however, was 'incompatible with Allied objectives'.

Murphy, who in Munich in 1923 had watched Hitler's abortive 'beer-hall putsch', would in due course watch the last and final failure of National Socialism to gain power. He recommended to Eisenhower that the 'Doenitz Administration' should be removed, as his 'conversations with Doenitz confirmed Eisenhower's suspicions that these Germans were trying to create a rift between Anglo-Americans and Russians'.

On the morning of 23 May 1945, a French fishing boat approached the tiny island of Minquiers, one of the Channel Islands group. It was the first time that the French fishermmen had sailed these waters for five years and they were looking forward to a record catch. But to the surprise of the French skipper, Lucien Marie, the island – a collection of low reefs – was inhabited. He announced to the crew of *Les Trois Frères*, 'It looks as if the Roastbeefs [he meant English] have taken possession.'

One of them cursed. Before the war the French and English fishing skippers had fought over the island and they had been doing so for over a century; the fish off-shore were very plentiful.

'Don't say they're out fishing?' someone else commented.

'No,' the skipper answered, eyeing the figures on the shore, 'they

---

12 Today many of those same scientists are American citizens

look like Tommies . . . I think they're wearing uniform. Let's have a look at 'em.'

A few minutes later the little boat weighed anchor off the nearest reef and the crew of Les Trois Frères waded ashore to be faced, not by British soldiers but by German ones, fully armed!

Bewildered by the sight of fully armed Boches, three weeks after the surrender, Lucien Marie wondered what to do. He didn't have to wait long though. The German sergeant in charge raised his pistol and said in fairly good Norman French, 'Hey you, come here!'

While the rest of the crew raised their hands, the skipper walked over hesitantly. 'What is it?' he asked.

'Listen Frenchman,' the German NCO said, 'We've been forgotten by the British. Perhaps no one in Jersey told them we were here.'

The skipper nodded, but said nothing, wondering what was coming.

'So we've had enough,' the Sergeant said. 'We're running out of food and water. You must help us.'

'How?' the skipper asked.

'Simple. I want you to take us over to England . . . We want to surrender.'

Numbly Lucien Marie nodded. Little did he know it, but he had accepted the surrender of the last soldiers of Admiral Doenitz still free west of the Elbe. Now it was the turn of their commander . . .

The last operations of Field Marshal Montgomery's men in the Second World War commenced at dawn when Brigadier Churcher's brigade in Flensburg was alerted for the task allotted to them. It consisted of the Cheshire and Hereford Regiments and the Shropshire Light Infantry, supported by 15/19th Hussars. While that unknown German NCO surrendered to the French fishermen, they took up their positions. As Doenitz drove up to the SS Patria for the very last time, no one presented arms and the Grand Admiral knew there was to be trouble. He could smell it in the very air.

On board Doenitz was faced by three Allied generals from SHAEF, an American, a Briton and a Russian. The American, General Rooks, rose and read from a paper in his hand. 'Gentlemen,' he announced in a voice that was awkward, as if he were not accustomed to reading aloud:

I am in receipt of instructions . . . from the Supreme Commander General Eisenhower to call you before me this morning to tell you that he has decided, in concert with the Soviet High Command, that today the acting German Government and acting

271

German High Command with several of its members shall be taken into custody as prisoners of war. Thereby the acting German Government is dissolved. . . . When you leave this room an Allied officer will attach himself to you and escort you to your quarters where you will pack, have your lunch and complete your affairs, after which they will escort you to the airfield at one-thirty for emplaning. You may take the baggage you require. That's all I have to say.

The interpreter put Rooks' words swiftly into German and then the American asked, 'Would you like to make a statement?'

Doenitz shook his head. 'Comment is superfluous' he snapped.

Almost at that same moment on land in the barracks, Schwerin von Krosigk, the 'Foreign Minister', had just opened his daily cabinet meeting when the door burst open and a heavily armed British soldier burst in. Swiftly the Germans were hurried outside, where they were frisked expertly. Then the interpreter commanded '*Hosen runter!*' – pants down.

Thus the last of the Nazi *prominenz* were forced to drop their pants, spread their legs and bend down, while a British sergeant of the Royal Army Medical Corps, finger encased in a surgical stool, searched their anuses for poison.

Even the hard-bitten war correspondents could not take the indignities heaped upon these elderly Germans. The staff reporter of the *Daily Express* could record that Doenitz was found to be wearing seven pairs of woollen underpants; no one ever found out why. Edward Ward, recently returned from a German POW camp himself, walked over to the Australian Chester Wilmot and said, sickened, 'You wanted to cover this story, Chester. As far as I'm concerned, it's all yours.' Then he walked away with Anthony Mann of the *Daily Telegraph*, whose face was as haggard as Ward's, for he, too, had been imprisoned by the Germans in Denmark ever since 1940.

That day Admiral von Friedeburg, that 'General Admiral', whose title had so amused Montgomery, committed suicide with the shame of it all. Later Churchill would write to Montgomery in protest, 'I did not like to see German admirals and generals with whom we had recently made arrangements being made to stand with their hands above their heads. Nor did I like to see the infantry component of the 11th Armoured Division used in this particular task.' He added, 'I understand that the whole was ordered by SHAEF.'

Churchill obviously knew that the whole business had been directed from Eisenhower's HQ with the clear intention of humiliating the Germans in the eyes of the Russians and to clarify any doubts the latter might have had about US intentions towards Doenitz.[13] But there was nothing more he could do about it, for on this same day Churchill tendered his office of Prime Minister of Great Britain to the King. Now he would prepare to fight the first general election the country had had in ten years; and those same soldiers of Montgomery's armies, whom he head inspired in those black years to fight for final victory, would ensure that Churchill would lose it . . .

---

13 A couple of years later, when London decided to bring FM von Manstein to trial as a war criminal on the basis of evidence supplied by the Russians, an appeal was launched through the *Daily Telegraph* to provide money to pay British lawyers to defend the ageing German. The first name to head the list was Churchill's. He had donated twenty-five pounds.

6

'The only German secret weapon not used.'

I

Just before the German surrender, Schwerin von Krosigk, Doenitz's 'Foreign Minister', had said to Himmler, 'What I recommend you to do is to go straight to Montgomery's HQ and say that you are Heinrich Himmler and that you want to take full responsibility for everything the SS has done.'

But SS Reichsführer Himmler, 'the most wanted man in the world' that May, was not going to do Doenitz and his 'ministers' that favour. He was not going to sacrifice himself that easily so that Doenitz could claim he had rid himself of the Nazis and give himself what the Germans of that time called a *Persilschein* – a Persil certificate, proving that they were politically clean.

Instead, accompanied by the head of his former bodyguard Macher and several senior SS generals, he set off to reach his home in far-off Bavaria to the south. But he didn't get too far. On 22 May, one day before the 'Doenitz Adminstration' was arrested, Himmler, together with SS Colonel Grothmann and Macher, was spotted walking down the main street of the small German town of Bremervoerde, not far from where Guardsman Eddie Charlton had gained the last VC of the war in what now seemed already another age.

Himmler could hardly have realised just how bizarre he looked. All three were clearly military men, wearing long *Wehrmacht* rubberised overcoats over a motley collection of civilian garments, with the man in the lead of the odd procession constantly looking back to see if the others were still with him. Indeed they were arrested even before they reached the guarded bridge across the Oste.

As yet the young sergeant who arrested the three had no idea of the catch he had made. Obviously the threesome's papers were forged and that was about it. So, as the soldiers heard that one of them –

Himmler – had a bad stomach, they took pity on him. As the three detainees prepared to spend the night in a grain store, serving as a temporary gaol, their captors brewed the most feared man in Europe 'a mug o' char'!

On the following day Himmler and his two bodyguards were transported by truck to the former naval POW camp at Westertimke. Now its purpose had been changed. It housed civilian internees. Still 'Sergeant Hitzinger', as Himmler was calling himself, was not recognised by those many hundreds of former Nazis who had once served under him. But that evening, as Himmler was moved to yet another internment camp at Kolkhagen, fate finally overtook him.

Ex-Gauleiter Kaufmann of Hamburg was watching the new arrivals springing down from the truck that had brought them when he noted an odd figure in military boots and breeches, with a civilian jacket. Suddenly the 'new boy' disappeared behind some bushes. When he reappeared, he had taken off the piratical patch he had been wearing and replaced it by that so-well-known pince-nez. There was no doubt about it. *It was Himmler!*

Half an hour later 'Sergeant Hitzinger', Grothmann and Macher were facing Captain Selvester of the Reconnaissance Corps, who was the camp commandant, and Selvester recognised him immediately. Himmler knew the game was up. In a very quiet voice, he said, 'Heinrich Himmler!'[1]

Things started to move fast. While Selvester ordered Himmler to be searched for the same kind of poison phial with which von Friedeburg had killed himself that very day in Flensburg, Colonel Murphy, Dempsey's Chief of Intelligence, arrived to take charge of the prisoner. Again Himmler was searched. Again no poison was found on him. But Murphy was not taking any chances. He ordered his doctor to stand by at HQ. Then, clad only in his underpants and shirt, but wrapped in a grey British Army blanket (Himmler had refused the offer of a British uniform), Himmler was whisked away to Luneburg. On the way the driver got lost and Murphy, himself not sure of the road, turned to ask his assistant the way. Quietly Himmler said, 'You are on the road to Luneburg.'

Captain C. Wells of the Royal Army Medical Corps started to examine Himmler immediately he was brought into the 2nd Army's Interrogation Centre at Number 31a Uelzener Strasse on the outskirts

---

1 There had been many and varied accounts of Himmler's arrest and death. For example, it was stated that Himmler asked to see the camp commandant personally, but it could well be that Kaufmann informed on him. The coincidence is too great.

of Luneburg,[2] while a Major Whittaker stood watch. He wasn't impressed by the man who had once terrorised Europe. 'There was no arrogance about him,' he noted long afterwards. 'He was a cringing figure who knew the game was up . . . He was quiet and co-operative.' With great care the medical officer examined his hands and feet for any sign of concealed poison, noting that 'His finger nails were cut to a point which in a man I had always coupled . . . with sexual perversion.' Then he examined his chest and buttocks, finally coming to Himmler's mouth.

Casually Wells asked him to open it, while Whittaker shone his standard lamp into Himmler's face to give the doctor more light. At first Himmler drew away, like people do when they are about to be examined by a dentist. But then the head of the SS did open his mouth and Wells noted that his teeth were 'goodish', with plenty of gold fillings. He also noticed 'A small blue tit-like object sticking out of the lower sulcus of his left cheek. That was something abnormal.' He immediately recognised it for what it was. The poison capsule! What was he going to do now? 'The real question and I realised it, was not what I had seen – but whether Himmler knew what I had seen? Had my face given me away?' It had.

As Wells inserted his finger once more, Himmler bit hard. 'We struggled for a moment. He wrenched my hand out of his mouth . . . swung his head away and then with almost deliberate disdain faced me, crushed the glass capsule between his teeth and took a deep inhalation.'

'My God, it's in his mouth . . . *he's done it on me!*' Wells shouted as Whittaker smelled the cyanide and acted immediately. 'We immediately upended the old bastard and got his mouth into the bowl of water which was there to wash the poison out. There were terrible groans and grunts coming from the swine.'

While all this was going on, Colonel Murphy was shouting urgently for needle and thread, as he and Whittaker took it in turns to hang on to Himmler's tongue. The needle was brought, and swiftly the thread was slipped through the tip of the dying man's tongue to keep it outside his mouth.

By now Himmler's face was suffused purple and contorted with pain. Sweating heavily, Wells tried artificial respiration, crying out as he laboured feverishly, 'Must have cardiac stimulants . . . For Crissake, *cardiac stimulants!*'

---

2 Today it's an old folks home – *Lebensabend* – the 'evening of life'. So it was for Himmler, too, but his evening didn't last very long.

Someone rushed to the phone, stepping over the writhing body with officers everywhere trying to help. No use! The phone was out. Hurriedly Whittaker dispatched an officer to get to the nearest MI Room to find the stimulant. He sped away.

Some minutes later, gasping for breath and dishevelled, he found one, where a doctor's farewell party was taking place. By now it was after eleven; the party was in full swing and the guests were well oiled. He burst in, shouting 'Must have a cardiac stimulant!'

Everyone thought it was a huge 'in' joke. Someone pushed a whisky at him. 'Come and have a drink, old man.'

Thus Himmler's life ended in a kind of tragicomedy at twenty to twelve that Thursday night, with more and more senior officers alerted by the news crowding, drinks in hand, into what had once been a prosperous middle-class German parlour to see the dead man. 'Jimmy the Dentist' badly wanted to pull a couple of Himmler's teeth for a souvenir. Firmly Major Whittaker said 'No!'[3]

Then it was all over and the body was left on the floor, the lower extremities covered by a blanket. On the morrow the Russian delegation attached to SHAEF would come to view it and ensure that not only the Americans but the Russians too knew that 'the most wanted man in the world' was at last dead.

While Himmler lay there, the 'Doenitz Administration', laden into an American DC4, flew into the unknown. Doenitz, sitting between packing cases and suitcases, his face a mixture of despair and cynicism, did not know or care where they were flying. Speer, still eager for new scenes and new events, thought they were flying to London, perhaps.

But most of the prominenz had relapsed into a silent cocoon of their own thoughts. Perhaps at last they were realising that they were no longer the leading actors in the great roles they had played in their nation's supreme drama. The grand illusion had collapsed. The colossal performance of the boastful '1,000 Year Reich', which had lasted exactly twelve years, four months and eight days, was over. In the bitter years to come they and their people would look back at this time now and again (but not very often) and wonder how they could ever conceivably have been taken in by that monstrous dream with its loud-mouthed effrontery, gold-braided vulgarity, jack-booted cruelty – the bloody nobility of its youthful sacrifices. It was all over . . .

3 Himmler's death mask and sketch of his teeth – complete, thanks to Major Whittaker – rest today in the Royal Army Dental Corps Museum in Aldershot.

It was dark when they arrived at the one-time *Luftwaffe* field just outside the capital of the tiny principality of Luxembourg. A cordon of US soldiers was drawn up outside. Each man had an automatic rifle aimed at the lane through which they would walk to the waiting, open American trucks. Speer thought he had seen 'such a reception only in gangster films when the criminals are led off to justice'.

They drove swiftly down into Luxembourg city, their lights ablaze. The mobs booed them. Then on up into the hills once more, heavy with the scent of pine. Six months before, during the Battle of the Ardennes, the pale-faced planner Colonel-General Jodl, now sunk deep in this own thoughts, had come within an inch of victory here. Now all was lost. On and on. Ever closer to Germany once more. The drivers slowed down, crashing home the lower gears. For now they were making a very steep descent. They were coming down to the River Moselle, the houses on the other side – the German side – a mass of ruins. Here the Americans and the Germans had fought for over three months in the winter. Finally the trucks stopped altogether. They were at Bad Mondorf, a Luxembourg spa-town right on the river, in front of the Palast Hotel, which boasted its own park.[4]

From outside Speer could see the other *Prominenten* of the Third Reich – Goering and the rest, who had been apprehended before them – pacing up and down the glass-fronted, but barred veranda, the *Wintergarten* as the Germans called it. They were all there, the ministers, the field marshals, the state secretaries. 'It was a ghostly experience,' he recalled afterwards, 'to find all those who at the end had scattered like chaff in the wind reassembled here.'

But he had not time to reflect further. The guards pushed them forward into what the Germans with their keen sense of their own social standing and prestige named the *Prominentenlager*. The contemptuous, cynical GIs who guarded them allowed their charges no such idle pretensions. With brutal directness they gave the hotel-cum-prison camp their own name. It was 'Camp Ashcan'!

It was long after midnight before they were all settled, tossing and turning on their narrow iron cots, the only sound the soft shuffle of their GI guards in their rubber-soled boots. They had gambled and failed – and 3,000 miles away in New York, American newspaperman Drew Middleton scribbled away furiously at the article which would

---

4 Today it is also an old folks home, but on the windows one can still see the traces of the bars from when it was used as the place of imprisonment for those who were going to be tried at Nuremburg.

be featured on the front page of the New York Times on the morrow. It would begin quite simply with the sentence: 'THE THIRD REICH DIED TODAY . . .'

The officers who had tried in vain to stop Himmler killing himself had now departed, disappearing into the officers' mess with worried looks on their faces. Now the half-naked body lay sprawled on the floor of the octagonal basement room. By now Sergeant Bill Ottery, a curly-haired member of the 2nd Army's Defence Company, had posted a guard on the room. Now he waited till the officers disappeared – 'the bastard's beat us,' he heard one of them say angrily – before he decided it was safe to have his own private look at the dead man.

Together with some of the 'other lads', he went into the heavily furnished room. There Himmler lay sprawled on his back, hands folded on his stomach above the blanket, with the white enamel bowl the doctor had used just near him. For a moment or two they gazed in silence at this insignificant-looking ex-chicken farmer, who had once been the cause of so many dying horribly. Then one of the 'lads' drew away the blanket to reveal Himmler's skinny pale legs and bare abdomen. 'The only German secret weapon not used,' one of them said with a snigger, indicating Himmler's flaccid organ.

A little later giggling parties of ATS from the Headquarters also came in to view the 'only German secret weapon not used' before the officers reappeared and dignity and order were restored. Now the question was – what to do with the body?

While the American observers came to confirm that this really was Himmler, followed by the Russians, who reluctantly agreed that it might be (somebody had taken Himmler's pince-nez as a souvenir and their absence puzzled the Russians somewhat), the top brass pondered the problem.

It took a whole day and the final decision was taken by the 2nd Army Commander General Dempsey himself. The body would have to disappear so effectively that it could never be found again and used in some possible post-war neo-Nazi movement.[5] But first there would have to be a cover story which would fool the press and the general public.

Thus it was that at five in the afternoon on 25 May a press conference was called at which the senior NCO of the Defence Company,

5 In the case of the war criminals executed at Nuremburg, their bodies were later secretly incinerated (under the cover names of dead GIs) and then at midnight their ashes were thrown into the River Isar at Munich to disappear for ever.

Sergeant-Major Austen, recorded his impressions for the BBC: 'After a struggle lasting a quarter of an hour, in which we tried all methods of artificial respiration, under the direction of the doctor . . . he died . . . and when he died . . . we threw a blanket over him . . . and left him.'

Later Austen was asked what had happened to Himmler. He said:

I wrapped him up in a couple of blankets. Then I put two of our army camouflage nets around him and tied him up with telephone wires. I put the parcel on the back of a lorry and drove off. I dug the grave myself and nobody will ever know where he is buried.

It made a great story, especially as Austen turned out to have been a corporation dustman before the war. Even as they rushed to the phones, the correspondents could see the headlines – 'DUSTMAN BURIES HIMMLER'. There was only one catch in the story. Sergeant-Major Austen could not even drive. So who *did* bury Himmler that day, and where?

In fact it was a small party under Major Whittaker, including Sergeant-Major Austen and two of his NCOs, Sergeants Reg Weston and Bill Ottery, who carried out Colonel Murphy's instructions to 'put the body under the earth in the morning. As few as possible to know the location.' As Whittaker noted in his diary:

Took the body out in a truck for its last ride. Hell of a job to find a lonely spot. Anyhow we did find one and threw the old basket into the hole which we had dug. We had wrapped the thing in a camouflage net. The press are still asking when we are going to have the funeral!

The press would continue to ask for many years to come, but Himmler was well hidden, the disturbed earth above him stamped down hard with British ammunition boots and then covered with leaves to hide the site. After that the NCOs, Austen, Weston and Ottery, enjoyed a well-deserved pint of beer brought to them by Major Whittaker. For they were all warm and sweating from 'all that digging when we had better things to do'.[6]

II

But now everyone had 'better things to do'. National Socialism was as dead as its main leaders – Hitler, Goebbels, Himmler and the like.

---

6 Twice after the war, the site was reported to have been discovered and Major Whittaker, who was sworn to secrecy, was hurriedly sent to Germany to check the report. But both times he discovered the site was undisturbed. He went to his grave taking this secret with him, as did Sergeant-Major Austen. Reg Weston and Bill Ottery were still alive in 1976, when they told their part of the story, but even then they did not reveal the site's location.

Now the task was to start putting the ruined country on its feet again. The other Allied soldiers who had conquered and ruined her would take no part in her rehabilitation. Bradley was already on his way home. Eisenhower would soon follow to become America's Chief of Staff, and Patton, Military Governor of Bavaria, would soon be fired on account of his controversial attitude to the Germans, whom he felt, would be needed in the war soon to come with Russia.

At the great military review of Allied might in Berlin, Patton succeeded in insulting the conqueror of the German capital, Russian Marshal Zhukov, and then he fell into a trap set for him by newspaper correspondents. One of them asked with seemed innocence, 'Isn't this Nazi thing really just like a Republican–Democratic election fight?' Patton replied, 'Yes, that's about it . . . It's just as if the Democrats in power at home threw out every Republican who held any kind of civic job or vice versa.' Next day the US headlines screamed 'AMERICAN GENERAL SAYS NAZIS ARE JUST LIKE REPUBLICANS AND DEMOCRATS'.[7] Patton was fired.

Montgomery, as vain, as arrogant and as opinionated as Patton, did not make gaffes like that whatever he thought privately. But he was the only Allied soldier at the top who saw that Germany was breaking down. There were millions of people running wild without an effective police force to restrain them. There was a horrific food shortage in the offing and it might not be long before the starving population started looting and rioting.

What was needed was not a long-range strategic and political solution, but a short-range tactical and economic one. That summer Montgomery saw that America was abandoning Germany and Europe. He was the first of any of the top European leaders, military or civil, to recognise the problem – and do something about it!

In the months that followed, under Montgomery's personal leadership and against the opposition of many back at home, including a laggard Labour Government under Attlee, the seeds would be sown which would lead to West Germany's 'economic miracle' and the establishment of a free and democratic society in that country.

Montgomery received the first bunch of civilian administrators from London himself. He told these men and women who would run the British Control Commission, that they were to operate exactly as if the war were still going on. They would handle all details themselves or take tham to his Chief of Staff. When they wanted to see Montgomery

---

7 Patton was trying to explain the Allied de-Nazification policy, which included firing all Nazi officials from post-war administration. He maintained he couldn't run Bavaria without using some of them.

himself, they would have to state their business within ten minutes. But for the present their major concern would be to get Germany's most populous and industrialised district, which made up the British Zone of Occupation, through the crisis.

Thereafter followed a series of 'ops', run on the lines of Montgomery's schemes for training his troops for the invasion of Europe – 'Operation Barleycorn' to demobilise German soldiers who volunteered to work on the land; 'Operation Coal Scuttle' to gather fuel for the coming winter and release soldiers prepared to work in the mines; etc.

Naturally in the chaotic Germany of the time, Montgomery's administration was not flawless. The problems were too great and Montgomery was not receiving the support he needed from the government back home. But he did establish law and order, and of the four zones of occupation the British was generally regarded as the best run. Unlike the French and Russians, the British were not out for revenge. As for the American Zone, it was led by incompetent administrators and by many refugees from German oppression who had now returned to the land of their birth to exact retribution.

Going up in a troop train with a group of 18-year-old reinforcements who were about to join the newly named British Army of the Rhine (BAOR),[8] war correspondent Tom Pocock noted how the boys were at first eager to sell their cigarettes and soap on the black market, but how that changed when the train ran into the shattered suburbs of Osnabrueck. There it was mobbed by skinny children, some of them with their feet wrapped in rags. 'They were pathetic little creatures with stick-like arms and legs, waxen faces and sunken eyes.' Suddenly the young soldiers' mood changed. Now they were 'vying with each other not only to give away any sweets they had, but also their own rations. As the train began to pull away, one boy, who had an armful of tins and packets of food, climbed out and jumped to the ground, distributed it and clambered back on to the last carriage.'

On the whole, that was typical of the average British soldier's attitude, and that of their Commander-in-Chief, Montgomery. He was quite unmoved by notions of revenge – or non-revenge for that matter. Abstract emotions – mass emotions – just had never touched him in the least. So Montgomery got on with the job, as usual throwing himself into it heart and soul, of ensuring that his twenty-three million Germans would survive the summer and the winter to come.

---

8   Before, Montgomery's army had been named 'British Liberation Army' (BLA). The soldiers quipped that the initials meant 'Burma Looms Ahead'!

As Helmut Schmidt, one day to become General Federal Chancellor, then an ex-*Wehrmacht* artillery officer recently released from a British POW camp, remarked many years later of his first experiences with the English in his native Hamburg, 'For me in Autumn 1945, a few Englishmen gave the hope of a new democracy . . . I knew something of English common sense, English pragmatism and fair play. Therefore, I was happy that my hometown Hamburg and a large part of North Germany had been placed under a British military government.'

He was not alone in those feelings. The man who had inflicted some of the country's most crushing defeats on the Germans would be the first to raise them from the depths of their despair and offer them hope for the future. For a while, some of them would remember him and his soldiers – *die Tommies*. The skinny-legged children who received their daily ration of free cocoa from the British Army; the many war-crippled for whom Montgomery made the provision of artificial limbs a number-one priority; the workers of Wolfsburg, who by that autumn were already producing the first post-war Volkswagens at Montgomery's command; the starving children of shattered Berlin flown out to be fattened in special camps in Montgomery's British Zone of Occupation . . . For a while at least, they would remember.[9]

Montgomery had conquered them; now he tried to restore their lives with the limited means at his disposal. But in his remote *Schloss*, Montgomery's mind was turning to his own affairs, his own future, too. That autumn he wrote to the King, stating:

I am a poor man. I have no money of my own. All my belongings have been destroyed during this war by enemy bombing . . . Every single thing I possess has gone; it was all stored in a big depository in Portsmouth and was lost in a bombing attack on that city in January 1941. I have no home; even if I had a house, I have nothing to put in it. I have nowhere which my stepson and my own boy can come to and call 'home' . . . I must honestly confess that I look forward to the future and the 'evening of life' with some concern.

Montgomery then humbly requested that he should be offered a home. 'Could you give me a small house and equip it with what is necessary so that I can have a home. Quite a small house . . . and it need not be gifted, it could be only for my lifetime. I would not ask it a gift which I could leave for my descendants.'

Montgomery pointed out that he could make a fortune by writing

---

9 It is interesting to note that many younger Germans who did not experience the war think that Hamburg, Bremen and the rest of North Germany were captured by the US Army.

his account of the war – he had already been offered half a million dollars from America to do so. But he didn't want to do that; nor did he want to go into the City and take up directorships. All he wanted was a home, 'for my lifetime. I hope I have made myself clear?'

He had. But the King, whose throne he had played a large part in saving and who had often solicited invitations to Montgomery's HQ during the war, refused. Like Churchill and Brooke (who had to sell his collection of bird pictures to make money to live on), Montgomery would have to take to writing – 'stirring up the mud', as he called it – in order to live.

Thus he started to pass from the scene. For a while he would be Chief of Staff. After that he would serve as the deputy head of NATO virtually exiled to Europe for several years. He would be heaped with honours, created a viscount, before slipping into obscurity. But he would never fight another battle. That final dash across the Elbe and the race for the Baltic had been Monty's last battle.

Thus he ended his life, bedridden and 'to all intents and purposes gaga' – as Field Marshal Templer, one of those who had served under him in Germany, put it – forgotten by the nation he had served so well. In the early hours of 24 March 1976, three decades after he had fought that last battle, his heart gave out and the news was flashed round the world, 'MONTY IS DEAD' . . .

ENVOI

'When you go home,
tell them of us and say:
For your tomorrow,
we gave our today.'

On 5 May 1945, the day after Montgomery and the Germans signed the surrender document, an oak plaque was erected on the spot where the tent had stood and the site was renamed 'Victory Hill'. Three days later the plaque was stolen. Another replaced it and in September it, too, was removed by persons unknown and found some 400 yards away daubed with paint.

It was decided the wooden marker, which could be removed so easily, had to go. In November 1945 it was therefore replaced by a permanent stone memorial weighing 9 tons. A little later a guardroom was erected nearby and five Germans were employed to guard the place at eighty-nine pfennigs an hour, then the equivalent of ten pence.

But by April 1955 things had changed drastically in the relative status of Germany and Britain. The former country was booming, rationing and hardship long forgotten; Germany had its 'economic miracle' and the 'hard D-Mark'. Britain, the victor, on the other hand, had only just got rid of rationing and, as usual in those days, the pound sterling was weak. It was decided to remove the guard for economic reasons. One month later the bronze plaque on the stone memorial to British victory was stolen and an unknown German wrote on the stone itself, 'Due to this victory, Communism could spread in the heart of Europe. After ten years it is time to recognise the common danger. Let us forget the past.'

As we know, the British do not readily forget their past: a past, incidentally, which the Germans definitely wanted to forget. They soldiered on and the local British military commander made the local burgomaster Carl Basse responsible for the security of the monument. For three further years all went well and the monument remained untouched. But in 1958 the area in which it stood was designated to become a training and battle school for the new German Army, *die Bundeswehr*. It was decided the monument would have to be removed.

Field Marshal Montgomery was consulted. He decided it should be removed to the safety of Sandhurst. This was done and the monument was re-erected on New College Square opposite the Royal Military Academy's officers' mess. In his re-inaugural speech of 29 November 1958, Montgomery explained why he had selected Sandhurst. He said, in that clipped precise voice of his, with those lisped 'w's:

The Stone commemorates the climax of over five years of hard fighting at sea, in the air, and on land . . . It now stands where what it says can reach the right men . . . the future officers of the armed forces of Britain. They are the right men, because the key to all which happened was leadership.

In Germany, 'Victory Hill' disappeared and the site of the great victory reverted to its original German name, Timeloberg. Today, nearly half a century later, all that remains of the victory on that historic, rain-swept May afternoon are the two concrete supports for the long-vanished memorial on 'Victory Hill'.

It is pretty much the same everywhere in North Germany where that last battle took place. There is little tangible evidence of all that tremendous effort, those scenes of desperate action, where young men, British, American, Canadian and German, fought, suffered and died. The fields and low hills, once littered with the ghastly debris of war, rusting, shattered tanks, abandoned guns and equipment, still figures in khaki and field-grey, have long reverted to their former state. The black German names on the yellow road signs, which once meant horror and terror – the sudden blast of the 88mm cannon, the blue angry flame of a flame-thrower, the obscene howl of a multiple mortar, the 'moaning Minnie' – are once more just indicators of the way to go. No longer has the path ahead to be bought with young men's lives.

Here and there one can catch a glimpse of that long-forgotten time. At Artlenburg, where the cumbersome dukhs waddled into the Elbe with their freight of infantry, the older red-brick houses along the water's edge are still marked with the rough scars of the German shells fired from the other side. Just outside Schwarzenbek, in the long stretch of rough woods beyond the new housing estate, one can still find the weapon pits with their rusting fragments, from which the guns fired that knocked out Corporal Pinder's section of frightened young men. At Westertimke, a few of the old huts which once housed thousands of British naval prisoners of war are left. Last year, so the local villagers relate, forty of the place's 'old boys' came back to celebrate a reunion in the village. But they are very old now and one of them suffered a fatal heart-attack because of the excitement. The villagers think they won't come again. If they do, what is left of 'their' camp will have vanished. As always – and rightly so – time and nature will have drawn a green cloak over the scenes of that terrible time.

The cemeteries are there, of course. Here the last of Montgomery's soldiers rest. For the most part they were teenage reinforcements who made up his infantry divisions in the end: boys of 18 and 19 killed at the very moment of victory, dead before they had even begun to live. Unlike the victorious American Army, which ordered that all American soldiers who had been killed in action in Germany should be dug up after the war and re-buried in the nearest Allied country – Belgium, France, Holland – the British Army left its dead in the heart of the defeated enemy country.

But these are not Kipling's 'silent cities' of the First World War, huge sprawling acres of white crosses, nor the great cemeteries of the Western Desert such as the one at El Alamein. 'I couldn't sleep last night,' Montgomery confessed on his death-bed. 'I can't have very long to go now. I've got to go to meet God – and explain all those men I killed at Alamein.' These cemeteries in North Germany – near Celle, near Munster, and so on – are small, quiet, reflective places.

And the dying Field Marshal need not have been troubled that he had led these young men to their deaths. At the zenith of the British Empire, they had achieved the high hopes he had set upon them. Against the odds stacked against him – and them – after the defeat of Dunkirk, they had finally vindicated the British ethos and had vanquished the cruel and unworthy.

Bibliography

Barclay, C. *The History of the 53rd Welch Division in World War Two* (London, 1956)

Blake, G. *Mountain and Flood: The History of the 52nd (Lowland) Division* (Glasgow, 1952)

Cameron, J. *The History of the 7th Argylls, 1942–45* (London, 1956)

Cassidy, G. *The Story of the Algonquin Regiment* (Toronto, 1948)

Cunliffe, M. *History of the Royal Warwickshire Regiment, 1919–53* (London, 1956)

Doenitz, K. *Zehn Jahre und Zwanzig Tage* (Bonn, 1954)

Dunlop, J. 'The Capitulation of Hamburg, 3rd May 1945', *Journal of the Royal Institute*

Ellis, L. *Welsh Guards at War* (Aldershot, 1946)

Fitzroy, O. *Men of Valour: History of VIII King's Royal Irish Hussars* (Liverpool, 1961)

Gill, R. *Club Route in Europe* (Hanover, 1946)

Die Geschichte des Panzerkorps Grossdeutschland (Neckargemund, 1956)

Gunning, H. *Borderers in Battle: The War History of the King's Own Scottish Borderers* (Berwick-on-Tweed, 1948)

The History of the Fourth Armoured Brigade (Gluckstadt, 1945)

Horrocks, B. *A Full Life* (London, 1960)

Kemp, R. *The Middlesex Regiment, 1919–52* (Aldershot, 1952)

Ludde-Neurath, *Die Regierung Doenitz* (Göttingen, 1956)

Moeller, K. *Das Letzte Kapitel: Geschichte der Kapitulation Hamburgs* (Hamburg 1947)

Montgomery, B.L. *From El Alamein to the Sangro* (London, 1948)

Pakenham-Walsh, R. *The History of the Royal Corps of Engineers* (Chatha, 1951)

Peters, R. *Zwolf Jahre Bremen* (Bremen, 1951)

Salmond, J. *The History of the 51st Highland Division, 1939–45* (Edinburgh, 1951)

Scarfe, N. *Assault Division: A History of 3rd Infantry Division* (London, 1947)

Speer, A. *Erinnerungen* (Berlin, 1969)

Stacey, C. *The Victory Campaign* (Ottawa, 1960)

Steiner, L.N. *Die 23 Tage der Regierung Doenitz* (Dusseldorf, 1967)

Verney, R. *The Desert Rats* (London, 1954)

War Report. BBC War Reports (London, 1945)

Woehlkens, E. *Uelzen in den Letzten Kriegstagen* (Uelzen, 1970)

Source Notes

BOOK ONE

Chapter 1

As with all histories of the campaign in Europe in 1944-45, the most important documentary sources are the official records of the individual units concerned. However, in the unofficial records are the divisional and regimental histories. In this chapter these include: *History of 7th Armoured Division* (Germany, 1945) (no author); Charles MacDonald *The Last Offensive* (US Department of Defence, 1972); J. Toland, *The Last 100 Days* (Random House, 1966); N. Hamilton, *Monty*, Vol. III (Hamilton, 1986); T.E.B. Howarth, *Monty at Close Quarters* (Leo Cooper, 1986).

Chapter 2

Hamilton (op.cit.); R.W. Thompson, *Men under Fire* (MacDonald, 1945); G. Schwarberg, *Der SS Arzt und die Kinder* (Sternverlag, 1986); H. Schwareaelder, *Der Britische Vorstoss an die Weser* (C. Schuenemann Verlag, Bremen, 1973); T. Pocock, *The Dawn Came up Like Thunder*
(Collins, 1982); D. Botting, *In the Ruins of the Reich* (Allen, 1985); *Daily Telegraph* and *Sunday Times* for April 1945; *Illustrated London News*, 21 April 1945.

Chapter 3

A. McKee, *The Race for the Rhine Bridges* (Souvenir Press, 1971); S. Ambrose, *The Supreme Commander* (Doubleday, 1970); R. Butcher, *My Three Years with Eisenhower* (Hutchinson, 1946); Toland (op.cit.); C. Ryan, *The Last Battle* (Simon & Schuster, 1966); G. Roberts, *From the Desert to the Baltic* (Kimber, 1987); Schwarberg (op.cit.).

Chapter 4

Thompson (op.cit.); J. Haines, *Maxwell* (MacDonald, 1988); B. Horrocks, *A Full Life* (Leo Cooper, 1974); O. Bradley, *A General's Life* (Simon & Schuster, 1983); B.L. Montgomery, *Memoirs* (Cassell, 1958); Hamilton (op.cit.); *After the Battle* No. 49, Rosse and Hill; *The Guards Armoured Division*, Bles 1956; M. Hastings, *Bomber Command* (Michael Joseph, 1979).

Chapter 5

H. Gunning, *Borderers in Battle: The War History of the King's Own Scottish Borderers* ; N. Scarfe, *Assault Division* (Collins, 1953); L.N. Steinert, *Die 23 Tage der Regierung Doenitz* (Econ, 1972); Hamilton (op.cit.); Howarth (op.cit.); Toland (op.cit.); D. Irving, *The War between the Generals* (Allen Lane, 1983); J. Gavin, *On to Berlin* (Viking, 1978); *The Times*, June 1986.

BOOK TWO

Chapter 1

H. Essame, History of the 43rd Division (Clowes, 1952); Scarfe (op.cit.); Hamilton (op.cit.); Schwareaelder (op.cit.); C. Ryan, A Bridge too Far (Simon & Schuster); Toland (op.cit.).

Chapter 2

Steinert (op.cit); P. Padfield, Doenitz: The Last Führer (Gollancz, 1984); Haines (op.cit.); Gunning (op.cit.); BBC War Report (Collins, 1945).

Chapter 3

H. Saunders, Green Beret (Four Square, 1955); Schwareaelder (op.cit.); A. Speer, Memoirs (Collins, 1971); Ryan (op.cit.); Steinert (op.cit.).

Chapter 4

Daily Mirror 28 April 1945; J. Grimond, Memoirs (Collins, 1970); Saunders (op.cit.); Padfield (op.cit.); History of 7th Armoured Division (op.cit.); Gavin (op.cit.); M. Ridgway, Soldier (Simon & Schuster); J. Johnson, Wing-Leader (Hamlyn, 1973).

Chapter 5

Gavin (op.cit.); Hamilton (op.cit.); MacDonald (op.cit.); C. Whiting, The Hunt for Martin Boorman (Ballantine, 1974); Padfield (op.cit.); R. West, Anatomy of Treason (Pan, 1970); Daily Telegraph, 4 November 1988; M. Wolff-Moenckeberg, On the Other Side (Pan, 1979).

BOOK THREE

Chapter 1

Gavin (op.cit.); The Saga of the All American, 82 AB Association, 1946; Mission Accomplished, XVIII, 1945; The History of 28th Infantry Regiment, Washington Infantry Journal Press, 1946; Padfield (op.cit.); History of 7th Armoured Division (op.cit.).

Chapter 2

Haines (op.cit.); Hamilton (op.cit.); Gavin (op.cit.); Roberts (op.cit.); Steinert (op.cit.) Pocock (op.cit.); Toland (op.cit.); Thompson (op.cit.).

Chapter 3

Haines (op.cit.); Wolff-Moenckeberg (op.cit.); Hamilton (op.cit.); Thompson (op.cit.); Toland (op.cit.); Ridgway (op.cit.).

Chapter 4

Hamilton (op.cit.); P. Marrinan, Colonel Paddy (Ulster Press, 1972); Thompson (op.cit.); Alan Moorehead, Eclipse (Collins, 1946); M. Lindsay, So Few Came Through (Arrow, 1952); Horrocks (op.cit.); Essame (op.cit.); Pocock (op.cit.); L. Atwell, Private (Dell, 1946); Flowers, Anatomy of Courage (Cassell, 1968).

Chapter 5

Hamilton (op.cit.); D. Niven, The Moon's a Balloon (Coronet, 1971); R. Maughan, Jersey under Jackboot (Corgi, 1961); Der Vlis, Tragedie op Texel (Langeveld, 1958); R. Murphy, Diplomat Among the Warriors (Collins, 1958); J. Mordal, Hold-Up Naval à Granville (Editions France Empire, 1963); R. Hansen, Das Ende des Dritten Reiches (Klett, 1964); Pocock (op.cit.); Hamilton (op.cit.).

ENVOI

After the Battle, 1976 and 1977; Pocock (op.cit.); Hamilton (op.cit.); C. Whiting, Nordeutschland, Stunde Null (Droste Verlag, 1978).

Index

Achim 89–91, 109
Adair, General 84
Adams, Sergeant Major 70
Alexander, Field Marshal 80, 234
Aller 54
Alps, resistance in 69, 175
Ambrose, Stephen E., *Supreme Command* 19
Arctic 266
Arnhem 59–61, 63–64, 75, 117
  city zoo 61
  First Battle of 63
Arsten 111–113
Artlenburg 115, 156–157, 286
Athen 80
Athens 80
Atkinson, Lieutenant Harry 93
Attlee, Clement 231
Atwell, Private Lester 247, 256
Austen, Sergeant Major 280
Avonsdorf 115

Bad Doberan 206
Bad Mondorf, Palast Hotel 278
Bad Oldesloe 207
Bad Salezelmen 26–27
Baldwin, Squadron Leader 226–227
Baltic, race for 66, 79, 81, 95, 101–102
Barby 33–34, 37
Barker, General 15, 50, 75, 78, 82–83, 114–115, 131, 139, 164, 167, 189
Battles
  Bulge, of 47, 165
  Arnhem, First of 63
  Hurtgen Forest, of 165
Bavaria 53
BBC, *War Report* 134

Beagle 264–265
Beck, Rainer 262–263
Becker, General 129–131, 137, 140
Beckhurst, Major 136–137
Becklingen, British Military Command at 87
BEF 15–16
  Second Corps 15
Belchem, General 243
Belgian communist resistance 80
Belsen 50–53, 56, 100–101, 193–194, 232, 260
Berlin 55, 65–66, 73, 81
  bunker 96, 120
  Gateway to 30
  preparation for airborne attack on 102
  Templehof Airport 102, 56–57, 145, 177
Bernadotte, Count Folke 56–57, 145, 177
  meeting with Himmler 98–100
Bertram, Captain 210, 221, 227–228
Bierden 91
Billingslea, Colonel Charles 214
Bittrich, General 117
Blackman, Lieutenant 133
Blaskowitz. General Johannes 60, 265
Bleckede 106, 164, 170
Blumenson, Martin 21
Blumentritt 17
Boehme, General 262
Bogarde, Dirk 260
Bols, General 180
Bomber Command 88–89
Bormann, Martin 173–175, 195–196
Bornholm 79,147–148

Borucki, Doctor 221
Bourke-White, Margaret 207–208
Bradley, General 33–36, 40–41, 53, 67,
    69, 78, 103–104, 168, 234, 261, 281
    A General's Life 17–18, 166–167
Braun, Eva, suicide of 173
Bremen 42, 45, 46, 54, 75, 77–79, 85, 87,
    111, 122, 124–125, 246
    assault on 88–94
    capitulation of 137
    defence of 128–130
    tidy up of 139
Bremerhaven 247
Bremervoerde 274
Brest 261
Breuninger, Captain 148–149
British forces
    3rd Division (Iron Division) 111, 114,
        129–131
    1st Airborne Division 59, 75, 117
    5th Airborne Division 159
    6th Airborne Division 159, 166, 168,
        179–180, 203–205, 207, 212, 238, 255
        3rd Brigade 203
    3rd Anti-Aircraft Division 152
    7th Armoured Division 75, 77, 96,
        124–125, 144, 153, 162, 197, 199–201
    11th Armoured Division
        49–50, 69, 75, 82, 115–116,
        158–159, 168, 172, 193–194, 196,
        207–208, 250
        131st Infantry Brigade 162, 250
    79th Armoured Division 60
    Guards Armoured Division 141,
        245
    Army Group (21st) 53
    2nd Army 53
    8th Army 81
    Cameron Highlanders 159, 172
        C Company 172
    Cavalry Reconnaisance Squadron
        (87th) 212
    Commando Brigade (1st) 155,
        158–159
    12th Corps 75
    30th Corps 44–45, 77, 87, 89, 109,
        139, 247
    Devons (2nd) 125–126

Dorsets (4th) 110
Duke of Cornwalls 109
    Light Infantry 111
Duke of Wellingtons Infantry 61
    C Company 61
Durham Light Infantry 162, 201
179 Field Artillery Regiment 109
Fife and Forfar Yeomanry 207
Glasgow Highlanders 128–129,
    159
Hampshires (7th) 109
Hampshires Regiment 265
Hereford Regiment 271
8th Irish Hussars 75–77
11th Hussars 82–83, 223, 240
    No 4 Troop 241
13/18 Hussars 45
15/19 Hussars 207, 271
23rd Hussars 50
1st Infantry 249
3rd Infantry Division 89–90
3rd Highland Infantry Division
    77
5th Infantry Division 190, 207
15th Scottish Infantry Division
    115–116, 155–156, 158–159,
    164, 169, 172
43rd Infantry 89–90, 109
43rd Infantry Division 59, 61
51st Highland Infantry Division
    77, 89–90, 245–246
52nd Lowland Infantry Division
    47, 89–90, 109, 131, 140, 246
53rd Infantry Division 47, 83, 155,
    159
Irish Guards 84
    Armoured Division 84
        No 1 Squadron 84–85
King's Own Scottish Borders
    (4th) 114, 131, 157–158, 208
    6th Battalion 91–92
        A Company 91, 93
        C Company 91–93
        D Company 94
King's Shropshire Light Infantry,
    4th Battalion 69–70
Leicesters (1st) 62
Lincolns (2nd) 129–130

C Company 129
Manchester Regiment (1st) 47
  history of 49
  158 Brigade 47
  160 Brigade 47
3rd Parachute Brigade 206
7th Battalion Parachute Regiment
  239
12th Battalion Parachute
  Regiment 188
13th Battalion Parachute
  Regiment 188
Queens (1st/5th) 76–77, 125
Reconnaissance Regiment (43rd
  Division) 42–45, 90, 109–111,
  131, 137, 140, 247, 249
  129 Brigade 131
Rifle Brigade 77
Royal Army Educational Corps
  118, 120
Royal Army Medical Corps 275
Royal Army Service Corps 84
Royal Scots 156
Royal Scots Fusiliers 156
Royal Scots Greys 93–94, 188
Royal Tanks (1st) 76
Royal Tanks (3rd) 156, 208
Royal Tanks (4th) 113
Royal Ulster Rifles 113–114
SAS, D Squadron 244
Scots and Welsh Guards 142–143
Scots Guards (3rd) 84
Seaforth Highlanders 173
Sherwood Rangers 133
Shropshire Light Infantry (7th)
  112, 207, 271
  Y Company 112
  Z Company 112
Somerset Light Infantry (4th)
  45–46, 131, 135
  C Company 135
TAC Air Force 89
Tactical Air Force (2nd), 83rd
  Group 159
Welch Regiment (1st/5th) 47–48,
  127
  Royal Welch Fusiliers 49, 202
  159th Brigade 49

West Somerset Yeomanry 245
Wiltshires (5th) 131–133, 140
  A Company 132
    13th Platoon 133
  C Company 132
    4th Platoon 133, 136
Worcestershire Regiment (1st)
  42–44
  A Company 44
  D Company 43–44
Yorks and Lancs Infantrymen
  60–61
Buchenwald 101
Budapest 65
Bukreyev, Major Vassili 57–58, 228
Bulldog 264
Bullendorf 69
Bullenhuser damm 71
Bunz 218
Burchard, Doctor 162
Busch, Field Marshal 95, 123–124,
  143, 152–153, 168–169, 172–173,
  191, 200
Butcher, Captain 66
Byrom, Paramedic James 255

Caen 47
  massacre at 48
Calder-Marshall, Arthur 251
Canadian forces
  Argyll and Southern
    Highlanders, Second Corps 46,
    49, 157
  Canadian Parachute Battalion 203
  First Army 53, 54, 59
    5th Armoured Division 60
    11th Armoured Regiment
    60–61
Cap Arcona 194–195, 210, 221,
  225–228
capos 51
Carroll, Sergeant 46
Carver, Lord 99
Celle 244
Chalmer, Major W. J. 248
Charlton, Guardsman Eddie 83–87
Churcher, Brigadier 49, 250, 271
Churchill, Winston 17, 34, 54, 60, 80,

102, 117, 148, 198, 234, 254–255, 267, 275
  Eisenhower, and 64–67, 272–273
  'Iron Curtain' Telegram 268–269
  on Montgomery 40
  relationship with Russia 20–21
  writings of 284
Clapham, Captain 112
Clapton, Captain 158
class system, British 117–119
Colverson, Major 132
Cologne 103–104, 259
Compiègne 252
Cooley, Staff Sergeant 27–28
Corby, Colonel 133
Coventry 232
Cox, Geoffrey 266
Crabhill, Colonel Edwin 33
Cremer,Lieutenant Commander 96, 176–177
Crete 55, 266
Crossingham, Lieutenant 44
Crozier, Colonel 47
Cruden, Captain 158
Czechoslovakia 249

Danish Peninsula 66, 138
Danzig 95
Davidson, Colonel 92
Dawnay, Colonel 224, 231–232
Day, Private Bob 62
D Day 84, 111, 115
de Grineau, Captain Brian 48
de Guingand, Freddie 41
Delmenhorst 90
Dempsey, General 164–166, 200, 223–224, 279
Denmark 54, 79, 95, 102, 124, 143–144, 147–148, 241, 262
  liberation of 17, 53, 57–58
  resistance in 69
Derry Cunihy 110
'Desert Rats' 75, 77, 125, 127, 222
Deutschland 194, 227
Diepholz 79
Disney, Colonel Paul 25–26, 32
Dittmar, General Kurt 68–69
Doclik, Doctor Bogmuil 57

Doenitz, Grand Admiral Karl 123–124, 143–145, 148, 153, 161, 174–178, 193, 195–201, 209, 215–216, 232, 234, 250–251, 260, 262–264, 266–267, 272–273
  'Administration' 268–270, 277–279
  Hitler, and 97–98
  personality of 96–97
Donnison, F.S.V. 119
Dorfer, Bruno 262–263
DPs 105, 191, 209
Dreye, taking of 111–113
Dunkirk 15, 50, 55, 76, 78, 251, 261, 265, 287
  Medal 17
Dunkley, Private Reg 61–62
Dunnett, Robert 63
Dutch Government in exile 59
Dutch forces, 34th SS Division 60–61

'ear' battalion 92
Earle, Major Peter 81–83, 98
Eden , Anthony 102
Edwards, Captain 135
Ehrlich, Paul 229
Eisenhower, Dwight D. 33–34, 38, 53–55, 71, 78–79, 81, 102–104, 106, 122, 128, 144, 200, 210, 225, 234–236, 249–254, 256, 267, 280, 281
  biographer of 19
  Bremen, surrender of, and 89
  relationships, with Churchill 64–67
    with Montgomery 40–41
El Alamein 55, 117
Elbe, river, assault on 138–139
  crossing of 26–38
Elmenhorst 190
Emden 53, 95
Ems, river 46, 54
Erdmann, General 43, 161, 208
Essame, Brigadier 140, 247–249
  The Battle for Germany 19, 111
Ewart, Colonel 231, 233, 240

Fahrmbacher, General 263–264
Fallingsborstal 55–56, 75
Festungen 260
Fischer, Doctor 123–124
Flensburg 209, 216, 224, 234, 243, 250, 259, 262, 270–271
  'Enclave' 266
Focke-Wulf apprentices 128–129
Foster, Colonel 116, 120, 159–160, 167–168, 172
Foulkes, General 60, 265
Frahm, SS Sergeant 72–74
Franklin, Major General, *Across the Rhine* 18
fraternisation 105, 256, 258–259
Friedl, Major 231, 240, 242
Friesoythe 46, 49
Frisius, Freidrich 261, 265
Fuhrmann, Claus 149

Gadesbuch 187–188
'Gateway to Berlin' 30–31
Gavin, General James 18, 104–106, 164–165, 167, 171–173, 189, 211, 213–215, 217, 237
German forces (*see also* Hitler Youth and Werewolf movement)
  8th Airborne Division 161
  21st Army 213–215, 217
  Flak Artillery 131
  8th Flak Division 140
  Infantry, 102nd 205–206
    245th 172–173
    280th 92
  2nd Marine Division 44–45, 85, 161
  Panzer Army, 1st 120
    3rd 120, 145–146, 150
    7th 121
    15th 245–246
  15th Panzer Grenadier Division 85–87, 141
  8th Parachute Division 208
  Paratroop Command 43
  12th SS Panzer Division 47, 68
  SS Panzer Corps 117
  SS Training Regiment, 12th 161–162
    18th 111, 127
  Vistula 120, 144–147, 189, 231–232
Geschonnek, Erwin 227–228
Gilbert, Major Glyn 129–130
Glasmacher, Heinrich 262
Godt, Admiral 195–196
Goebbels, Doctor Josef 80, 173–174, 195, 252
Goering 102, 160
Gort, Lord 15
Gott 82
Granville 264
Gray, Piper Jock 131
Greek communists 80
Grigg, Sir James 20
Grimond, Jo 155
Grothmann, Colonel 274–275
Gulag 79

Habenhausen 114
Hall, Major 44
Halton, Matthew 62
Hamburg 42, 53–54, 56–57, 70–71, 73–77, 85, 115, 123, 125–126, 143, 197, 222
  destruction of 95
  road and rail links with Bremen and 87, 109
Hamburg/Harburg 76–77, 125
Hamilton, Nigel 18
Harding, Lieutenant Colonel 245
Hargreaves, Flight Lieutenant J. 226
Harris, Air Marshal 207, 209, 222
  Bremen, and 88–89
  personality of 88
Hasbrouck, General 211
Healey, Captain 108
Healey, Major Denis 118
Heath, Lieutenant Peter 250–251
Hechthausen 245
Heine, General 264
Heinrici, General 120–122, 144–146, 150–152
Hela peninsula 262
Hermann von Wissmann 260
Himmler, Heinrich 73–74, 144–145, 152, 176–178, 193,

196–197, 251
disposal of body of 279–280
meeting with Count Bernadotte
100–103
suicide of 274–277
Hinds, Brigadier General Sidney 29,
37
Hitler 68, 73, 95–96, 102, 145
Doenitz and 97–98
planned kidnap of 100
suicide of 173–174, 198–199
'Hitler Youth' 47–49, 76, 82, 110,
117, 120–122, 126, 187, 191,
206–207, 220
Holland 54, 59, 106, 265–266
clearing of 53
liberation of 63
Prince Bernhard of 265
Hollenstedt 77
Hollingsworth, Major James 25–29
Horrocks, General Brian 16, 44–45,
77–78, 109, 139–141, 247
Bremen, and 87, 89–90
Horsford, Captain 233
Howarth, Major T.E.B. 38, 99
Huffmeier, Admiral 261, 264–265
Hungary 47
Hunter, Doctor Robert 99–100
Huntzinger, General 252

Illustrated London News, 21 April
1945 Issue 48
'Instrument of Surrender' 242
Italian front 54
Italy 60, 84
Canadians in 60
Salerno landings 62

Japan 130
Jodl, Colonel General 224, 250–254,
262, 267, 278
Johnson, Johnnie 167–168
Jones, Sapper 206
Joyce, William 152, 178–180
Jugoslav communist resistance 80

Kaiser Wilhem Canal 209, 215
Kamptz, Commander 147

Kankelan 190
Kaufman, Gauleiter 95, 123–124,
143–144, 151–153, 161–163, 176,
194, 197–198, 222–223, 275
Keitel, Field Marshal 73, 145–147,
150–151, 250–251, 253–254
Kesselring, Field Marshal 250
Kiel 53–54, 95, 215, 244
Kinzel, General 234, 242–243
Klein, Doctor 52–53
Knight, Captain Jack 26–27
Knowlton, First Lieutenant Wiliam
212–213, 236–237
Koehler, General 153
Koehn, Wilhelm 262
Kramer, Josef 50–51
Kropp, Lieutenant 262
Krueger, Else 174
Krylov, Ivan 149–150
Kuhstedt 245
Kunzig, Colonel 212
Kwapinski, Tadensz 194–195

Labour Government 281
Labour party 84
Langer, Magdalene 221
Lauenburg 69–70, 138–139, 158,
170, 234, 287
bridge at 69, 71, 75, 115
Lethe, river 42
Lever, Harold 120
Lewin 18
Liddell, Captain L.O. 87
Lindemann, General 262
Lindsay, Colonel Martin 246
Lingen 87
Lloyd, Lieutenant Peter 114
Lord, RSM 75
Lorient 263
Loudspeaker Unit One 50
Lübeck 17–20, 54, 95, 100, 102–103,
115, 138, 165, 190, 192–193,
206–207, 209, 287
bay at 194–195, 226
Lubz 213
Ludwigslust 214
Luedde–Neurath, Commander 96,
175–177, 195–196, 209

Luneburg 50, 82, 115, 252, 275, 287
   surrender of German army at 19
Luxemburg 278
Lyne, General 144, 163, 200

MacDonald, Captain 60–61
Macher, Colonel Heinz 177, 275
McKee, Alexander 63–64
Macon, General 33
Magdeburg 29, 67
   bridge at 69
Manchester Police Force 84
Mann, Anthony 272
Marie, Lucien 270–271
Marshall, General George 64–65,
   102–103
Masur, Norbert 74
Maxwell, Captain Robert 76, 125,
   197, 222
Mayhew, Christopher 118
Mecklenburg 79, 144, 211, 231
Mehringer, Heinrich 226–228
Mende, Major Erich 206
Meyer, General Kurt 48
Military Medal 93
Mills-Roberts, Colonel 158
Minquiers 270–271
Moelln 191–193
Montgomery, Field Marshal
   Bernard Law 37–39, 52–55,
   58–60, 66–67, 69, 75, 78–82,
   96, 102–103, 106, 153, 164–166,
   200, 219, 224–225, 230–236,
   241–243, 249–250, 252, 254,
   259–261, 267
   Anglo-American rivalry and
      19–20
   Belsen, and 53
   biographers of 18
   'bouncing the Rhine' 59
   British Control Commission, and
      281–283
   caravan 54–55, 80
   Charles Sweeney, and 268
   death of 284
   Eisenhower, and 40–41
   El Alamein, and 117
   Elbe assault, and 138

'eyes and ears' of 38, 81–82, 268
   General Brooke, and 16
   General Simpson, and 34
   homosexuality, rumours of 99
   'Instrument of Surrender', and
      242
   John Poston, and 98–100
   last operations 17–21, 271–273
   Lübeck mission, and 103–104
   Lucien F. Trueb, and 99
   mother 99
   Ninth army, and 34
   personality 16–17, 39–41
   popularity 40
   request to King for house
      283–284
   surrender of Bremen, and 89
   upper-class sporting image 118
Moorehead, Alan 18, 52, 247
Moscow, German drive on 79
Mosley, Leonard 52
Muehlen-Richsen 188
Mueller, Colonel 140
Murphy, Colonel 224, 270,
   275–276, 280

National Redoubt 53, 68–69
National Socialism 63, 96–98
Neuengamme 56, 71, 73, 100,
   123–124, 197–198, 209–210
Neumunster 244
Neustadt 193, 220–221
Nicholls, Corporal Thomas 15
Nijmegen Home Guard 59–60
Niven, Lieutenant Colonel David
   257–258
NKVD 57
Norman, Captain 142–143
Normandy 78, 84, 106, 110, 117, 262
Norway 79, 231
   liberation of 17, 57
   resistance in 69

O'Cock, Major Mick 85–86
Ochtumsand 244
Odeme 81
Oder, river 120
Operation Barleycorn 282

Operation Eclipse 105
Operation Coal Scuttle 282
OST labourers 139–140
Ottery, Sergeant Bill 279–280
Oxenius, Major 252

Pahl, Captain 262
Parchim 213
Parry, Private 48–49, 127
Patton, General 33–34, 53, 66, 104,
    235, 249, 254
    firing of 281
    Montgomery and 40–41
Pauly, Max 56–57
Pershing 104
Pinder, Lance-Corporal 190, 286
Ploen 94, 96, 98, 123, 144, 152–153,
    161, 174, 193, 196, 219, 247, 256
Pocock, Tom 283
Pollek, Colonel 242
Pope, Major 136–137, 140
Poston, Major John 81–83, 138
    death of 98–100
Potsdam 36
Prague 66, 254
Prussia, East 95

Quickborn 240
Quinan, Lieutenant Barry 85–86

Raeder, Admiral, resignation of 96
Read, Major 112–113
Red Cross nurses 214
Reichhelm, Colonel 68
Remagen, railway bridge at 26, 69
Remington-Hobbs, Colonel 172
Rethem 47
    massacre at 49
Rheims 33
Rhine 18, 26, 60, 75, 105
    bridge at Arnhem 59
Ridgway, General Matt 18, 79,
    103–106, 122, 164–166, 168, 189,
    210–211, 236–238
Ridler, Sergeant 244
Ritchie, General 16, 75, 77–78
Roberts, General 50, 69–71, 75, 82,
    115–116, 173, 189, 191, 208, 250

Roesdahl, Doctor 71
Rokossovsky, Marshal Konstantin
    39, 79, 120, 144–145, 147, 149
Rooks, General 271–272
Roosevelt, Theodore 64, 200
Ross, General 155
Rosslau 30
Rostock 165
Rotenburg 85
Rothenburgsort 71
Rotterdam 62
Route 4 115–116, 158
Rubel, Colonel George 211–212
Rumbold, Squadron Leader Martin
    225–226
Runcie MC, Lieutenant Robert 143
Russia, agents 79
    Churchill bargaining with 34
    cold war, and 104
    front 106
    race for the Baltic 20
    participants in Second World
        War 35, 37, 55, 57, 66, 73,
        80–81, 101–103, 120–122, 144,
        147, 190, 200–201, 235
Russian forces
    2nd Belorussian Army 79, 148,
        176, 216, 236
    Georgian Infantry Battalion,
        822nd 261
    Red Air Force 148
    Red Army 55, 79, 148–149, 166,
        217–218
        breakthrough on Oder 120
    Red Navy 79

Sahms 190
Saunders, Pilot Don 226
Sawtell, Corporal Dick 86
Schaefer, Doctor Albert 162–163
Schellenberg, General 100, 145
Schmidt, Helmut 283
Schnakenbek 115–116, 157
Schoor, Gerhard 228
Schoenebeck 25–27, 33
Schultz, Private 106
Schwarzenbeck 190, 286
Second Army's Interrogation

Centre 275
Selvester, Captain 275
SHAEF 55, 235, 242, 250, 252–253, 271
Sibert, Major General 131, 137
Silesia, coalmines in 55
Simpson, General 33–38, 55, 67
Sington, Captain Derrick 50–51
Sissonne 104
Smalley, Sergeant Major Sam 130
Smirnov, General 237
Smith, Bedell 249, 252–253
Smith, Lieutenant 43
Snow, Brigadier 264
Soegel, fight for 46
Speer, Albert 96, 151–152, 195–198, 277–278
Spindler,Captain 205–206
Spurling, Brigadier 162, 201
SS *Patria* 251, 271
Stacey, Colonel C.P. 59
Stalin 65–66, 79, 147, 254
Stalingrad 79
Starr, Captain James 26–27
Steiner, General 120–121
Stemann, Peter 147–148
Stettin 20, 102
Stevens-Guille, Captain 16
Stewart, Major 91
Stewart, Sergeant 188
'stomach' battalion 92, 94
Stroh, General 165
Strong, Brigadier Ken 234–235, 249, 253
Strong, General 269–270
Stuart, Admiral 264
Suchowiak, Bogdan 228–230
Summersby, Kay 65
Susloparoff, General 235
Sweden 57, 79, 101, 124, 143–144, 147, 153
Swedish Red Cross 56
Sweeney, Charles 16, 268
Swinemünde 150–151
Switzerland 57

Tallett, Private Joe 106
Telegraph Cottage 67

Templer, Field Marshal 284
texel 260–261, 265–266
Thielbek 221, 227, 229
Third Reich 68, 78, 101–102
  final surrender of 17
Thomas, General 109, 131, 247–249
Thomas, Wynford Vaughan 134–135
Thompson R.W. 18, 76, 242, 246
'Thousand Year Reich' 29, 63, 277
Timeloberg 285
Tito 80
Tobruk 55
Tokyo 104
Toland, John, *The Last Hundred Days* 17
Tonkin, Major 244
Torgau 166, 210
Tostedt 76
Trittau 191
Trueb, Lucien F., and Montgomery 99
Truman, Harry S. 30, 64
  'Iron Curtain' Telegram, and 268–269
Trzebinski, Doctor 72–73

Unemployment, in Germany 99
United Nations 242
Uphusen 90–91, 93–94
US forces
  8th Corps 75, 82–83, 114, 116, 120, 131, 156–157
    Airborne
      82nd Airborne 102–104, 189, 211, 213–214, 217
      325th Glider Infantry 214
    Airborne Corps, 18th 79, 103, 105, 122, 166, 189, 220
    Armored
      Armored Infantry Regiment, 41st, 1st Battalion 29
        3rd Battalion 29, 32
      Ninth Armored 26
      Second Armored 25, 28–33, 35, 37, 67, 79, 95, 143, 148, 215
        combat command B 25
      Seventh Armored 166, 168, 211, 222, 238

740th Tank Battalion
211–213
Infantry, 8th 165
30th 67–68
35th 35
83rd 32–35
Parachute Regiment, 504th 189
505th 106, 170, 189

Vahrendorf 125–127
Vandeleur, Brigadier Joe 131,
135–136
VE Day 255
Vegesack 88
veneral disease 259
Verden 90
Victoria Cross 87
Victory Hill 284–286
Vienna 66
Villiers, Brigadier 169, 172–173
von Buelow, Leutnant Hans-
Juergen 85–86
von Friedeburg, Admiral 209,
215–216, 223–225, 231–233, 240,
242, 250, 252, 272
von Jungenfeld, General Ernst 213
von Krosigk, Count Schwerin 216,
267, 272, 274
von Laun, Leutnant Otto 162
von Manteuffel, General 120–122,
145–146, 150–152, 189
von Tippelskirch, General 120, 151,
189, 213–215
von Trotha, General 144–145
von Varnbuhler 213–215

Wade, Captain 206
Wageningen 265
Wagner, Admiral 242
Wainman, Colonel Bill 223
Wallenberg, Jakob 144, 149
Ward, Edward 272
Warren, Colonel 224, 230–232,
240–241

Warsaw 65
Watts, Major 135, 205
Wegener, Gauleiter 95, 124–125, 197
Weidemann, Margot 220
Weimar Republic 97
Weitzmuhlen 47
Wells, Captain C. 275–276
Wenck, General 30, 68
Werewolf movement 187, 238
Weser 46, 54, 75, 77, 89–90
dam across 89
Westerhusen 29
Western Desert 81, 141
Westertimke 141, 247, 275, 286
Weston, Sergeant Reg 280
Wheaton, Captain R. 245
White, General Isaac 26, 29, 32
Whittaker, Major 276–277, 280
Wiesbaden 35–36
Wigle, Lieutenant Colonel 46
Wilhemshaven 53, 55, 95
Wilmot, Chester 168–169, 272
Winschoten 38
Wismar 18, 203, 205–207, 238, 255
advance to 188
Wistedt 85, 87
Witt, Frau 127
Wolff-Moenckeberg, Frau 199, 223
Woltz, General Alwin 126, 152–153,
161–163, 198–201, 223
Wood, Private 113
Woodward, David 52

Zeven 85
Zhukov, Marshall 281
Zimmerman, Lieutenant
Commander 264
Zone of Occupation, American
259, 282
British 259, 282–283
French 282
Russian 66, 102, 238, 282
Zwolle 63